PRAISE FOR
MANAGING CONFLICT

'This is an incredibly useful guide to underst.
David Liddle helpfully combines the theory and psychology behind conflict with
hands-on, practical tips for managing conflict, all brought to life in case studies.
Whilst the author is clearly an expert in conflict and shares many examples
of situations he has been involved in, this guide is accessible to all. I will be
recommending it to my team, managers and employees – in fact to anyone
involved in managing conflict.' **Kirsty Devine, Head of US HR and Global
Projects, *Financial Times***

'Conflict is inevitable – indeed a healthy level of conflict enables organizations to
grow. It is when conflict becomes unhealthy that it stifles the organization and
the employees within it. David Liddle's book is a practical and essential guide to
understanding and managing what is often regarded as a taboo subject. With
case studies from a wide range of industries, handy tips and questions that any
HR professional should be asking themselves, *Managing Conflict* is required
reading.' **Martin Blackburn, UK People Director, KPMG**

'After the Dispute Resolution Regulations (2004) were repealed following my
report ten years ago, it was widely hoped that a system of Alternative Dispute
Resolution (ADR) would emerge across the UK. In *Managing Conflict*, David
Liddle has highlighted some innovative and highly effective approaches and
he has gathered first-hand evidence about the powerful and lasting impact
of ADR. Moreover, he has also set out some very significant challenges (and
some pragmatic solutions) that should be addressed by HR, unions, business
leaders and policymakers if we are going to see a real shift in culture and
policy regarding the management of conflict at work.' **Michael Gibbons CBE,
Independent Reviewer of the Dispute Resolution Regulations (2004) for
the Secretary of State, Department of Trade and Industry, 2007**

'This is a very useful and, in many ways, radical resource for employers
managing conflict within the workplace. The book advocates a "holistic and
integrated conflict management system" and provides a wealth of resource
materials in order to establish and implement such a system. Employment
lawyers should note the book's trenchant comment criticizing the traditional
adversarial and rights-based grievance procedure and the range of conflict
management processes that are recommended in its p

being fully compliant with current legislation. There is cogent evidence that a significant number of employers are now implementing internal workplace mediation schemes with high success rates and that many others are likely to follow this trend.' **Peter Frost, Partner and Head of Employment Disputes, Herbert Smith Freehills LLP**

'Every workplace generates chronic conflicts, yet few organizations have rethought the way they work, or used conflict resolution techniques to transform the sources of conflict at work, or examined their "conflict cultures" to discover how disputes are being generated and prevent their recurrence. Fewer still have conducted "conflict audits" to reveal where these streams of conflict originate, or designed complex, multilayered, integrated systems to strengthen their capacity for conflict prevention, resolution and transformation. David Liddle has written an incredibly useful book that shows how to measure the costs of conflict in any workplace and how to prevent and resolve it. It is insightful and immensely practical, and I recommend it highly.' **Kenneth Cloke, co-author of** *Resolving Conflicts at Work: Ten strategies for everyone on the job*

'David Liddle's book is honest, thoughtful, engaging and practical. Conflict has been a big part of my 40 years as a union officer, during which I have learned the hard way of the benefits of getting below the surface and recognizing the demons at work inside everyone round the table and moving beyond process and game playing. My demon has always been that by taking such a risk I will be scoffed at because "of course it won't work". Well it does, and this important book shows that it does. I hope the wisdom on every page will give courage, hope and help to a new generation freed from the traditions of dispute resolution.' **Jim McAuslan, ex-General Secretary, British Airline Pilots' Association**

'This book offers a welcome relief from traditional approaches to managing conflict. The arguments for shifting to a more integrated, person-centred and values-based approach are set out simply and plainly. The models and toolkits that David Liddle has created are easily applied and will be of benefit to all organizations.' **Andy Keeling, Chief Operating Officer, Leicester City Council**

'Having had to implement grievance and disciplinary procedures in various business, public and third sector settings, I have often wished for a more humane and less exhausting process. This book not only shines a light on what is going wrong, it offers practical and proven alternatives. Not only does it supply ideas on what to do, but also how to do it. The layout is helpful for busy managers who wish to dip in and out of the book and there is a very useful Resolution Resources section. I wish this book had been available years ago.' **Nancy Radford, Business Coach and Mediator, Roundtuit Ltd**

'This book draws on extensive research to deliver a comprehensive and accessible framework for managing the broad spectrum of conflict situations facing organizations today. A highly recommended read.' **Rachael Tyler, Development Director, Healthcare People Management Association (HPMA), London Academy**

'There will no doubt be a time in every person's life where they will feel overwhelmed, dismayed and perplexed by either a personal or organizational conflict. Read and apply what *Managing Conflict* has to offer and that statement could become a thing of the past. A must-read for any HR professional, leader, manager or team member.' **Caroline Waters OBE, Founder, CW Consulting Box**

'This book challenges traditional thinking on managing conflict in the workplace and makes us consider the broad benefits a positive approach to conflict resolution could bring, as well as supplying practical tools and guidance to facilitate the reduction of conflict.' **Philip Edwards, Head of ER and Policies, Financial Services**

'This book provides everything that leaders and HR professionals need to build the case for a different approach to managing conflict. It provides real-world examples that show the benefits to the individual and the organization of mediation, plus practical tools to build skills. It is a full-on challenge to the HR function to change its role during conflict – from policing and process to dialogue and understanding. If you have witnessed the damage that conflict inflicts on individuals, teams and organizations and you want to learn about a better, top-to-bottom organizational response, this book will help you in so many ways.' **Debbie Sanders, Head of Employee Relations, National Air Traffic Services (NATS)**

'If there is one book you must read it is David Liddle's *Managing Conflict*. David has been at the forefront of dispute resolution for years, and this book does what it says on the cover. As ever, David brings a practical, no-nonsense and empathetic approach to his subject. One to trust, dip into at any time and return to, again and again.' **Andi Hargreaves, Head, People Policy and ER, Department for International Trade**

'*Managing Conflict* provides a well-structured and hugely practical insight into understanding, preventing and resolving workplace issues. From understanding mediation to positive psychology, the author covers relevant topics in a thorough and accessible style, completing the book with an invaluable resources section.' **David D'Souza, Head of Engagement and London, CIPD, Experienced HR/OD/Change Leader**

'This book lives up to the description of being a practical guide. It covers a wide range of conflict situations with very "doable" ways of dealing with them. This is an extremely valuable guide for HR professionals and others who need to manage conflict on a daily basis.' **HR Leader, Mercer**

'This is a really comprehensive review of what causes conflict in an organization and different methods to address it. I was really struck by the whole-systems approach taken and the focus on different forms of mediation, particularly for addressing incidents of bullying and harassment. An ideal resource for HR professionals and organizational leaders.' **Rachael Etebar, Group HR Director, Department for Transport**

Managing Conflict

A practical guide to resolution
in the workplace

David Liddle

KoganPage

Publisher's note

Every possible effort has been made to ensure that the information contained in this book is accurate at the time of going to press, and the publisher and authors cannot accept responsibility for any errors or omissions, however caused. No responsibility for loss or damage occasioned to any person acting, or refraining from action, as a result of the material in this publication can be accepted by the editor, the publisher or any of the authors.

First published in Great Britain and the United States in 2017 by Kogan Page Limited

2nd Floor, 45 Gee Street
London EC1V 3RS
United Kingdom

c/o Martin P Hill Consulting
122 W 27th St, 10th Floor
New York NY 10001
USA

4737/23 Ansari Road
Daryaganj
New Delhi 110002
India

www.koganpage.com

© David Liddle, 2017
© for Chapter 4, Laura Farnsworth, Chris Smith and Laurence Mills of Lewis Silkin LLP, 2017

The right of David Liddle and of each commissioned author of this work to be identified as an author of this work has been asserted by him/her in accordance with the Copyright, Designs and Patents Act 1988.

ISBN   978 0 7494 8088 2
E-ISBN   978 0 7494 8089 9

British Library Cataloguing-in-Publication Data

A CIP record for this book is available from the British Library.

Library of Congress Cataloging-in-Publication Data

Names: Liddle, David (Mediator) author.
Title: Managing conflict : a practical guide to resolution in the workplace / David Liddle.
Description: 1st Edition. | New York : Kogan Page Ltd, [2017] | Includes bibliographical references and index.
Identifiers: LCCN 2017035672 (print) | LCCN 2017027712 (ebook) | ISBN 9780749480899 (ebook) | ISBN 9780749480882 (alk. paper)
Subjects: LCSH: Conflict management. | Interpersonal conflict–Prevention. | Personnel management.
Classification: LCC HD42 (print) | LCC HD42 .L53 2017 (ebook) | DDC 658.4/053–dc23

Typeset by Integra Software Services, Pondicherry
Print production managed by Jellyfish
Printed and bound by CPI Group (UK) Ltd, Croydon, CR0 4YY

CONTENTS

05   Measuring the costs of conflict 89

06   The psychology of conflict and conflict management 112

07   The resolution spectrum 136

Bonus online-only materials are available at the following url (please scroll to the bottom of the web page and complete the form to access these):

www.koganpage.com/ManagingConflict

ACKNOWLEDGEMENTS

A massive thank you to the following people and organizations who contributed to this book and without whose help it would not have been possible:

The Chartered Institute of Personnel and Development (CIPD)

The Institute of Administration Management (IAM)

The TCM Group

The Professional Mediators' Association (PMA)

Arcadia Group

Tesco

London Ambulance Service

Hastings Borough Council

Red Funnell Ferries

University of Greenwich

The Royal Marsden NHS Foundation Trust

St George's University Hospitals NHS Foundation Trust

Hertfordshire Police Federation

Royal Lancaster London Hotel

Capgemini

Northumbria Healthcare NHS Foundation Trust

University of Westminster

Geoban (part of the Santander Group)

Parcelforce Worldwide

Onesoure (outsourced back office functions for the London Boroughs of Havering and Newham)

The Arbitration and Conciliation Advisory Service (ACAS)

The Trade Unions Congress (TUC)

The Confederation of British Industry (CBI)

Angie Juttner-Hart

Marie Coombes from Royal Mail

Owen Bubbers

Bola Oginni

John Ford

Paul Latreille and Richard Saundry

Victoria and Albert Museum

BNY Mellon

A special thanks to the TCM team in London who managed to do amazing work while I have been working on this book and also to my wonderful wife, Jayne and my three beautiful children Daniel, Ethan and Imogen, who have been so supportive and understanding – thank you all xxx.

Introduction

Conflict is in the news every minute of every day of every week. It has probably always been that way. However, the news over the past few years seems to have been about rapidly rising levels of division, disengagement and dissatisfaction, within the United Kingdom and further afield. The banking crisis and the worldwide impact that this has had, the EU referendum in the United Kingdom, the breakdown in trust with our once cherished institutions, the presidential election in the United States, the rise of the far Right, the bloody civil war in Syria, terrorist atrocities across the world, the seemingly irrepressible nature of Daesh and the myriad other wars and conflicts, all make the world feel a little less stable and a bit more unsafe than it has done for many years, certainly in my lifetime. Conflict, it seems, is rife.

From my 25 years working as a mediator and a conflict management professional, in one form or another, I have become used to working with emotionally charged and complex conflicts: where two or more sides are engaged in a battle of wills with a focus on winning that seems to impede their ability to remain rational and that significantly distorts their perspectives. I have seen the best of conflict and I have seen the worst.

Beating the bullies

Over the past 25 years, I have set up and run a charity that specializes in mediating in community disputes and I've set up mediation and restorative justice (victim/offender mediation) programmes across the United Kingdom, including a scheme I established that aimed to tackle bullying in schools by training young people to act as peer mediators. The project became known as The Conflict Resolution in Schools Programme (CRISP). CRISP was ground-breaking in its approach to tackling bullying and it had a real impact, not just on the young people who were trained as mediators or who engaged in mediation, but also on the teaching staff and parents. In 1998, CRISP featured in a powerful and thought-provoking BBC1 documentary called 'Beating the Bullies'.[1]

My toughest mediation ever

People often ask me: 'David, what was your toughest ever mediation case?' I remember vividly the toughest assignment that I ever mediated. I was invited to mediate in the aftermath of a young girl's unlawful killing by her ex-boyfriend, who went on to commit suicide that same night. The two families were devastated and diametrically opposed. A shrine set up in the boy's memory had been desecrated and the entire community had been torn in two.

The inquest had been scheduled and the police's family liaison officer (FLO) requested mediation to help calm the dangerously strained relations between the two families. I spent several weeks shuttling between them before, one Saturday, bringing them together to meet each other in a local hotel. The mediation was one of the most emotional experiences of my life and, without a shred of doubt, theirs also. Slowly, the two families began talking and it was evident that they had a lot they needed to say to each other. On the day of the inquest, the father of the dead girl stated, via the local newspaper, that he understood the other family had experienced a loss too and he had sympathy for the boy's family. Prior to the mediation, he and his wife saw the boy (and his family) as the devil incarnate. I use that case as a benchmark – if those two families can come into a room together and begin to resolve their differences, then anyone can.

Total Conflict Management

Inspired by the impact of mediation in complex and seemingly intractable community disputes, I saw a growing need for organizations to adopt a similar approach for resolving conflict in the workplace. After studying an MBA, in 2001 I set up a specialist consultancy to help organizations, big and small, to embed person-centred and values-based approaches for managing conflict, change and crisis – I called this new approach Total Conflict Management (TCM).

TCM is a system for embedding constructive remedies to conflict across the entire organization. Since 2001, I have worked with numerous HR professionals, managers and leaders, lawyers, union officials and many others, to help them to redesign the landscape of conflict management and to embed a TCM approach. This has included helping organizations to transform their traditional approaches to conflict and challenging the conventional wisdom that conflict can be resolved by simply applying a policy or a procedure or, worse, by avoiding it and hoping it will go away.

This book draws on evidence from a growing number of organizations that are rejecting the traditional grievance and dispute resolution processes in favour a greater focus on early resolution, roundtable facilitation and mediation. These include the London Ambulance Service, Topshop/Topman, Capgemini, Parcelforce Worldwide, University of Westminster, Tesco, The Royal Lancaster Hotel, London Borough of Newham, The Association of Administration Management and Northumbria Healthcare NHS Foundation Trust.

The challenges of managing conflict

In Spring 2015, the Chartered Institute of Personnel and Development (CIPD) published two ground-breaking reports into the causes, costs and consequences of conflict in the workplace. These reports examined the limitations of the traditional approaches for managing conflict at work and explored the role of innovative new approaches for tackling conflict such as mediation (CIPD, March 2015; April 2015). Where the CIPD defined the nature of the problem, I have, within this book, attempted to provide a clear solution.

My journey of organizational conflict management has brought me into contact with many interesting fields, including management and leadership, human resources, employment law, employee wellbeing and engagement, labour relations and organizational development. I have come up against a plethora of challenges to overcome in terms of embedding a compassionate and collaborative approach for managing conflict. However, for those organizations that have had the courage to embrace a new form of conflict management the results have been incredible: enhanced employee wellbeing, increased employee engagement and customer experience, leadership capability, performance management, reputation management, risk management and of course employee productivity and happiness.

It's not been easy. We often think that it won't happen to us, that conflict is something that only happens in badly managed, poorly organized and dysfunctional teams. Conflict is viewed by many as a destructive and damaging phenomenon – an unpleasant by-product of working life. For others, conflict is seen as someone else's problem: an HR professional maybe, or a line manager, or a union official or perhaps a stress counsellor who will magically fix it and make it go away. Some view conflict as a risk and have designed meticulous policies and processes to mitigate the risk and reduce the damage or the threat of future litigation. Of course, these risk management systems (also known as rules and HR procedures) protect the organization from a small percentage of the working population. Paradoxically, the majority of employees are left with a policy framework that is at best cumbersome and at worse adversarial and divisive. In other cases, conflict is used by the protagonists as a tool to help get the work done and achieve their objectives. While we have seen a relative decline in collective disputes over the past 40 years. it is self-evident that some of the protagonists in many of the recent, high-profile industrial relations disputes use conflict strategically. The parties appear to purposefully maintain high levels of conflict to give their roles meaning and to give their cause a boost. Labour relations conflict is used as a proxy for wider political discord. Irrespective of the cost or the damage caused to themselves, to colleagues, to customers or to society as a whole, the protagonists have a vested interest in the conflict perpetuating and perhaps even worsening. As someone once said, 'That's a heck of a way to run a railroad.'

During these uncertain times, the need to manage conflict better has never been greater. Organizations, like society more widely, are adapting quickly to the promises and the threats arising from the digital revolution, climate change, increasing life expectancy, a shift to a knowledge-based economy, greater globalization and cultural diversity. In a 'post-truth' world where trust in our leaders, in accepted norms and in our institutions is being severely challenged, the skills and processes to manage conflict effectively are no longer a 'nice to have': they are a 'need to have'.

The world is less certain than it was and our organizations are microcosms of this uncertain world. Conflict is at the heart of that uncertainty: both a cause and a symptom. Organizations, again as with society, are experiencing unprecedented levels of volatility, uncertainty, complexity and ambiguity – these are VUCA times. However, this uncertainty, as with conflict, presents huge opportunities as well as huge threats. Managing conflict effectively can result in the development of positive and lasting relationships that are resilient and sustainable. Conflict, when managed well, can result in the most powerful of outcomes – flow and insight. Flow and insight are the basis for human and business growth. Insight is the foundation for innovation, collaboration and competitive advantage; flow is about being ready to engage in adult-to-adult dialogue and being open to change. To generate flow and insight, our organizations need to value emotional intelligence as a core competence of leadership.

Organizations need to enhance leaders' and managers' levels of self-awareness; their ability to develop empathy with others; their ability to predict emotionally charged situations and to manage them effectively – to be emotionally intelligent. We also have to equip managers and leaders with the tools they need to model a calm, engaged, collaborative and compassionate approach during times of change, conflict, crisis or controversy. We need our managers and leaders to 'walk the talk': leadership behaviours have to become aligned with the organization's values.

Redefining resolution

This book challenges the existing paradigms for managing conflict. It is hard to do so without being honest and critical in one's appraisal of the traditional processes for managing conflict and, in particular, the traditional grievance, discipline and anti-bullying policies that are embedded in so many employee handbooks. My intention is not to blame or point the finger at any person or group. What this book aims to do is to shine a light on what I, and others, believe is going wrong and to offer practical and proven alternatives. However, my view, expressed in this book, could not be clearer: the traditional policies and practices for resolving workplace disputes are worsening conflicts and, rather than facilitating their resolution, they are perpetuating division and damaging relationships.

The cost of conflict

According to many scholars, as well as contributors within this book, unresolved conflict has a significant human as well as a financial and a reputational impact on their organization. They report a decline in employee wellbeing, employee engagement, performance and overall effectiveness as a result of unresolved conflicts. For businesses as a whole, conflict is a drain on resources, in particular time and money. Conflict is also described by many contributors as a threat to business effectiveness, reputation, customer experience, major projects, teamworking and competitive advantage – and the scale of the problem is becoming clearer every day:

- According to a major report published by the CIPD in 2015, four out of every 10 employees in the United Kingdom has experienced some form of interpersonal conflict within the past 12 months.[2]
- According to recent ONS data, the United Kingdom has one of the lowest productivity levels of the G7 nations.[3]
- The United Kingdom is ranked ninth out of 12 leading industrial nations for employee engagement.[4]
- Unresolved conflict costs the United Kingdom economy a staggering £33 billion a year according to CEDR/CBI.[5]

These statistics are not coincidental – they are, in my view, directly linked, although more research needs to be done to explore the relationship between conflict and overall business performance. Nonetheless, for something that presents such a clear risk, it is a surprise that so few organizations take the issue of conflict seriously. Even fewer have coherent conflict management strategies in place that can help them to prevent conflicts escalating, or have effective mechanisms in place to manage the conflicts that do.

A lack of a conflict management strategy undermines efforts to resolve it

Conflict is often treated as an afterthought. Organizations' policies and systems for handling it are reactive; boards and senior management teams ignore it, yet they expect their HR teams and line managers to deal with it. It is handled on a case-by-case basis and organizations are woefully ineffective at gathering data and learning the lessons from previous conflicts.

There is a myth that organizations have a legal or a statutory duty to have a 'grievance procedure'. This is not the case, nor has it ever been the case. However, this is the procedure that many organizations rely on to resolve a dispute at work. The grievance procedure seems to have a mythical quality, which means that it is rarely questioned or challenged. Chapter 4, prepared by partners at the law firm Lewis Silkin, critiques this approach and advocates, as do I, the development of a more progressive policy framework.

The book provides a tried and tested framework for organizations that wish to redefine resolution including, in Chapter 9, a unique and innovative policy template for managing conflict – the resolution policy. The Capgemini, Newham Council and Royal Lancaster Hotel case studies included in the book exemplify the benefits of adopting a resolution policy framework.

Dealing with the 'F words' of the modern organization

This book provides practical tools and tips to assist with the management of the 'F words' that seem to be overlooked in much of the management literature. Yet, when handled effectively, these F words are vital to personal, collective and business success:

- *Fights* – how to resolve conflicts courageously, constructively and collaboratively.
- *Feelings* – how to respond to strong emotions and give them meaning and relevance. Critically, how, with empathy, to use feelings to better understand another person's needs.

- *Fear* – how to have confident conversations, how to overcome our own fears and how to manage others without the use of fear.

- *Failure* – how to handle mistakes and learn from them while avoiding blame and retribution.

- *Forgiveness* – how to move on and how to let go.

- *Flow* – how to engage in a dialogue with others that opens up connections, promotes understanding, creates meaning and delivers insight.

An emerging role for mediation

This book profiles the best of contemporary conflict management approaches and includes practical tools and advice for organizations (big and small) that are considering implementing or expanding a conflict management strategy. The main focus is on mediation, as I believe (and the evidence increasingly supports this), that mediation is one of the most effective forms of dispute resolution available.

Mediation is an incredibly powerful remedy to conflict. It can, and should, be used to resolve a lot more disputes in the workplace than is currently the case. Ultimately, mediation is a process in which two or more disputing parties have a dialogue with one another to resolve a dispute with the help of a neutral third party. Mediation is not rocket science yet it is still widely misunderstood. This book aims to resolve that. Academic research plus numerous case studies contained within this book suggests that mediation is successful in as many as 9 out of 10 cases.

When one compares that with the miserable and damaging experience that most people have when they encounter the current systems for managing conflict it seems, to quote Winston Churchill (1954), that 'Jaw, jaw is always better than war, war.'[6] This book examines how more and more organizations are developing internal mediation schemes and training in-house mediators. At the end of the book, there are several practical toolkits and templates that will enable you to develop a mediation scheme within your own organization.

Introducing the 'resolution spectrum'

Regardless of its effectiveness, mediation is not always going to be the best (or the preferred) option. This book also explores a range of alternative options that organizations can apply at times of conflict, including:

- resolution triage assessment;
- early resolution meetings;

- facilitated roundtable conversations;
- early neutral evaluation;
- mediation; and
- team conferencing.

These approaches are the 'resolution spectrum'. Embedding a variety of proactive and empowering approaches for securing a constructive and lasting resolution delivers significant benefits, for small businesses and global blue-chip corporations. This book examines the applications, the benefits and the impact of the resolution spectrum in relation to:

- workplace conflict;
- bullying and harassment;
- labour relations and collective disputes;
- boardroom disputes;
- shareholder disputes;
- customer or consumer disputes;
- work and project team conflict; and
- conflicts arising from mergers and acquisitions.

This book doesn't make any wild assertions or tap into fashionable HR or management ideology. The book is about one simple principle: dialogue. Without dialogue, conflicts worsen. With dialogue, they can be resolved. It's simple – or at least it should be. This book will explore why many organizations are failing to create adult-to-adult dialogue at times of conflict and what can be done to bring dialogue back into the vernacular, the culture and the mindset of the modern workplace. This book will change the way that you think about conflict. Welcome to the resolution revolution!

Resolution reflection

- What prompted you to pick up this book?
- What do you need this book to deliver for you?
- As you think about resolving conflict, what are you most excited about?

- What fears do you have about managing conflict?
- If you had no constraints whatsoever, how would you tackle conflict within your organization?
- What is stopping you from achieving these aspirations right now?

Objectives of this book

In this book I share my own experiences of what I believe works (and doesn't work) and I draw on case studies and insights gathered during numerous in-depth interviews with HR professionals, business leaders, policy makers, trade unionists, managers, scholars, mediators and, of course, employees whose lives have been changed by conflict. The book aims to redefine our understanding of conflict and to promote conflict management as a strategic imperative for policy makers, business leaders, HR professionals, lawyers, union leaders and employees – for each and every one of us. The objectives that I had in mind as I was writing this book were:

- To demonstrate that there are two types of conflict, of which only one is damaging and harmful: *dysfunctional conflict*. The other is valuable, productive and healthy: *functional conflict*.
- To encourage organizations to make conflict management a strategic priority.
- To help leaders, policy makers and others to create organizational systems, processes and cultures that promote, encourage and embrace healthy (functional) conflict rather than harmful (dysfunctional) conflict.
- To provide a clear explanation of what conflict is and how it escalates, following a broadly predictable lifecycle.
- To shine a light on the human and the organizational causes of conflict.
- To showcase best practice in conflict management from organizations that have begun to think differently about conflict management.
- To examine the costs of conflict and to provide guidance for organizations that wish to measure those costs.
- To provide guidance for organizations wishing to create a resolution policy as an alternative to their traditional grievance procedure.
- To provide guidance on the legal framework for managing conflict currently in place within the United Kingdom.

- To provide an international perspective of conflict management.
- To provide practical tools, tips and templates for HR, unions, lawyers, leaders and managers to help them secure better outcomes from conflict.

How to use this book

- Each chapter includes opportunities for personal reflection; these are called: 'resolution reflection'.
- Resolution recommendations provide handy hints and tips.
- References and other sources are listed at the end of many of the chapters.
- The chapters contain a range of practical tools and tips for use. These can be adapted and modified to meet the specific needs of your organization.
- Part Three of the book contains a number of practical tools and templates that you are free to amend and use within your organization to support the development of your conflict management strategy.

References

CIPD (2015) *Conflict Management: A shift in direction?* CIPD, London
CIPD (2015) *Getting Under the Skin of Workplace Conflict: Tracing the experiences of employees,* CIPD, London

Notes

1 Documentary available to watch from http://truevisiontv.com/films/details/87/beating-the-bullies

2 www.cipd.co.uk/Images/getting-under-skin-workplace-conflict_2015-tracing-experiences-employees_tcm18-10800.pdf

3 www.ons.gov.uk/economy/economicoutputandproductivity/productivitymeasures/bulletins/internationalcomparisonsofproductivityfinalestimates/2014

4 http://engageforsuccess.org/wp-content/uploads/2015/09/The-Evidence.pdf

5 https://www.cedr.com/news/?item=Conflict-is-costing-business-GBP-33-billion-every-year

6 http://www.bartleby.com/73/1914.html

PART ONE
Putting conflict into context

What's wrong with contemporary conflict management and what can organizations do about it?

Grievances kill the employment relationship. (Head of employee relations, global drinks company, CIPD, March 2015)

KEY LEARNING POINTS IN THIS CHAPTER

- Workplace conflict is a taboo subject and it is widely misunderstood. This makes it hard for organizations to acknowledge it and to manage it.
- Conflict is inevitable and unavoidable. It will always exist and it affects every one of us.
- There are broadly two types of conflict: dysfunctional (unhealthy and destructive) and functional (healthy and constructive).
- Resulting from organizations' focus on managing the risks and fallout from dysfunctional conflict, the potential to transform conflict into functional, healthy and constructive dialogue is often missed.

- Rights-based, adversarial, divisive and confrontational policy frameworks such as the traditional grievance procedure and bullying policies are ineffective at managing workplace conflict. Evidence suggests that these policies are harming employees, teams and organizations as a whole.

- Over the past 10 years, there has been a lack of coherent guidance from policy makers for organizations that wish to adopt innovative systems for managing conflict such as resolution triage assessments, early resolution, facilitated roundtable conversations or mediation.

- Simply referring to mediation in the introduction of the ACAS Code on Discipline and Grievance fails to deliver the message that mediation and associated ADR (alternative dispute resolution) approaches offer a valuable and highly effective remedy to workplace conflict.

- There is a common myth that organizations have a statutory (legal) duty to have a grievance procedure. They do not and they never have done.

Putting conflict into context

Sarah and Mike were in a long running dispute following a comment that Mike overheard Sarah making one day on the phone. She accepted that she described him as 'disorganized and unprofessional' but she maintains that it was said as a joke. Mike didn't see the funny side and refused to speak to Sarah for six months. One Tuesday, Mike got cross with Sarah about a relatively minor issue. He allegedly shouted at her and was verbally abusive. Sarah put in a grievance against Mike. The issue was investigated over a period of six weeks and a panel was convened to reach a determination. The outcome was that there was no case to answer. Sarah felt that no one believed her and that she wasn't trusted – she left the business shortly after. Mike felt let down by the whole process and he became reclusive and quiet. He didn't bother applying for a promotion, believing that this was a stain against his name.

Workplace conflict is one of the most enduring taboos

Workplace conflict is something of a taboo subject. No one really likes to talk about it. Organizations are often loath to admit that it is a problem and I hear very few people boasting that their organization benefits from it. Organizational conflict management strategies are generally vague (if indeed there are any) and many organizations rely on HR processes such as grievance procedures and bullying policies to resolve interpersonal disputes or workplace conflicts.

Some organizations, particularly in smaller businesses, where there may be less of a policy framework in place, depend on the discretionary activity of managers who may (or may not) have the courage, the confidence and the competence to deal with the underlying issues effectively and to help the parties achieve a resolution. Other organizations deny that conflict exists, suppress it and avoid dealing with it. In these cases, the conflicts can manifest in a number of ways that I will explore in more detail in Chapter 2. Suffice to say that suppressed conflicts can have the most damaging and destructive impact imaginable and when the volcano erupts it can have a significant impact on all concerned, not to mention the 'collateral damage' that can be caused. In those cases, conflict becomes a threat and a major risk to the individuals involved, their colleagues, their managers and potentially to the whole organization.

So why is this still happening?

Conflict is a complex subject and it requires a sophisticated and nuanced approach. The best response is to promote dialogue between the disputing parties. However, too many organizations still turn to formal processes for managing conflict in the belief that these will spit out two happy people and a lasting resolution. They don't.

Our reliance on formal processes to resolve conflict at work is anathema. In 2007, Michael Gibbons was commissioned by the UK government to undertake a root and branch review of workplace dispute resolution. I was actively involved in that review and I vividly recall sitting in consultation meetings at 1 Victoria Street in London (home of the then Department for Trade and Industry) hearing numerous tales of failed approaches to resolving workplace disputes that had resulted in significant escalation and great business and human cost. Gibbons' seminal report *Better Dispute Resolution* (Gibbons, 2007) paved the way for the repeal of the Dispute Resolution Regulations.

Gibbons highlighted that organizations relied too heavily on formal approaches for managing conflicts that could have been resolved at an informal level. He suggested that organizations' reliance on formal approaches had a serious and a negative impact:

Problems escalate, taking up more management time. Employees find themselves engaged in unnecessarily formal and stressful processes...the use of formal processes in cases where other approaches would be more appropriate affects the climate for resolution, and makes parties defensive and more likely to consider an employment tribunal from the outset. (Lederach, 2003)

It is now 10 years since the Gibbons review and the subsequent repeal of the Dispute Resolution Regulations. Yet the above paragraph could still be applied to most employees' and managers' experience of conflict management within our organizations today. However, in his report, Gibbons (2007) set out the case for mediation and ADR perfectly clearly:

It is clear that the earlier a dispute is settled, the better it will be for all concerned, eg in terms of disruption to businesses and lives, and associated costs. Early resolution can also involve outcomes not available through the tribunal system such as a positive job reference, an apology and changes in behaviour. Mediation and other alternative dispute resolution techniques are effective means of achieving early resolution.

The question persists: why are such approaches, and in particular mediation, still so underutilized? – a question that I will come back to in Chapter 10.

Resolution reflection

- Does your organization have a conflict management strategy that pulls together your various efforts to manage customer complaints, employee grievances and team disputes?
- If not, what impact does this have?
- What benefit would a conflict management strategy offer to your organization?

One particularly interesting piece of research that begins to shine a light on the problems with contemporary conflict management was published in 2016: *Managing Individual Conflict in the Contemporary British Workplace*. I draw on this and other pieces of research throughout this book. That report states:

The problems facing organizations in managing conflict... stem from the lack of conflict competence among frontline managers; the erosion of structures of employee representation; and the increasing remoteness of HR. This, in turn, reflects the failure of employers to recognize the strategic importance of effective conflict management. (Saundry *et al*, 2016)

The research suggests three factors that contribute to conflict in the workplace are:

1 Lack of the skills that managers need to possess to manage conflict.

2 Erosion of the structures by which employees can have their voices heard either through unions or informal means.

3 An HR function that focuses increasingly on transformational and strategic activities rather than the traditional personnel activities of transactional people management. In the new paradigm people management has been delegated to managers – but see point 1.

These three factors are valid and they are a call to arms for organizations; I will address each of these factors throughout this book. However, the authors appear to miss a key point in their analysis. There is a fourth factor and, for some reason, we seem afraid to talk about it. The fourth and possibly most significant factor at play in terms of conflict management is our reliance on a policy framework comprising formal rules and processes for managing conflicts, complaints, disputes and allegations of bullying. The traditional policy framework has a chilling and harmful effect on employees who become increasingly infantilized, disengaged and disadvantaged; on working relationships that become increasingly polarized, hostile and tense; on work teams that become increasingly divided, fractured and less resilient; and on organizations as a whole that become less efficient, less productive and a lot less harmonious.

While giving an outward appearance that conflicts and disputes are being taken seriously, that there is a consistency of approach, that the approach is legally compliant and that the organization is delivering 'procedural fairness', the reality of traditional discipline, grievance and bullying policies is:

- The underlying issues are not being resolved.
- Relationships are being irrevocably damaged.
- There is substantial inconsistency in the application of the rules by managers who are not trained or supported adequately.
- A blame culture emerges that can translate into a culture of conflict avoidance.
- The policies take far too long to generate an outcome.
- The parties, the teams and the overall business needs are overlooked and ignored.
- Opportunities for insight, dialogue and transformation are missed.
- The policies generate increasing levels of stress, anxiety, depression and the associated absence.

In a report published by the Chartered Institute of Personnel and Development (CIPD) in 2015 entitled *Conflict Management: A shift in direction?* the authors state:

> Most employers say that once an issue has entered the grievance procedure, it generally becomes much more difficult to resolve... the use of the grievance procedure can be emotionally wearing for both employer and employee. (p 12)

The CIPD report cites a number of stories from senior human resources professionals and business leaders who have a less than positive perspective of the traditional grievance process:

> Grievances [are often] based on misperceptions; grievances are tough for the individual. We see discipline and grievance processes as a last resort. (Head of HR, global asset management)

> Managers worry if they deviate from the procedure in the Code. (Managing associate, law firm)

The last statement is the one that I find interesting and disturbing. Surely managing conflict is about taking risks, being innovative and crafting new solutions to complex problems? How and why do managers and HR fear deviating from The ACAS Code on Discipline and Grievance? Why do they adhere to a policy framework that they know is doomed to failure? After all, the ACAS Code sets out a minimum standard for employers to follow; it is not a manual for managing complex interpersonal conflict in the workplace.

The fear of future litigation is destabilizing our organizations and the more that can be done to address this issue the better. As illustrated in Chapters 4 and 9 of this book, organizations simply need to provide a statement that sets out the mechanism for employees to raise a grievance against their employer. There is no statutory requirement to have a grievance procedure and there is absolutely no requirement to address interpersonal issues via such a mechanism. The room for innovation in how we manage conflict is vast.

The ACAS Code on discipline and grievance sets out a recommended minimum framework and the tribunals welcome any attempts to resolve issues at an early stage. In fact, a growing number of employment judges have been trained to act as mediators through a process called 'judicial mediation'. I always felt that the term 'judicial mediation' was an oxymoron but it is great to see the judiciary subscribing to the principles of ADR and I celebrate this development.

Thankfully, while many lawyers still believe that the threat of litigation is a stick that can be used to leverage a deal, some are now rejecting litigation in favour of a more compassionate and less costly remedy to conflict.

Camilla Palmer QC is an employment lawyer who saw plenty of conflict during her time as a litigator:

> I saw the appalling impact on an employee of bringing a claim: their life was put on hold, it was expensive and it was stressful… the only ones who benefited were the lawyers, but the clients were the ones who paid out. Even if the employee wins, they don't necessarily get what they want and it can negatively impact their future careers and their reputations.

Camilla has now rejected litigation in favour of non-adversarial dispute resolution. She is the joint CEO of a fast-growing charity that promotes non-adversarial remedies to employment disputes: YESS Law (Your Employment Settlement Service). Camilla explained to me what drove that change for her:

> While litigation is important in some cases, on the whole litigation delivers a lose/lose outcome. Lawyers and litigation ratchets up the fury. It has a damaging impact on the parties. Barristers are taught to go into battle – litigation is a deeply adversarial process. Grievances are much the same, they ratchet things up, are rarely upheld and they inhibit a resolution. The parties do not benefit from these processes. What employees often want is an apology. Lots of grievances and litigation could be avoided if the word 'sorry' was used more often.

Camilla has a clear vision for the future of dispute resolution:

> We should replace grievances with a more conciliatory approach and the ACAS Code of Practice should be amended to focus on raising issues and resolving them based on the structure and principles of the resolution policy. There needs to be more emphasis on finding solutions; employees should be encouraged to raise issues as an early stage and HR should be focused on securing resolution. The culture of an organization should encourage employees to raise issues at an early stage.

The only real benefit that I can see of such rigid rules and processes for managing conflict is that the perceived legal risk to the business is minimized, in so much as key players can state at any future legal process: 'We were just following the stated procedure.' Such approaches treat conflict as though all conflict is harmful and dysfunctional. This is a shameful waste of a good opportunity. Organizational policies for managing conflict are, in and of themselves, divisive, reductive and binary, ie they divide the parties into camps; they reduce conflict to right/wrong, win/lose, attack/defend and they require black and white evidence so that a case can be proven or not proven. Such rules and processes do not acknowledge that conflict can be creative, healthy and positive – that conflict can be functional and even transformational – when it is managed well. The CIPD (March 2015) agrees:

> There may be some truth in the view that… formal procedures are ineffective because they encourage parties to set battle lines, fostering a zero-sum game mentality and making views more entrenched, instead of encouraging a more balanced and positive win-win outlook.

The bottom line is that, for the parties in conflict, it can be one of the most dreadful, painful and depressing experiences they have ever had. For those people required to manage a conflict, it can be baffling, complex, stressful, costly and time-consuming.

Resolution reflection

Think of a conflict that you have experienced at some point in your life:

- How did it start and how did it end?
- How did it feel?
- What impact did it have on the other person?
- Was anyone else affected by it and how?
- Did you use a formal process such as a grievance procedure?
- What impact did it have?
- How was it resolved?
- If you could go back in time and give yourself a piece of advice to help resolve the conflict, what would it be?

Here's my hunch: I bet you didn't go back in time and suggest that you take out a grievance against the other person or that you stop talking to them. Can I be so bold as to assume that you may have said 'act earlier' or 'talk to them' or 'listen to them'?

If early resolution, talking and listening are so innately the best way to resolve conflict, why are we so afraid of doing it? Perhaps it's the nature of conflict, perhaps we are confused about what conflict is and that leads to fear and paralysis, which inhibit the opportunities for dialogue.

What is conflict?

Conflict occurs when one person (or a group) perceives that another person (or a group) is preventing him or her achieving his or her needs or is blocking him or her from expressing his or her values and beliefs in a way that he or she thinks is reasonable. Conflict is a perfectly normal part of being a human being. It can be internal – inside our heads, or it can be external – with others. Often, internal and external conflicts feed off each other – that's why it can be hard to sleep when you are in conflict with a colleague.

In the above definition I use the word 'perceives'. Conflict pivots between functional or dysfunctional conflict based on our perceptions. Conflict management is about helping people to modify or 'reframe' their perceptions of themselves and of the other person. For example:

- 'They did it on purpose' becomes 'It's impacted negatively on me but I don't really know what their intentions were.'

- 'They are wrong' becomes 'Neither of us is entirely wrong nor entirely right.'

- 'They are a bully' becomes 'They have hurt me and I need them to stop.'

Conflict can be toxic, harmful and destructive. It can also be a powerful driver of change, learning and growth. We can choose to ignore it, complain about it, blame someone for it, or try to deal with it indirectly by gossiping and dropping hints. Or we can be direct, clarify what is going on, and attempt to reach a resolution. The key phrase in this sentence is that *we can choose* how to deal with it. There are numerous definitions of conflict and it is something of a complex area spanning social psychology, behavioural sciences and neuroscience. However, cutting through that complexity is important if organizations and their people are going to embed effective systems for managing it.

As mentioned earlier, as human beings we experience two forms of conflict. The first is the kind of conflict that goes on inside our minds – *internal conflict*. We may experience it when we have a difficult choice to make; when we are faced with a moral dilemma; or when we are tackling a tough personal problem such as ending an addiction or ending a relationship. The internal conflict occurs when part of you disagrees with the other part of you. This dissonance, or tension, can create strong feelings and emotions such as guilt, self-blame, shame, frustration and anger. We may feel like we are going crazy and that we can't make sense of the situation. The outward symptoms of a difficult internal conflict can include:

- Not sleeping properly (insomnia).
- Inability to 'switch off' or relax.
- Feeling tired all of the time (often because of the lack of sleep and inability to relax).
- Struggling to concentrate on tasks and during conversations.
- Irritability or mood swings.
- Physiological symptoms may include irritable bowel syndrome (IBS), eczema, weight gain/loss, increased propensity to pick up cold and flu bugs, feeling run down, backache and painful shoulders or necks, etc.

However, over time, we generally figure out how to resolve the internal conflict and we reach a decision or a resolution. Over time, sleep returns, the stress and anxiety dissipate and the issues, which seemed so tough and intractable at the time, mysteriously disappear and are forgotten. We move on and, hopefully, along the way we learnt something useful about ourselves. Unfortunately, in some instances of internal conflict, the resolution doesn't happen and it can lead to long-term mental health issues or worse.

Resolution reflection

Reflect on an internal conflict that you have experienced:

- What impact did it have on you?
- How did you resolve it?
- What did you learn from it?

The second kind of conflict that we may experience is conflict with others – *external conflict*. Managing eternal conflict is the main focus of this book. However, it is important to stress that external conflict can, and often does, result from an unresolved internal conflict. As a mediator, I understand that it is important to give all parties in a conflict time to work out their own internal issues: before, during or after they have worked out their differences with a colleague, a co-worker, a union representative, a boss or a customer. External conflict occurs when an individual (or a group of individuals), believe that another individual (or a group of individuals) is preventing him or her from achieving his or her needs or goals; preventing access to the resources he or she requires to achieve his or her needs or goals; or preventing him or her from expressing his or her values or beliefs in a way which he or she considers to be reasonable.

When we are gripped by conflict (internal or external) our brain becomes a bit like a mad scientist's laboratory. A small almond-shaped part of our brain called the amygdala gets very excited and we experience a range of complex chemical events. In particular, we experience the release of a variety of hormones such as adrenalin and cortisol. (We are going to get to know these two hormones well and I will cover them in more detail in Chapter 6 along with some valuable insights and useful steps for you to use to help you resolve conflict using the principles of positive psychology and emotional intelligence.)

Conflicts can exist at any level of an organization and at any stage of its development. Conflict between two employees may arise from a disagreement about how to complete a particular task or a clash between their personal values, goals or expectations. Within a work team, conflicts can result from a change process, revised working practices, a lack of role clarity or a lack of coherent leadership. Within a project team, conflict may be due to differing priorities, competition over scarce resources, unclear objectives or remote working patterns. (See Chapter 3 for more detail relating to the causes of conflict.)

According to John Paul Lederach, distinguished conflict transformation expert and scholar: 'Conflict is normal in human relationships and conflict is a motor of change' (Lederach, 2003). He recognizes, as do I, that conflicts, when managed effectively can bring about lasting change – internally and externally. Lederach is one of the key drivers in the area of conflict transformation, a process that I describe simply as being a positive and lasting change in the way that we perceive ourselves and others.

Carl Gustav Jung, the Swiss psychologist and psychotherapist, also suggests that we need conflict in our lives to create stronger relationships:

> The most intense conflicts, if overcome, leave behind a sense of security and calm that is not easily disturbed. It is just these intense conflicts and their conflagration which are needed to produce valuable and lasting results. (Jung, 1875–1961)

Jung and Lederach demonstrate deep insight into the nature of conflict and its potential impact on each and every one of us. They recognize that only if they are overcome can we realize the true benefit of conflict. For many of us, 'overcome' can sometimes seem a million miles away. My hope is that mediation and the concerted efforts of organizations to manage conflict better make the 'if overcome' clause more accessible, real and meaningful.

The two types of conflict

Table 1.1   The two types of conflict

Conflict state	Descriptor
Dysfunctional conflict	This is destructive conflict. It is harmful, stressful and costly. Dysfunctional conflict generates little, if any, benefit for the parties, their colleagues or the organization as a whole. Dysfunctional conflict may also be called affective conflict, bullying, mobbing, intimidation, harassment, oppression, discrimination, violence or confrontation. This kind of conflict rarely ends well.
	If left unresolved, dysfunctional conflicts will have a significant impact on the psychological, emotional and physiological wellbeing of employees and managers. It can be insidious, subtle, hard to define and hard to manage. It may be mistakenly written off as 'banter' or 'letting off steam'. Team leaders and managers need to explore ways of responding to dysfunctional conflict swiftly and robustly and be trained in setting boundaries and helped to address the language and the behaviours associated with dysfunctional and destructive conflict.
	This kind of conflict takes (and keeps) the parties into the 'ZONC' – The Zone of Negative Conflict.
	In Chapter 5, I explore the costs and the effects of destructive conflict in greater detail.
Functional conflict	This is constructive conflict. The parties are engaged in dialogue and they are focused on achieving an outcome that is mutually acceptable. The parties seek win/win outcomes and neither party wishes to cause harm to the other. it exists where the parties are willing to engage with one another to generate enhanced levels of insight, understanding and learning, Functional conflict requires open and honest dialogue, empathy, self-awareness and a willingness to change – to transform ourselves and our relationships with others.
	Functional conflict may also be called healthy disagreement, creative conflict, cooperative conflict or cognitive conflict.
	This is the kind of conflict that promotes flow and gets the parties into the ZOPA – the Zone of Possible Agreement. Functional conflict is most commonly associated with open and honest dialogue.

Functional conflict is a key component of high-functioning and high-performing teams (see Table 1.1). Conflict arises from differences between people; the same differences that often make diverse teams more effective than those made up of people with similar experiences. An office full of robots won't experience conflict but, conversely, they won't display high levels of innovation, insight and judgement. When people with varying viewpoints, beliefs, experiences, skills and opinions are tasked with a project or a problem to solve, the combined effort can far surpass what any group of similar individuals could achieve. Team members must be open to these differences and not let them turn into full-blown disputes.

Resolution reflection

You become aware of a conflict in your team between two colleagues:

- What do you do?
- What are your fears about dealing with the conflict?
- How will you understand the root cause of the conflict?
- How will you assess the impact of the conflict?
- What steps would you advise them to take to resolve it?

Understanding and appreciating the various viewpoints involved in conflict are key factors in its resolution. These are key skills for all team members, and their leaders, to develop. The important thing is to maintain a healthy balance of constructive difference of opinion, and avoid dysfunctional conflicts that can become destructive and disruptive.

Resolution recommendations

Effective conflict management is about giving people the space, time, support and resources to resolve their internal conflicts as well as their external ones. Getting to, and maintaining, that balance requires well-developed leadership skills, particularly the ability to resolve conflict when it does happen, and the ability to keep it healthy and avoid conflict in the day-to-day course of teamworking.

Conflict mode analysis

In 1974, Kilmann and Thomas identified five styles, or modes, for handling conflict that have become part of the vernacular of conflict management. They help us to understand how we and others relate to others during conflict. The styles are defined by how much our own needs and goals matter to us versus how much the needs and the goals of the other party matter to us:

1 Force.

2 Avoid.

3 Accommodate.

4 Compromise.

5 Collaborate.

Figure 1.1 represents the conflict mode analysis that I use when I am training mediators and leaders to manage conflict effectively, while Table 1.2 expands on Kilmann and Thomas's five styles or modes for handling conflict.

Figure 1.1   Conflict mode analysis

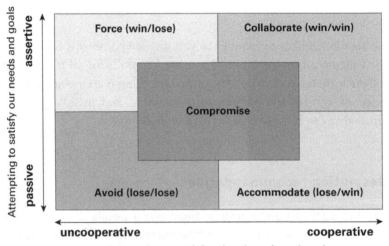

SOURCE Adapted from the Thomas Kilmann Mode Instrument

Table 1.2 The five styles or modes for handling conflict

Avoid – 'The turtle' (withdrawing)

Turtles withdraw into their shells to avoid conflict. They give up their personal goals and relationships. They stay away from the issues over which the conflict is taking place and the people they are in conflict with. Turtles believe it is easier to withdraw (physically and psychologically) from a conflict rather than face it.

Compete – 'The shark' (forcing)

Sharks try to overpower opponents by forcing them to accept their solution to the conflict. Their goals are highly important to them and their relationship is of minor importance. Sharks seek to achieve their own goals at all costs. They are not concerned about the needs of other people. They do not care if other people like or accept them. Sharks assume that one person winning and the other person losing settles conflicts. Sharks want to be the winner. Winning gives sharks a sense of pride and achievement. Losing gives them a sense of inadequacy and failure. They try to win by attacking, overpowering, overwhelming and intimidating others.

Accommodate – 'The teddy bear' (smoothing)

To teddy bears the relationship is of great importance while their own goals are of little importance. Teddy bears want to be accepted and liked by other people. They think that conflict should be avoided in favour of harmony and believe that if the conflict continues, someone will get hurt and that would ruin the relationship. Teddy bears give up their needs and goals to preserve the relationship. Teddy bears say: 'I'll give up what I want and let you have what you want in order for us to get along.' Teddy bears try to smooth over the conflict and avoid causing harm.

Compromise – 'The fox' (middle ground)

Foxes are moderately concerned with their own goals and about the relationship with other people. Foxes seek compromise. They give up a part of their goals and persuade the other person in conflict to give up part of his or her goals. Foxes seek a solution to conflict where both sides gain something – the middle ground between two positions. They are willing to sacrifice part of their goals and relationships in order to find agreement for the common good.

Collaborate – 'The owl' (building consensus)

Owls highly value their own goals and relationships. They view conflicts as problems to be solved and seek a solution that achieves both their own goals and the goals of the other person. Owls see conflict as an opportunity for improving relationships by reducing tension between two people. They try to begin a discussion that identifies the conflict as a problem to be solved. By seeking solutions that satisfy both themselves and the other person, owls maintain the relationship. Owls are not satisfied until a solution is found that achieves their own goals and the other person's goals and until the tensions and negative feelings have been fully resolved.

Resolution reflection

Based on the five styles for managing conflict:

- Which of the five creatures in Table 1.2 represents your primary conflict style most closely?
- Do you have different styles at home and at work? If so why?
- Do you have a secondary style that you use if your primary style is unsuccessful?
- What triggers you to switch between different styles?
- If the owl is the most effective at managing conflict, what changes can you make to help you be an owl as often as possible?

Conclusion

Dysfunctional conflict is bad for business, it is bad for anyone who is required to manage it and it is most certainly bad for the disputing parties. The traditional systems for managing conflict are proving, time and time again, to be ineffective. Yet there seems to be a reluctance by organizations to fully embrace new approaches for managing conflict such as early resolution, resolution triage assessment, facilitated roundtable conversations and mediation. These approaches, are, as this book will demonstrate, proven remedies to conflict.

As the CIPD research has identified, and my own experience confirms, many managers and HR professionals are worried about working outside of a formal structured process for fear of damaging their prospects at a future hearing or litigation. Conversely however, they understand that their traditional discipline, grievance and bullying processes are ineffective and the evidence is incontrovertible. This Catch 22 situation could well be the catalyst for change.

There is a middle ground. It is possible to create a policy framework that also promotes resolution. That way organizations get the best of both worlds – they have access to a coherent procedure that is compliant with the ACAS Code and relevant employment legislation plus a policy framework that promotes dialogue, understanding and resolution.

One size doesn't fit all

Conflict at work is complex and multifaceted. It can span a relationship breakdown between two colleagues in a depot, and a labour dispute over pay and conditions across an entire railway company. Yet behavioural, relationship and contractual issues are dealt with using the same litigation-inspired, quasi-judicial, rights-based remedies. Our reliance on a single grievance procedure to resolve all the intricate, diverse and complex issues that a modern, progressive organization faces is both unrealistic and untenable. This is the root cause of dysfunctional conflict in our organizations and it is the reason I have written this book.

References

CIPD (2015) *Conflict Management: A shift in direction?* CIPD, London, p 12

CIPD (2015) *Getting Under the Skin of Workplace Conflict: Tracing the experiences of employees,* CIPD, London, p 13

Gibbons, M (2007) *Better Dispute Resolution: A review of employment dispute resolution in Great Britain,* DTI, London

Jung, C G (1970) *Structure and Dynamics of the Psyche: Vol 8, Collected Works of Jung,* eds G Adler, M Fordham and H Read, Princeton University Press, Princeton, NJ

Kilmann, R and Thomas, K W (1977) Developing a forced-choice measure of conflict-handling behavior: The 'mode' instrument, *Educational and Psychological Measurement,* 37, p 309

Lederach, J L (2003) *Little Book of Conflict Transformation,* Good Books, Skyhorse Publishing, New York

Saundry, R *et al* (2016) *Managing Individual Conflict in the Contemporary British Workplace,* ACAS, London

The lifecycle of a conflict 02

How and why conflicts escalate

You are not stuck in traffic – you are traffic. (TomTom satnav advert)

KEY LEARNING POINTS IN THIS CHAPTER

- Conflict has a distinct lifecycle that is broadly predictable; it comprises five stages: pre-conflict, early conflict, mid-conflict, late conflict and post-conflict.

- There are a variety of conflict management interventions that can be used at each stage of the conflict lifecycle.

- Conflict avoidance is not a good management strategy – it generally leads to an escalation and simply puts off the inevitable.

- There are several antecedents to a conflict at the pre-conflict stage. Planning conflict management into processes such as project teams and change programmes can be a useful way of preventing dysfunctional conflict from escalating.

- Conflict is nothing to be feared – when it is managed well, at any stage of the conflict lifecycle, it can be a positive and deeply affirming experience for the parties and for the person managing it.

- Corporate conflict management strategies should take account of each stage of the conflict lifecycle and appropriate remedies and resources should be put in place to resolve conflict at each stage.

Introduction

In case you wondered why I used the TomTom quote (with permission, of course) at the start of this chapter, let me explain. I was sat on the M4 one day coming into London. Crawling along in heavy traffic, I looked up and I saw that phrase in an advert on a digital billboard. I'm not saying that sat on the M4 in heavy traffic was my epiphany, but I do remember that moment clearly. I wasn't sat in traffic, I *was* traffic. There was no point in blaming others for the queue that I was sat in: I was that queue. All the other cars, vans, lorries and taxis – they were all going in the same direction as I was and they were all experiencing the same problem that I was. Suddenly the traffic jam became a shared experience, something that we had in common. At that moment, I was part of something bigger than one car stuck in traffic crawling into London – I was traffic.

The same is true of conflict. We are not stuck in conflict, we are conflict. It's not the difficult colleague, the bullying manager or the aloof business partner. We are all experiencing this together and we all understand what it means to be in conflict. Blaming others, pointing the finger and seeking retribution – it's ultimately futile and pointless. The only way to address conflict is to find a shared meaning, a shared solution and a way forward – together.

Conflict is complex and confusing. That's what makes it so hard to manage and, as a mediator, so enjoyable to resolve. In my experience, two of the biggest barriers organizations face when they are managing conflict effectively are: a lack of understanding about what conflict is, and a fear of conflict. In many respects, this entire book is about defining conflict and attempting to make it less daunting and scary for the parties and the people managing it.

Resolution reflection

Consider a conflict that you have been involved in, as a party, an observer or as an intermediary. This may be a workplace conflict, a conflict with friends, a conflict within your family or a conflict with a stranger when you are driving, or in a restaurant or a bar.

- What were the causes of the conflict?
- Were there any observable stages at which the conflict escalated?
- What were the triggers for the conflict escalating?
- What other factors influenced the lifecycle of the conflict?
- How and when was the conflict resolved?

The lifecycle of a conflict

Every conflict, it seems, has a definite lifecycle and most track the same course. Each stage of the conflict presents an opportunity for resolution but also a risk of escalation if it is not dealt with appropriately. My experience has led me to believe that the more that is done to manage conflict at the earliest stages, the less negative impact it will have. Some people describe this as 'nipping conflict in the bud' and I am yet to come up with a better term. It can also be described as conflict prevention.

However, that is not to say that conflict can't also be resolved at the later stages. At the later stages, the parties are often exhausted and many of the routes to resolution have been exhausted also. As the parties stare into what I call 'the precipice of doom', they realize that resolving it now is better than falling over the edge into the unknown. Nothing focuses a mind better than a precipice. In these cases, the parties may have to walk backwards in order to walk forwards – but at least they are moving.

As mediators, we recognize this and that is why we don't blame or judge people – no matter how divisive, damaging and destructive the conflict has become. We support the parties as they make new choices and open their minds to new possibilities. One of those possibilities will now be about engaging in constructive and meaningful adult-to-adult dialogue. During this dialogue the parties become more empathetic and are able to reflect on their underlying interests, needs and goals rather than the strengths of their relative positions.

Over the next few pages, I will explore the five stages of a conflict (shown in Figure 2.1; the five types of team conflict are shown in Figure 2.2). I also set out a series of practical tools and tips to assist you at each stage of the conflict.

Resolution recommendation

When conflict is handled in a supportive and collaborative way, the opportunities for resolution are greater. When conflict is avoided, the risks of escalation are greater. Therefore, we have a better chance of securing a positive resolution by doing something than by doing nothing. Conflict avoidance is not a sustainable or effective long-term conflict management strategy.

Figure 2.1 The five stages of conflict

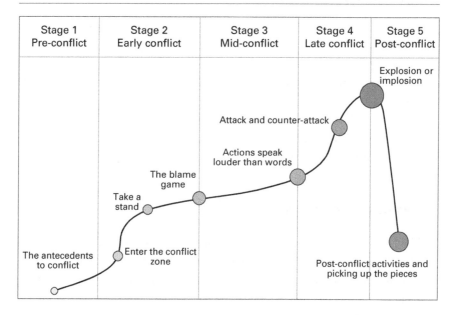

Figure 2.2 The five types of team conflict

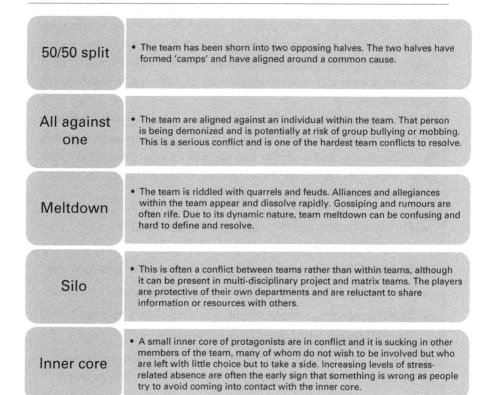

50/50 split	• The team has been shorn into two opposing halves. The two halves have formed 'camps' and have aligned around a common cause.
All against one	• The team are aligned against an individual within the team. That person is being demonized and is potentially at risk of group bullying or mobbing. This is a serious conflict and is one of the hardest team conflicts to resolve.
Meltdown	• The team is riddled with quarrels and feuds. Alliances and allegiances within the team appear and dissolve rapidly. Gossiping and rumours are often rife. Due to its dynamic nature, team meltdown can be confusing and hard to define and resolve.
Silo	• This is often a conflict between teams rather than within teams, although it can be present in multi-disciplinary project and matrix teams. The players are protective of their own departments and are reluctant to share information or resources with others.
Inner core	• A small inner core of protagonists are in conflict and it is sucking in other members of the team, many of whom do not wish to be involved but who are left with little choice but to take a side. Increasing levels of stress-related absence are often the early sign that something is wrong as people try to avoid coming into contact with the inner core.

Stage 1 The pre-conflict stage

This stage relates predominantly to the underlying or root causes of conflict. For instance, change and conflict are inextricably linked and one often drives the other. Other factors include the role of leadership, functional, systemic and structural factors, cultural and political factors, or factors relating to the distribution of resources or rewards. These factors act as an antecedent to the conflict. Conflict is predictable and organizations and their employees benefit by anticipating conflict and making it clear that conflict is a healthy expression of working life.

Resolution recommendation

Planning for conflict arising is the most proactive and often the most effective way of managing it. Designing and embedding collaborative and constructive dispute resolution approaches into HR policies, project teams, role designs, change programmes and leadership behaviours can prevent conflicts from escalating and can create the right conditions for functional conflict. The energy of any potentially dysfunctional conflict can be better spent on crafting innovative solutions rather than on destructive and damaging interactions.

It is advisable to identify potential conflict hotspots and to constantly monitor and track your organization for factors that could give rise to conflicts. These may include a merger or acquisition, a major change process, a change in leadership, new working practices, or attempts to harmonize pay and conditions.

Project managers, team leaders, change agents, employee relations (ER) specialists and organizational development (OD) specialists should be encouraged to embed a conflict management statement within their plans and frameworks. The conflict management statement should include the following statements:

- That we anticipate that this project/process may result in some disagreements and conflict.
- That we will aim to resolve conflicts constructively and collaboratively.
- That we encourage all parties to aim for win/win outcomes to conflict.
- That the system for managing conflict will include face-to-face meetings between the parties wherever possible.
- That project managers and change agents will facilitate dialogue where possible and where it is not possible, external support will be sought.

I have designed the following statement for use within employee handbooks and as part of wider conflict management strategies:

> This organization recognizes that, occasionally, we won't agree on something and that our different beliefs, values, needs and goals may clash. This is perfectly normal and this organization views conflict as a healthy part of working life.
>
> This organization has planned for such conflicts arising and we take them seriously when they do. This organization has created a culture and climate where conflicts can be resolved in a constructive and supportive way.
>
> We ask all of our employees, managers, human resources professionals, union officials and others to work together to find mutually acceptable, win/win outcomes to conflict.
>
> This organization will actively encourage and support such resolution processes and we will do everything that we can to promote and facilitate dialogue. Where dialogue doesn't work, or is not suitable, we will always seek the most appropriate and effective remedy to the conflict for all concerned.

Stage 2 The early conflict stage

This stage develops as the parties experience the initial stages of the conflict – often referred to as 'fight, flight, freeze or fall'. The parties' positions may harden and communication become limited and disrupted. Alliances and cliques begin to form and the parties blame each other for the problem.

As parties enter the 'Zone of Negative Conflict' (ZONC), divergence between one or more of their needs, goals or expectations begin to emerge. This leads to a sense of frustration and anxiety for the parties and the early warning signs may include:

- reduced communication;
- hostility and aggression;
- inappropriate behaviours; and
- attempts to isolate one another.

The parties adopt a series of rigid positions to communicate their own points of view, which can become mutually exclusive and seemingly irreconcilable. This adds to the frustration, anger and a sense of mistrust for all parties as their positions are not accepted or realized. At this stage, the parties frequently lose sight of common ground and focus on the factors that have driven them apart.

Resolving differences at this early stage and encouraging the parties to 'let off steam', step back and talk the issues through can be very valuable. By engaging the parties in a process of open and honest dialogue, positions can be softened, behaviours changed, attitudes realigned and dialogue developed. However, many managers miss this vital opportunity to 'nip the conflict in the bud', leaving the conflict to fester so that it requires only a spark to ignite it and throw all parties into an uncontrollable and destructive spiral of stressful and damaging dysfunctional conflict.

As the conflict escalates, the parties begin to take a stand. They are now deeply immersed in the ZONC. Though they may still be prepared to engage in dialogue, if their efforts to seek a resolution are fruitless, they will start to doubt that a solution can be found and they will question the 'reasonableness' of the other party. As the conflict escalates and rational communication is replaced with emotional confrontation, the parties may become more forceful in pushing their positions. All focus is now on winning.

At this stage, the protagonists may try to forge alliances with people they believe will support and strengthen their position. Inflexibility and stubbornness become the staple diet of the conflict and tactics may appear confused, irrational and increasingly aggressive. These behaviours, however, reflect the parties' perceptions of reality – their 'truth'. In conflict, our sense of the 'truth' is extremely powerful, and any attempts to force parties to accept another 'truth' may be viewed with suspicion. It is hard for parties to listen at this stage. They are planning their strategy, and the ability to empathize is seriously undermined.

Resolution recommendation

Top tips for managing conflict at the early conflict stage

A resolution triage assessment can be a valuable tool in helping identify the most appropriate route to resolution. (Details of how to carry out a resolution triage are included in Chapter 7.) This is a time to engage the parties in assertive yet empathetic adult-to-adult dialogue. Encourage the parties to take a break from the conflict and give them the space (a safe space) they need to work the conflict out. Ideally, the safe space for dialogue to happen should be neutral and away from the main place of work.

Early resolution meetings (direct talks) between the parties are a valuable way to promote dialogue. In some cases, the parties may benefit from a third-party intermediary to facilitate the conversation – these meetings are called 'facilitated roundtable conversations'. The third-party intermediary may be a manager, an HR professional or a union rep. (More details of how to set up an early resolution meeting and the skills required to facilitate a roundtable meeting are provided in Part Three of this book.)

It is important for the parties to have time to let off steam and they should be encouraged to sit down with one another to discuss the situation, to explore the issues, to describe their impact and to agree a way forward. It is also important at this stage to keep the conflict in perspective and to maintain lines of communication. Line managers, in particular, should be skilled at spotting and resolving conflicts at this stage.

Stage 3 The mid-conflict stage

This stage often sees the parties engaging in coercive or destructive tactics to 'win' the conflict (I win/you lose). Often this is a very challenging period for managers and HR, and is typified by increased grievances, allegations and absence, and stress for all parties.

The blame game

As the conflict escalates, the parties' tactics are aimed at gaining and maintaining the upper hand. Both parties are convinced they are in the right and that the threat to their values, needs, goals or expectations is real and substantial. The language of blame becomes the language of the conflict:

'You should back down... you are wrong.'

'They always behave like this and should be punished.'

'If it wasn't for them...'

'You're the manager; you do something about them...'

This language is aimed at presenting the other party as the wrongdoer and influencing decision makers to take sides. It can become increasingly threatening, sometimes even aggressive and violent. The parties are being driven by their emotional responses and may experience symptoms of stress and anxiety. They may try to project an image of righteousness and strength while absolving themselves of responsibility for the conflict. The blame game prevents protagonists from looking inward, and maintains an unhealthy focus on the tactics and games being played. Any reasonable attempts to engage the parties in communication may result in bickering, arguments and hostility. It is unusual for either party in a conflict to win the blame game.

Actions speak louder than words

Not unsurprisingly, as the conflict escalates the communication and dialogue tail off, with the parties beginning to feel further debate is unlikely to resolve anything. The parties develop strategies that will make the other side back down and yield to their demands – they aim to block the opposition from attaining their needs, goals and expectations while enabling theirs to be met. As communication fades into distant memory, it is replaced with a series of non-verbal signals and actions. The protagonists form stereotypical views of their counterparts based on assumptions and prejudice. Typically, these are wholly inaccurate but they are used to rationalize and justify their own behaviour and activities. Tactics include:

- Provoking the other person to act in a particular way.
- Trading insults and negative comments.
- Preventing the other party from accessing information, files, records, etc.
- Issuing threats and ultimatums.

Attack and counter-attack

These threats and ultimatums become increasingly rigid and inflexible. As the conflict continues, the parties start to view each other as almost sub-human. They react violently to one another and may experience high levels of anxiety in each other's presence. Given the codes and norms of the workplace, it probably won't be easy for them to engage in open hostility, so the attacks and counter-attacks become increasingly subversive and devious.

The parties may start to feel out of control and their alliances begin to fail as the conflict becomes more serious and threatening. They may lose sight of their strategy and begin to demand immediate actions from their counterparts, some of which will leave them with little room for manoeuvre. If it hadn't already, the conflict will now have taken over and the parties are entirely locked in. To back down now would end in a loss of face, submission and failure. At this stage, the parties may seek external assistance, sometimes as a tactic to strengthen their position, sometimes as a genuine cry for help and support. Rising sickness levels are one clear symptom of conflict at this stage.

Resolution recommendation

Top tips for managing conflict at the mid-conflict stage

It is vital that a resolution triage assessment is carried out as quickly as possible to understand the issues and to explore potential routes to resolution. It is now time for the parties to start talking and listening to each other with the objective of achieving a mutually acceptable resolution. This is the time for adult-to-adult dialogue.

The impact and the consequences of the worsening conflict may be apparent to everyone except the parties. If the conflict continues it will worsen and the impact could be far greater than it already is. It is important that the parties are made aware of the potential impact of the conflict, the consequences of that impact and the organization's commitment to promoting constructive and collaborative dialogue for resolving issues. Organizations would be right to assert that they now require the parties to engage in dialogue with each other.

We know that the parties are experiencing strong feelings, that they are gripped by 'fight or flight' and the conflict has polarized them. The parties may be worried about being seen to be backing down. Any formal processes that encourage win/lose behaviours, language or mindsets should be avoided. 'Backing down' can be perceived as a sign of weakness, so it is important to position adult-to-adult dialogue as a positive step that the parties can sign up to without being seen to be weak, to have failed or to be somehow giving in.

Stage 4 The late conflict stage – explode or implode

This stage may see the conflict erupt and become all-consuming. Alternatively, the conflict could slowly 'eat away' to such a great extent that a previously well-performing team begins to fail and implode. Either way, the cost of the conflict can be significant and extensive.

At this stage, the 'fight or flight' response is extremely powerful and the basis of the parties' activities is survival at all costs. In the workplace the parties are at war. The smallest spark could result in an all-out offensive and the normal rules of engagement have been tossed in the bin. The parties engage in often brutal and increasingly desperate attacks and seek to inflict as much damage on the other as possible. They will seek to harm their opponent's reputation, integrity, power base and alliances. They may lash out blindly and may even seek to inflict damage upon other staff, managers, representatives, mediators or negotiators.

As the conflict grows in intensity and sucks other people in, the pressure increases and the parties experience extreme levels of stress. Then *bang* – suddenly, like a volcano, it explodes or, like a collapsing building, it implodes. Now, the conflict will be potentially highly dangerous with very little consideration of personal needs; it is about winning at any cost – mutually assured destruction (MAD). This can have a number of outcomes, including: both parties being subjected to disciplinary action; one or both parties pursuing grievances; one or both parties being dismissed; a criminal investigation; or litigation by the parties or the organization.

Resolution recommendation

Top tips for managing conflict at the late conflict stage

This stage requires a calm and rational response. If you are in any way conflicted yourself, ask a colleague to step in to help. Knowing our own boundaries and our own internal 'unconscious' biases can really help. If you don't have anyone available to help you, try to suspend judgement and actively avoid taking sides or being drawn into the issues. At this stage, it is very easy to get drawn into the conflict and the parties will want you 'on their side'.

This could be a good time to involve a mediator. Trained internal mediators can provide a valuable resource or you may wish to access an external mediator. (See Chapter 10 for more details about the mediation process and guidance on how to introduce mediation to the parties.)

Stage 5 The post-conflict stage – the aftermath

Of course, someone must still meet the needs of the customers, answer the phones, deliver the services, heal the patients, sell the goods, drive the lorries, deliver the parcels, etc. It is often up to HR and managers to pick up the pieces and to retain a balance between the needs of the parties and the needs of the business. This is never an easy task, yet it is made even harder when the parties believe that they are right and everyone else is wrong.

My experience has led me to believe that this stage – the aftermath – is a rich source of learning and insight. There can be no doubt that the conflict will have been punishing: it could have created lasting damage and may have created some incredibly powerful emotions. Things may have been said that have hurt and upset others, some people may still feel vulnerable and others may be experiencing a sense of guilt about how they behaved during the conflict.

There will be any number of stories doing the rounds and the conflict may have been the hot topic of the day, internally and in some cases externally too. Nonetheless, it's over and it's time to move on and heal the hurts. It is time for everyone who was involved in the conflict to:

1 Sit down and reflect on what they have learnt.

2 Talk and listen.

3 Agree a mutual way forward.

4 Forgive each other for the mistakes they have made.

The biggest mistake that organizations make is just assuming all will be well and people can move on after a big conflict. Maybe they can, but it's a risk. Taking the time to reflect on the conflict gives everyone the chance to explore how it has impacted on them, what they have learnt and what changes they will make going forward. It can bring people together and real transformation can take place. It also means that the learning can be embedded into the organization's memory rather than being lost as just another blip.

The aftermath of a difficult conflict, when handled well is, in my experience, one of the most fertile opportunities to re-establish team boundaries, agree new behaviours and frame how conflicts will be managed in the future. Organizations generally benefit from having a skilled facilitator to manage this reflective process, but it is possible for teams to undertake such a piece of reflection themselves with a skilled and confident manager facilitating the session.

Resolution recommendation

Top tips for managing conflict at the post-conflict stage

This is an opportunity to promote a turnaround or transformation initiative in the team. It is now time to move on. See over for some critical questions that need to be asked of the whole team, either on an individual basis or, preferably, in a joint meeting with everyone present:

- Are there any burning issues that still require a resolution?
- What have you learnt from the conflict?
- What are our shared goals and objectives for the future – our common cause?
- How do we want to behave towards each other in the future?
- What does a good day look like for our team?
- What collective and individual actions will we take to prevent a similar situation occurring again?
- What support do we need now to achieve our actions as well as our shared goals and objectives?
- What early warning systems do we need to tell us if we are going off track?
- What do we need our leaders to do to helps us achieve our goals and objectives?
- Are we all ready to move forward – together?

Unresolved conflict in teams

Management gurus and well respected psychologists such as Bruce Tuckman (1965) tell us that conflict is inevitable and indeed it can be healthy and entirely necessary. Tuckman originally identified four stages of team development (he added a further stage of 'adjourning' a few years later):

1 *Forming.* The team is in its infancy. There are very few clear structures and the aims and the objectives of the team are being defined and formed. There is a high risk of dysfunctional conflict due to the relatively high levels of confusion and a lack of clear direction and the unclear nature of leadership.

2 *Storming.* Decisions don't come easily within the group as team members attempt to establish themselves and define their roles. The team's purpose and aims are being developed. Cliques and factions form and there may be power struggles. The potential for dysfunctional conflict is very high.

3 *Norming.* The team members are forming clearer boundaries around roles and relationships. Dysfunctional conflicts are being transformed into functional dialogue. The aims and the objectives are much clearer and the role of the leader has been defined. There is an emerging shared

culture and team identity. There is a greater chance for functional conflict to occur if leaders are equipped to handle conflict effectively.

4 *Performing.* The team has purpose and is performing against its stated goals and objectives. Conflicts can still occur but they are potentially resolved more collaboratively and constructively. At this stage, leaders may stimulate some conflict to drive innovation. In these cases, leaders need to be aware of the process of preventing dysfunctional conflict and promoting functional conflict.

The storming stage is particularly relevant in terms of conflict management as this is the point that the team begins to experience conflict and to shape the written and unwritten rules that will come to govern them in the future. During the storming stage, team members still see themselves as a group of individuals rather than a team with a core goal or a common purpose. The leader may perceive such dissent as a challenge to his or her role and an attack on his or her status and position within the team.

Conflict within teams can have a significant impact and it can undermine the efforts of all team members at each stage of the team development. Not all team conflicts are the same: I have identified five types of team conflict, shown in Figure 2.2 on page 33. Part Three of this book contains practical hints and tips for managers and leaders to help them resolve a team conflict.

Conclusion

My experience has taught me that all conflicts follow a similar lifecycle: they escalate in a broadly predictable way and do so due to similar factors. These are explored in more detail in Chapter 3, which examines the 10 main causes of conflict, and in Chapter 6, which examines the psychology of conflict. By developing the appropriate resources and remedies for each stage of a conflict, organizations will be better placed to prevent conflicts from escalating and, when they do, to respond in an appropriate and effective way.

Resolution reflection

Bearing in mind the conflict lifecycle discussed in this chapter:

● What practical steps will you take to manage conflict at each stage of the conflict lifecycle?

- What factors can cause conflict to escalate from one stage to the next of the conflict lifecycle?

- Drawing on your personal experience of conflict, what are the key challenges to be aware of at each stage of the conflict lifecycle and how will you handle them?

- How will you support others to manage conflict at each stage of the conflict lifecycle?

Reference

Tuckman, B W (1965) Developmental sequence in small groups, *Psychological Bulletin*, **63** (6), pp 384–99

The causes and the sources of dysfunctional conflict

03

Irrespective of how conflict manifests itself, when you peel back all the layers of the onion, in 99.9 per cent of the cases, ultimately, it comes down to relationship breakdown and a lack of understanding of each other.
(Helen Roden, Head of Employee Relations and Engagement for Geoban, part of the Santander Group)

KEY LEARNING POINTS IN THIS CHAPTER

- There are complex and varied causes of conflict, many of which are routinely ignored or misunderstood.

- The causes of conflict can be categorized into two broad areas: human and organizational.

- Conflict arises from unmet needs, which creates powerful emotions, perceptions and reactions.

- To resolve conflict we must first understand its root cause.

- Risk-averse, confrontational and adversarial organizational rules and procedures are the most significant causes and perpetuators of dysfunctional conflict. Such policies are about attributing blame and managing risk. They do not help us to understand the root cause of conflict and they inhibit dialogue rather than facilitating it.

- Organizations can create rules, policies, systems and structures that reduce the potential for dysfunctional conflict and encourage transformational conflict.

Introduction

When Kogan Page first asked me to write this book, I began reflecting on the causes of conflict that I have personally experienced over the past 25 years. Not the ones that I have read about in the management literature or in articles and blogs; I wanted to share my own personal reflections about the human and the organizational causes of conflict that I have witnessed first-hand. I started by making a list of the main causes of conflict that I see every day. They make for challenging reading and my intention here is not to attribute blame, but to shine a light on problem areas of the modern workplace that I believe are routinely overlooked, yet are easily remedied. Several practical remedies will be offered in subsequent chapters of this book.

Resolution reflection

- What are the main causes of conflict in your workplace?
- What tools do you use to evaluate the causes of conflict?
- Do you learn from previous conflicts to prevent them occurring again?

In Chapter 6 I examine the psychology of conflict and the role of positive psychology and emotional intelligence in helping to resolve conflict. In this chapter I examine the root causes of conflict from an organizational and a human perspective. These two perspectives are very closely aligned and they feed off each other in an elaborate feedback loop. That's to be expected given that our organizations comprise human beings. However, as this seems like such a prosaic and obvious statement, it is a constant source of sadness and surprise to me when I see organizational responses to conflict that dehumanize the parties or lose sight of the human impact of a conflict and try instead to make sense of it and resolve it via mechanistic and procedural approaches.

A recent CIPD report (2015), identified several causes of conflict: 'Conflict can be as varied and complex as the relationships we have with colleagues. It focuses on a wide range of issues and often has its roots in more than one.' However, the report goes on to state that: 'by a clear margin, the single most common cause or contributor is differences in personality or styles of working'. In my view, albeit that the CIPD report does examine some of the other causes of conflict, this analysis is an over-simplification. It places the blame for conflict at the door of the parties.

My view is that organizations need to take a step back and consider the systemic, cultural, procedural and structural issues at play as being the key drivers and antecedents of conflict. People are people: they fall out and they always will. We can't stop that happening. However, organizations are dynamic – they are constantly learning and adapting. In terms of managing conflict, this means that there is massive potential for them to get a lot smarter, a lot more efficient and a lot more effective at managing conflict. If we are going to take conflict and its management seriously, organizations (by which I mean HR, management and unions) need to take a long hard look in the corporate mirror.

The top 10 causes of dysfunctional conflict

1 A lack of a coherent conflict management strategy

Conflict is confusing, full of paradoxes and, without doubt, it can be incredibly difficult to manage. It is precisely at times of challenge and complexity that we look to our leaders to provide a clear steer and guidance – a strategy. However, very few organizations have developed a robust conflict management strategy that provides a clear map for resolving conflict which, in turn, drives the necessary culture and the behaviours of the organization.

This lack of a clearly defined conflict management strategy creates and perpetuates confusion and results in situations escalating into dysfunctional conflict rather than being predicted and managed at source. A lack of a strategic conflict management framework leaves issues hanging in the air and it makes the management of conflict an opaque, complex and costly business. The potential for dysfunctional conflict is far greater and opportunities for functional conflict are at best hit and miss. It breeds a culture of avoidance and, when conflict can be avoided no longer, of over-reaction.

Thus, a lack of a clear and coherent conflict management strategy, driven from the very top of the organization, generates a reactive conflict culture that results in operational management and HR perceiving conflict as a threat – a negative and time-consuming activity they generally avoid dealing with. It also creates dissonance: if organizations' boards don't take conflict seriously – they are reactive and, in some cases, they exhibit the worst of the dysfunctional conflict behaviours – how and why is it reasonable to expect operational managers, HR and others to take conflict seriously? In addition, a lack of a clear conflict management strategy and the associated perception of risk means that policies and procedures must be designed to ameliorate the situation. In such cases, it is rare for HR or managers to view managing conflict as a positive and rewarding activity that can deliver tangible business benefits. A lack of a corporate conflict management strategy is fuelling a proliferation of rules, policies and procedures that act as a 'safety net'. It is also fuelling the use of litigation and other formal dispute resolution processes.

Resolution reflection

- Is conflict treated as a strategic priority in your organization? If so, what impact does this have? If not, why?
- What would the benefits of a conflict management strategy be to your employees, your managers and your customers?
- What steps need to be taken to develop a conflict management strategy?
- Who needs to be involved and how will you secure their engagement?

---

2 The modern triumvirate (HR, unions and managers) pulling in different directions

The following analysis relates predominantly to unionized organizations. However, it could equally be applied to any other type of organization with works councils or other forms of employee representation.

I have worked with HR teams, union officials and senior and mid-level managers for many years. I enjoy working with them, I have learnt a lot from them and in some cases, I have found their insight and their judgement to be a source of inspiration. I am a huge advocate for the role of the union in the modern workplace, I can see a real benefit of having a well-resourced and well-organized HR function and I recognize the value that managers play in delivering effective employee relations. I refer to the HR, union and management functions as the modern triumvirate.[1]

However, there is problem at the heart of this modern triumvirate which is creating conflict and it is laying the foundations for dysfunctional conflict in the future. Each part of the triumvirate has a vital role to play to support its constituency. For HR, it is the needs of the employer; for the union, it is the needs of its members; and for management, it is the needs of the business, its customers and its shareholders. These three interests are intrinsically linked but are often competing, particularly in relation to managing conflict. As such, there is a potential for a lack of trust, for suspicion and for a breakdown in communication between them. Each part of the triumvirate fights for its interests to be met but fails to recognize that the other two members are also fighting for their constituent's interests to be met also. In some cases, two of the members of the triumvirate may align against the third and a battle ensues. In other cases, none of the parts of the modern triumvirate are aligned and the organization experiences perpetual conflict that results in seemingly intractable disputes, high absence levels, low engagement levels, low performance levels and a prevailing culture of mistrust, suspicion and fear.

While collective disputes and industrial relations unrest are nowhere near the levels that we saw in the 1970s, there are enough collective disputes hitting the headlines with others rumbling just under the surface to suggest that all is not as rosy as it may seem. From my experience, I have found the lack of common cause within the modern triumvirate to be a source of frustration and concern. My team and I have mediated in so many cases where, had a manager spoken to an HR professional or an HR professional to a union official or a union official to a manager at an earlier stage, the situation would not have escalated to a full-blown dysfunctional conflict or collective dispute. Had the modern triumvirate been operating effectively, the conflict could have been more easily managed in such a way that it quickly transformed into a functional conflict manifested by open and honest dialogue, collaborative problem solving, mutual respect and transparency. Furthermore, when I set up mediation programmes in organizations, the ones that I know will flourish and succeed are those that are fully supported by all members of the modern triumvirate. Those mediation programmes that operate without a joined up strategic triumvirate struggle to get traction and will invariably fail due to a lack of support, a lack of confidence in the scheme or general antipathy.

Organizations including the London Ambulance Service, Tesco, Parcelforce Worldwide, Arcadia Group, Northumbria Healthcare NHS Foundation Trust and Capgemini have developed systems that bring the triumvirate together. They have used conflict management as a tool that creates common cause and unites rather than divides the triumvirate. This book uses those examples as a benchmark of how effective the modern triumvirate can be at spotting, preventing and resolving conflict at work.

Resolution reflection

- How do your HR, union and management colleagues work collaboratively to solve workplace problems?

- If you are non-unionized, how will you ensure that your employees have a voice?

- How could your HR, unions and management colleagues improve the ways in which they collaborate?

- What benefits might greater collaboration among the modern triumvirate deliver for your organization?

- Do you have a written collaboration framework or is it assumed?

- What are the benefits of developing a written framework for promoting collaboration among the modern triumvirate?

- How will you persuade the modern triumvirate that enhanced collaborative working is good for them, for their constituents, for colleagues and for your organization?

3 A rights-based and risk-averse policy framework that institutionalizes division, dysfunction and discord

Most of the 'dispute resolution' policies in use in modern organizations are intrinsically adversarial; they draw on a quasi-litigation model and they focus on the rights and wrongs of a dispute rather than the parties' underlying needs and goals. The more that conflict is perceived as a risk, the more risk-averse the organization becomes, which in turn makes the chances of conflict far greater. The beneficiaries, of course, are those who profit from risk-aversion or litigation-based remedies to conflict – because that is surely where it will all end.

When I first start working with an organization, I often get the chance to review its people policy framework or employee handbooks. The first section of most employee handbooks is the 'Welcome to our organization' section. It looks nice: it is welcoming and it reads well. This section, while generally brief, is quite positive and upbeat. One rather gets the impression that it has been written by the organization itself rather than using a template, an external consultant or a lawyer. It usually offers some positive commentary about the organization and how great it is to work there. It is generally values-based and person-centred. 'Welcome to your new job…'.

However, the next and subsequent sections of the typical employee handbook go downhill very quickly. Section two goes on to say how we will discipline and dismiss you. Section three is how to raise a grievance against one of your new colleagues or your new manager. The section after that is what to do when you are being bullied or being a bully. If you make it this far, the ones after that contain details about how your new employer will deal with you when you don't perform very well; when you go off sick; when you discriminate against someone, or are a victim of discrimination; or when you post something unpalatable on Twitter or Facebook. 'Welcome to your new job and, by the way, we don't trust you so we will bind you up in rules.'

It is no surprise that most employee handbooks are rarely read and go onto a shelf and are only ever referred to when a problem arises. The most damaging, and in my view the most pernicious and most divisive of the policies in the employee handbook, is the grievance procedure. The grievance procedure is designed for resolving workplace disputes. However, its actual effect on working relationships is chilling. Many of the case studies in this book demonstrate that there is a very real and a very urgent need to remove this policy and its associated vernacular from the employee handbook and to replace it with something more modern, more progressive and frankly more human – a resolution policy.

It is the employee handbook that sets the tone and acts as a reference point for the way that conflicts will be managed in the future. They remind me of a father or mother scolding a naughty child and they read like a legal or a statutory instrument. They talk about respect but show very little in return. They talk about the importance of relationships yet they undermine trust from day one. They talk about the importance of due process but they get bogged down in unnecessary complexity, clauses and sub-clauses. This is the tone of voice (which defines the organizational culture) that most employee handbooks set from day one of our new employees starting work within our organizations:

- adversarial;
- reactive; and
- risk-averse.

I am not an anarchist. I recognize as surely as anyone would that clearly defined rules, procedures and processes are vital for a healthy organization. They offer protection to vulnerable employees, they can prevent and tackle harm and they provide an assurance of consistency and fairness. They can deliver justice and they can ensure that the organization is meeting the required statutory duties and legal requirements. However, the current trend for excessive rules, policies and procedures is neither valuable nor useful.

Having reams of paper sat on a shelf or on an intranet site is not a useful resource. In so many cases, employees go into a policy expecting it to resolve a situation when the reality is that they are left feeling:

- bamboozled;
- out of control;
- let down;
- unfairly treated; and
- betrayed.

Expecting a complex procedure to spit out a happy and healthy person at the end of it is unrealistic and highly improbable. Such procedures are bruising and they are stressful. Senior HR professionals are beginning to recognize the limitations of these formal processes. Jaua Harris is the Strategic HR Policy lead at the Metropolitan Police:

> I've been in HR for over 20 years and I have learnt that while formal processes are absolutely necessary, often by the time they are initiated individuals and their managers can become entrenched in their positions and lose their objectivity. This can cause long-term damage to trust and confidence in an organization and the ongoing working relationship. Instead of focusing on the team work objectives, the focus becomes the dispute. The formal process can sometimes take a time to complete so there tends to be a lot of negativity around it. Even, before individuals go into the grievance process they can be wound up, sometimes distressed, and this can make issues much harder to resolve.

An organization that adopts an adversarial process of dispute resolution, such as the traditional 'grievance procedure' will, as sure as night follows day, experience an adversarial mindset amongst its employees – particularly at times of conflict. The organization drives the individual's responses and the individual's responses define the organization's reaction to the conflict. As I often say when I am presenting to a team of business leaders: we get the behaviours that we deserve.

Resolution reflection

Print off a copy of your current grievance procedure. With a red pen, highlight all the parts of your procedure that are:

1 Formal

2 Adversarial

3 Rights-based

4 Going to result in a win/lose outcome

5 Taking control away from the parties

6 About allocating blame

Now, with a green pen, highlight all the parts of your procedure that are:

1 Informal

2 About promoting dialogue and empathy

3 Person-centred

4 Promoting win/win outcomes

5 Giving control to the parties

6 About being collaborative

What does this exercise tell you about your grievance procedure?

A good dispute resolution policy should have more green pen than red. Does yours? (For more details about developing a resolution policy, see Chapter 8.)

4 The application of the Ulrich model of HR

The focus on the role of HR as a strategic partner is a great development for HR and a positive step forward for many organizations. However, transactional people management activities (many of which used to be supported by the personnel function) are being delegated to line managers to handle. Many of these managers are ill-equipped and unprepared for the challenges of handling complex people management issues such as dysfunctional workplace conflict.

Human resources, as defined by Dave Ulrich, architect of the modern HR function, comprises four key areas, where HR is a strategic partner, an administrative expert, a change agent and an employee champion. In a seminal text published by Ulrich in 1997, he deals with what he describes as the old myths and new realities of HR (p 18). This text formed the basis of the Ulrich HR model and its variants that have been embedded in so many organizations across the United Kingdom and further afield.

The first of these new realities is that: 'HR departments are not designed to provide corporate therapy or as social or health-and-happiness retreats. HR professionals must create the practices that make employees more competitive, not more comfortable.' If this new 'reality' is being embedded in modern HR departments, it is perhaps no wonder that conflict is having such a significant and damaging effect on so many. Competition is great, up to a point, but too much competition or badly managed competition is harmful and counter-productive. And if it's not HR's role to make employees comfortable – I interpret 'comfortable' to mean safe, valued, secure, supported, nurtured, encouraged, engaged and respected – whose role is it?

Others are arriving at the same conclusion. Lucy Adams, former Director of Human Resources at the BBC and author of the book *HR Disrupted*, suggests that the culture of HR and the associated rules and regulations perpetuate parent-child relationships at work. Lucy argues that:

> HR often play the role of 'mum and dad' rather than looking to build trust with their employees. The parent-child relationship between HR and employees creates an environment in which people are unprepared to challenge authority; speak up; try something new and take risks. (Adams, 2016, p 28)

She offers a damning indictment of traditional HR policies and approaches when she states:

> Time and again, I witness situations in which people are disempowered at work because they are treated as children. This has a knock-on effect as employees become more infantilized; they feel less ready to make responsible choices and they expect their employer to make all of the decisions around their welfare. (p 29)

It doesn't have to be this way

The good news is that it doesn't have to be this way. Many organizations across the United Kingdom and further afield are changing the way that they handle conflicts by reframing their existing HR policy framework and employee handbooks. These organizations are developing a tone of voice that is values-based and person-centred. The result is that their employees adopt the same tone of voice and the same method when they are in conflict – adult-to-adult dialogue.

Resolution reflection

- Has your organization adopted the Ulrich model of HR?

- In what ways does your HR team act as employee advocate and what benefits does this deliver?

- Does your HR strategy include provision for the management of conflict, mediation or alternative dispute resolution?

- Do your employee relations, employee engagement and employee wellbeing programmes promote effective conflict management?

- How do you ensure that your managers and leaders are managing conflicts and disputes effectively where they are required to do so?

- What people management support does your HR team provide to managers and leaders to help them manage conflict and disputes?

- What could your HR do more or and less of to help secure better outcomes to conflict?

5 Managers who lack the courage, the confidence or the competence to manage conflict

The next cause of conflict that I have identified is the role that managers and leaders play. I have identified three aspects of management and leadership that are central causes of dysfunctional conflict:

a A lack of courage to deal with conflicts and relationship issues due to fear that the situation could escalate, that one or both parties could become uncontrollably emotional, that they may be blamed, and/or that a grievance or allegation of bullying may be brought against them.

b A lack of confidence arising from poor management recruitment processes, a confusing HR policy framework, lack of clear management job design and reactive and task-focused appraisal systems.

c A lack of competence arising from a lack of appropriate training and support.

Managers are often stuck between a rock and a hard place when it comes to managing conflict. As Kate Cooper, Head of Policy at the Institute of Leadership and Management (ILM) explained to me recently:

Managers are expected to undertake a growing range of people management activities, often without the appropriate training, support or sufficient time to do so... As a result, managers experience overload. ILM research (ILM and QA, 2014) has told us that many managers find managing conflict difficult. Over half of managers also recognize that managing relationships is an increasingly important part of their role. However, our research tells us that organizations place conflict management training very low down the list of priorities. That creates a real disconnect. What organizations are saying is that we know that conflict is a problem but when it comes to making our managers better at handling it, it is a case of let's not think about that – that's just too difficult.

The problem, as I see it, is that most line managers haven't been told that managing conflict and building stronger working relationships is a part of their job. They are left confused about what they should be doing and how they should be doing it. This confusion creates inaction and that can allow a conflict to slowly fester at a time when, with confident management support, the parties in a conflict could sit around a table and find a resolution.

Conflict competence

Many managers that I talk to lack the competence to manage conflicts and disputes and they rely instead on instinct and what has worked (or often not worked) elsewhere. This is often a result, as Kate Cooper from ILM says, of organizations not prioritizing conflict management training. Organizations and their managers benefit by developing conflict-competent managers who can:

- Mirror the organization's values within their own behaviour.
- Spot a conflict early and prevent it from escalating.
- Listen actively.
- Balance the need to be empathetic with being assertive.
- Manage strong emotions.
- Handle confrontation.
- Take parties out of the ZONC and into the ZOPA (from the zone of negative conflict to the zone of possible agreement).
- Create a safe space for the parties to talk.
- Facilitate dialogue between conflicting parties.
- Identify, agree and implement clear goals.
- Use principled negotiation methods to secure a win/win outcome.

One organization that has been addressing this issue is St George's Universities Hospital NHS Foundation Trust in south London. Mairead Heslin is Head of Corporate Training and Organizational Development for the Trust. She explains:

> In the past, conflict may have been accepted as an unavoidable part of organizational life and combined with a lack of understanding of the role of managers and leaders in dealing with conflict proactively. The essential message we are trying to get across is that managing conflict is part of the life of a manager and leader, and appropriate help is in place to support you to develop these skills. Alongside our internal mediation scheme, we are providing more sophisticated support to help managers and leaders develop the skills needed to create a harmonious work environment, in addition to spotting and resolving conflicts proactively when needed. By taking this approach we hope to gradually change how conflict is viewed and managed within the organization.

Resolution reflection

If you are an employer, use this space to reflect on the following areas:

- Do we have clearly defined leadership behaviours that relate to our core values?
- Do we identify conflict management skills within management and leadership role profiles?
- Do we invest in our leaders and managers to help them develop the prerequisite conflict management skills for delivering the people management parts of their roles?
- Do we value effective conflict management as part of hiring, rewarding and promotion processes?
- What impact do your answers to the above questions have on your organization?

If you are a manager or a leader, reflect on a conflict that you have had to deal with in the workplace. Please use this space to reflect on the following areas:

- Spotting a conflict early and preventing it from escalating.
- Listening actively.

- Balancing the need to be empathetic with being assertive.
- Managing strong emotions.
- Handling confrontation.
- Creating a safe space for the parties to talk.
- Facilitating dialogue.
- Securing a win/win outcome.

If you are a learning and development professional, reflect on the following:

- How effective are we at creating conflict-competent managers and leaders?
- How do we measure and evaluate conflict competence amongst our managers and leaders?
- How effective is our organization at embedding the core competencies for managers to deal with conflicts and complaints?

Define your expectations of leadership behaviour

Many organizations have a set of clear values that are either written or assumed. In addition, increasing numbers of organizations are developing a suite of leadership behaviours that are aligned to the values of the organization. Here, the management function 'walks the talk' and is well equipped to handle the complexity of managing a diverse workforce during these volatile, uncertain, complex and ambiguous (VUCA) times. However, in many other organizations, this is not the case. These organizations find that a lot of their time is spent reacting to problematic, dysfunctional conflict.

Developing a set of leadership behaviours that aligns to the core values of your organization is not a panacea. However, it goes a very long way to addressing many of the issues that this book is dealing with. When these valued-based leadership and management behaviours are brought to life through recruitment, reward and retention strategies, positive and lasting change will not be far away.

6 *Poorly defined job roles and unclear objectives*

The pace of work is so fast nowadays that what worked yesterday may not work tomorrow. Many organizational changes are being driven by technology, the economic climate, changes to the demographics of the workplace, political factors and of course, the United Kingdom's exit from the European Union. It sometimes feels that change is happening faster now than it ever has. However, it was the Greek philosopher Heraclitus who was quoted as saying 'Change is the only constant in life'. He had to write that on a piece of stone as blogging hadn't been invented in 500 BC. Maybe it's not change that is the problem: perhaps the problem is how we manage it.

It is hard for people's roles to keep up with the changes, and slowly their role description can slip further and further away from the job they applied for and for which they were, at the time, suitably qualified. One thing is for certain – we need our employees to be flexible, adaptable and mobile. However, this can come at a cost. Flexibility, adaptability and mobility mean that life is less predictable; roles are often unclear and the systems for giving and receiving feedback need to be precise and operate in real time. We are human beings after all, and we do like things to be broadly predictable.

When our roles and working life are so fast paced and so uncertain, the uncertainty can lead to conflict, stress, anxiety and trauma. There are several things that managers and leaders can do to address this issue before it generates negative, dysfunctional conflict:

1 Before the employee starts, ensure that you have designed the role adequately and the purpose and the objectives of the role are clearly defined.

2 Undertake regular employee touch points and reviews: weekly or monthly rather than annually. They don't need to be long meetings but they create a safe space for feedback to be given and tweaks and adjustments to be made in real time.

3 Focus on the positives, the achievements and the opportunities, and apply emotional intelligence and positive psychology as part of review of job roles (see Chapter 6 for more details.)

4 Agree and monitor realistic short- and medium-term objectives. Make sure that these are matched against the broader strategy and objectives of the organization.

5 Review the role against the values of the organization and measure what the role is achieving – measure outputs (what is achieved) but also inputs (what the role puts into the business).

6 Don't be afraid to make the necessary changes (collaboratively) to the role to ensure that it is fit for purpose.

7 Seek feedback from the employee about your management approach and don't be defensive if it is critical. Employee reviews are often didactic, ie the flow of information is from a manager (parent) to an employee (child). Managers who actively seek feedback from their employees are engaging in more productive adult-to-adult dialogue. This can open a debate with the employee and present an opportunity to identify and resolve

challenges or issues at the earliest possible stage. It is then important to assimilate that feedback (where suitable) into your own management style. This kind of adult-to-adult dialogue models positive communication across a team, which is the genesis of a culture of openness and transparency. Feedback is a gift.

8 Thank the person for a good job, well done. Let people know you value them.

Resolution reflection

- How do you ensure that you match the role design to the needs of the business?

- What actions could you take to improve the way that roles are designed to prevent confusion and the potential for conflict?

- How do you ensure that role designs are flexible enough to align with the ongoing changes and adaptations within your organization?

- How much time is spent reviewing role design and how effective are managers at giving and receiving feedback during reviews?

- How well do you balance the way that employee reviews are undertaken and, in particular, the need to examine what happened yesterday and what needs to happen tomorrow?

---

7 Organizational integrity and the perception of employees

We each have a set of values, needs, goals, aspirations, hopes or beliefs that may be unconscious but which drive our everyday behaviours and interactions. When our values, etc are aligned with those of others in the workplace we feel a sense of belonging and togetherness that is hard to define but, in that moment, we know it works. If we add to this knowing that the organization values us and it is meeting our needs – it's like a perfect situation – the perfect workplace. The outcome is that we are collaborative, we are productive, we are engaged and we feel happy.

The Great Place to Work® Institute recently produced a fascinating report on how values can transform a business from good to great (Great Place to Work Institute, 2014). The report highlights numerous examples of organizations that are getting this right and of course, many of these have been designated 'a great place to work'. However, the report examines the impact of stated organizational values not being aligned to employee experience:

> for many organizations, their written statement of values simply doesn't hit the mark. Employees see the statement as something to which the organization and its management simply pay lip service… In such an environment, employees inevitably become cynical, perceiving that the values are without real meaning, and merely words plucked out of the dictionary.

The study also found that there is a relationship between a culture of strong values and organizational performance and customer satisfaction. Our values, needs, goals, aspirations and hopes drive us and, when they are being met, we may feel fulfilled. However, when they are not being met, we may experience a profound sense of loss, such as loss of purpose, loss of drive or a loss of control. Unmet needs, goals and expectations are at the heart of every conflict that I have ever mediated.

Where people see colleagues, managers or leaders acting in such a way that is in direct contravention of the stated values of the organization it sows mistrust and suspicion. There are numerous examples of institutions that have acted with a disregard for their own core values and the values of a healthy society. These organizations are being publicly named and shamed as institutions that lack integrity and are, rightfully, being held to account. There has never been a closer link between values, leadership behaviour and reputation. However, at a more human level – the kind of level that exists in offices, depots, factories and shops, this misalignment between values and behaviour generates mistrust, antipathy and disengagement. These are not the enablers of growth or productivity: they are the enablers of failure. There can be no doubt – unmet needs, not feeling valued, a lack of respect for our beliefs along with a perceived dissonance between the stated values and leadership behaviours – are all antecedents to serious and damaging conflict.

Resolution reflection

List your organization's values:

- What do these values mean to you?
- How does your organization bring the values to life?

- What do you do to make your organization's values a reality?
- How can you help others within you team or organization to bring the core values of your organization to life?

When you see colleagues or managers who are not demonstrating the core values:

- How does this impact on you?
- How does this impact on the business?
- How does this impact on your customers?
- What do you do to remedy the situation?
- What more could you do to 'walk the talk' at work?
- How do you react when someone challenges your deeply held beliefs or values?
- How can you get better at aligning your beliefs and values with someone with whom you are in conflict?

8 *A breakdown in communication*

A breakdown in communication is both a cause and a symptom of dysfunctional conflict. As the emotions become stronger and the battle lines are drawn, so communication becomes less regular and increasingly tense.

Effective communication comprises a series of stages:

1 The sender decides to send a message to a receiver.
2 The sender chooses a means by which to encode the message – talking, a memo, an e-mail, etc.
3 He or she delivers the message through the appropriate medium – speech, writing and delivering a memo or sending the e-mail, etc.
4 The receiver receives the message and decodes it – reading, listening, etc.
5 The receiver sends a message back to the sender to confirm that the message has been received and understood – he or she gives feedback or asks questions to elicit more information.

This creates a feedback loop in which the sender and the receiver interact and the two roles become interchangeable (see Figure 3.1). However, there are several factors that can inhibit effective communication; these include:

Figure 3.1 The communication process

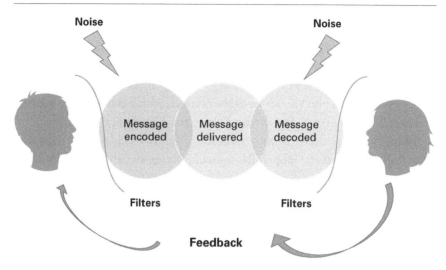

- *Noise* – an external or an internal factor that can distort the sending or the receipt of the message. In some cases, it can be a physical impact such as the noise in a factory or a busy office. Noise can also be subtler such as the impact of rumours and gossiping that affects the flow of communication. Noise can also result from a deliberate attempt to send an unclear message or to misinterpret a message that we receive.

- *Filters* – these are internal factors that can affect how we send or receive the message. They may be a result of our prejudices, assumptions or misperceptions. Filters are commonly called 'unconscious biases'.

- A *lack of feedback* – which means that the sender is unaware of whether the message has been received, understood and assimilated.

When the parties communicate during conflict, it can be stilted, hostile and often inflammatory. Face-to-face communication may be replaced by e-mails or other remote approaches. In some extreme cases, communication breaks down altogether and the parties resist any contact with each other.

Listening is a key part of the communication process: 'Most people do not listen with the intent to understand; they listen with the intent to reply' (Covey, 2012). In my experience, during conflict we often listen to the first 10 per cent of what someone is saying and we spend the next 90 per cent of the time they are talking watching their lips move and preparing our best defence to the first 10 per cent. I call this 'listening to defend'. However, when we avoid being reactive and defensive and listen instead to the whole 100 per cent of what the other person is saying, I call this 'listening to understand'. The more that parties in dispute can listen to understand rather than listen to defend, the more chance there will be of a moment of insight, shared understanding and mutual recognition. It certainly builds a more respectful, calmer, more empathetic and cooperative dialogue between the parties, even where the parties vehemently disagree on a particular point.

Communication breakdown feeds the conflict, which can lead to a significant breakdown in trust. As I often observe: the first thing that leaps out of the nearest open window is communication, followed closely by common sense, followed by trust. Hopefully, someone closes the window before the parties leap too!

Some practical tips for improving communication at times of conflict

- Reduce the opportunities for noise – find somewhere quiet and neutral to talk and to listen. It could be anywhere so long as it's a safe space for you to talk and listen.

- Avoid e-mailing – try to speak directly where possible. It is hard to communicate our emotions, needs, goals and beliefs in an e-mail and it is harder still to give nuanced and genuine feedback. Some people say, write the e-mail and send it to drafts and come back to it in a few hours when you have calmed down. That's great advice. I would go a step further: don't write the e-mail at all, go and put the kettle on, make two cups of tea and ask the person if he or she has 10 minutes for a chat.

- When you are having the discussion, avoid speaking over each other. Give the other person time to finish what he or she is saying before you start speaking. Ask him or her to do the same for you.

- Use positive body language, face the other person, maintain eye contact, avoid looking at the news headlines on your phone, etc.

- Thank the person for what has been said and affirm what he or she is saying as being valuable. Make him or her feel good about what he or she has to say and for having the courage to say it.

- Summarize back what you are hearing. This means that you can check that what you have heard is right and the other person knows that you have been listening. Summarizing is a key skill. I would go as far as to say this: if I could change one thing about how managers manage conflict, it would be for them to summarize back a lot more. Summarizing is like the gold dust of dialogue – the more you do, the more valuable it becomes.

- Ask a variety of open questions: 'please tell me more' or questions that start with who, what, where, when, how and why.

- Don't let the conversation move into personal attacks or hostility. Avoid using 'You did this or you did that' type language. 'Talk from the I'; this sounds like: I saw this; I feel this; I need this.

- Clarify and be curious. Let the other person know that you are interested and don't be afraid to ask the stupid question. The stupid question that everyone has been avoiding asking is often the killer question that everyone should have been asking.

- Keep the lines of communication open and be courageous. During conflict, it is the easy choice to stop talking or rely on e-mails. In virtually every mediation meeting that I have ever facilitated, at the end of the meeting, both parties have turned around to each other and said two things: This was not anywhere as bad as I thought it would be. Why did we not do this sooner?

Resolution reflection

- When communication breaks down at work, how do you react?

- How do you feel when someone doesn't say 'Good morning' to you?

- How do you react when you get a nasty e-mail from a colleague or a manager?

- What do you believe are the key ingredients of effective communication?

- What examples of noise have you experienced?

- What examples of internal filters have you experienced?

- Why is feedback important and how can you improve that in the way you communicate?

- Drawing on those key ingredients, how can you ensure that, in the event of a future conflict, lines of communication remain open?

---

9 Uneven or unfair allocation of resources

In the current economic situation and ongoing austerity, resources are increasingly scarce. In addition, lean business processes mean that organizations are striving to deliver more value for customers with fewer resources.

There is absolutely nothing wrong with this, but it can put strain on employee relationships, which means that people are acutely aware of what others are getting – or not getting.

Any sense of unfairness can be the first bit of grit in the system which, unless managed with tact and sensitivity, can quickly spiral into dysfunctional conflict. Conflict about the distribution of resources (or distributive conflict) can cause the whole system to begin to grind to a halt. The system can go 'from lean to mean' very quickly.

Perceptions of inequality and unfairness can lead to frustration and conflict across many levels, for instance between employees, groups of employees, teams and departments who are required to compete for a finite level of resources; and between employees and management where employees feel unfairly treated or don't trust that the management is providing the adequate resources for them to do their job. Distributive conflict can escalate at an alarming rate and may lead to allegations of discrimination or collective disputes and industrial relations problems. The costs and impact of distributive conflict are high and the repercussions can be felt for many years.

The national debate about executive pay, the introduction of the national living wage, and the various attempts being made to tackle the gender pay gap – distributive conflict is firmly on the front pages. In addition, recent high profile examples such as Uber, Amazon and Sports Direct have shown that in some cases of distributive conflict, the courts and even the UK government have been required to intervene to address the levels of unfair and unequal distribution of resources.

Resolution reflection

- Do you observe distributive conflict in your workplace?
- What impact does this have?
- What steps is your organization taking to resolve distributive conflicts and how effective are they?
- What more could your organization be doing to address distributive conflict?
- What role could mediation and other resolution processes play in tackling distributive conflict?

10 Organizational structures and culture

In our VUCA world, there are numerous systemic and structural factors that precipitate conflict. In Table 3.1 I have highlighted structures and cultures which, based on my own experience, I believe can perpetuate or cause dysfunctional conflict and those that can reduce dysfunctional conflict or help to generate functional conflict.

Table 3.1 The impact of organizational structures and cultures

Structures and cultures that can cause or perpetuate conflict	Structures that can help to reduce or prevent conflict
Rigid and inflexible structures and cultures that are slow to respond to employees' or customers' changing needs.	Flexible structures and cultures that can respond quickly to the changing needs of the workforce and the customer.
Overly hierarchical structures and cultures with several layers of management, which can block upward communication and innovation. Rigid hierarchical and bureaucratic structures can impede integration, collaboration, communication and flexibility.	Flatter structures and cultures that emphasize links between different parts of the organization and where management are seen as approachable and accessible.
Appraisal and accountability systems and processes that are seen as draconian, punitive or undermining.	Appraisal and accountability systems that measure and reward positive behaviours; demonstration of the core values; a focus on driving engagement; and promotion of adult-to-adult dialogue.
Structures and cultures where employees' voices are not heard by management, or where the senior managers and board are told that all is well because others believe that is what the board want to hear.	A structure and culture where the management of the organization are not viewed as sitting in an 'ivory tower' but are seen as an equal and valued part of the whole.
A structure or culture with no clear values or sense of common purpose.	A structure and culture based on a set of clear values and where the values and common purpose of the organization are clearly stated and visible in recruitment processes, new starter induction processes, the employee handbook, HR policies and procedures, internal appraisals and reviews and customer-facing activities.

(continued)

Table 3.1   (*Continued*)

Structures and cultures that can cause or perpetuate conflict	Structures that can help to reduce or prevent conflict
Complex organizational structures and cultures in which employees are unclear about their roles, responsibilities and reporting lines.	A structure and culture where reporting lines and levels of accountability are clear and the methods for reporting are consistently applied across the organization.
Risk-averse structures and cultures in which the needs, goals and aspirations of employees are out of line with the controls that the employer believes are necessary to maintain authority.	A structure and culture that embraces risk and minimizes the volume of rules and procedures. A structure where common sense prevails and in which people are treated as human beings.
Imposed mechanistic approaches to strategy formation with little involvement of internal stakeholders.	Organic and informal structures and cultures that encourage employees and managers to work together to develop the strategy and to agree common purpose. The structures can also be used to review progress and to evaluate effectiveness.
An over-reliance on technological or remote means of communicating.	Use of a variety of media to engage with one another, including roundtable briefings, laboratory workshops, one-to-one meetings, team meetings, town halls, etc. For remote teams, video conference technology can assist.
Structures and cultures that rely on combative and confrontational industrial relations between union and management as part of collective negotiation and collective bargaining.	An industrial relations structure including frameworks and partnership agreements that promote mutual, interest-based negotiation and problem solving.

Resolution reflection

Using Table 3.1 for reference, describe:

- Your organizational structure.
- Your organization's prevailing culture.

- Any sub-cultures that may exist.

- How does your structure and culture affect conflict at work?

- Is it clear what the lines of accountability are within your organization?

- What can be done to prevent conflict within the structures in your organization?

- Could your organizational culture be more resilient to conflict? If so, what changes need to be made?

Resources

While researching for this book, I came across a fascinating document produced by the US Department of Transportation Federal Highway Administration entitled *Achieving Multimodal Networks: Applying design flexibility and reducing conflicts*. This document is a great example of how systems (in this case a transportation system) can be designed specifically to reduce conflict. See www.fhwa.dot.gov/environment/bicycle_pedestrian/ publications/multimodal_networks/fhwahep16055.pdf

Note

1 The first triumvirate was an informal political alliance in Roman times comprising Julius Caesar, Pompeius Magnus ('Pompey the Great') and Marcus Crassus. The arrangement had no legal status, and its purpose was to consolidate the political power of the three and their supporters against the senatorial elite. See https://en.wikipedia.org/wiki/Triumvirate#Roman_triumvirates

References

Adams, L (2016) *HR Disrupted – It's time for something different*, Practical Inspiration Publishing, London

CIPD (2015) *Getting under the Skin of Workplace Conflict: Tracing the experiences of employees*, https://www.cipd.co.uk/Images/getting-under-skin-workplace-conflict_2015-tracing-experiences-employees_tcm18-10800.pdf)

Covey, S R (2012) *The 7 Habits of Highly Effective People*, Simon & Schuster, New York

Great Place to Work Institute (2014) *Organizational Values: Are they worth the bother? How values can transform your business from good to great,* Great Place to Work Institute, London

ILM and QA (2014) *2020 Vision: Future trends in leadership and management*; see https://www.i-l-m.com/~/media/ILM%20Website/Documents/research-reports/future-trends/ilm-research-reports-future-trends%20pdf.ashx

Ulrich, D (1997) *Human Resource Champions: The next agenda for adding value and delivering results,* Harvard Business Press, Boston, MA

Managing conflict

04

A legal perspective

LAURA FARNSWORTH, CHRIS SMITH
AND LAURENCE MILLS, LEWIS SILKIN LLP

KEY LEARNING POINTS IN THIS CHAPTER

- There are several legal claims that can be brought against an organization, including: unfair dismissal, direct and indirect discrimination, and whistleblowing.

- The differences between a grievance/disciplinary procedure and mediation as a form of workplace dispute resolution.

- The difficulties for organizations caused by court-based litigation, and how alternative dispute resolution should be considered even in 'traditional' litigation.

- The strategic benefits to engaging in workplace mediation for organizations facing an employment dispute.

- The legal and practice considerations for organizations when preparing for a workplace mediation.

Introduction

This chapter considers conflict management from an English employment law perspective. It is split into three sections:

1 The connection between mediation and employment law, starting by giving an overview of the common legal issues that arise in the

employment relationship and how they are dealt with, before commenting on the way in which mediation can play a role in resolving disputes as part of an employer's internal grievance or disciplinary procedure.

2   The role that mediation plays within the employment legal dispute process and how mediation broadly (as an out-of-court form of alternative dispute resolution) can assist both parties to resolve their legal dispute. This section will focus on the procedural imperative to consider mediation, the possible strategic benefits it can offer and the key legal considerations for organizations when approaching mediation.

3   The position of companies that are seeking to avoid the costs and exposure of employment litigation, and the practical points they should bear in mind when considering alternative dispute resolution (ADR), and more specifically mediation, as a means of resolving workplace issues.

This chapter is authored by Lewis Silkin LLP, a leading employment law firm with offices in London, Oxford, Cardiff and Hong Kong.

Mediation and employment law

The web of contractual and statutory rights and obligations that forms the employment relationship between an employer and employee is a complex one. At any given moment there is a myriad of contractual and statutory obligations being fulfilled and rights enjoyed. For example, employees have the contractual right to be paid a salary and the statutory right not to be subjected to discriminatory treatment, while at the same time being subject to the contractual obligations to arrive at their place of work on time and carry out the duties of their particular role. However, in addition to being a legal relationship, employment is a human relationship in which people's feelings, thoughts and ambitions are manifested on a daily basis. Against this intricate (legal and personal) background, it is perhaps unsurprising that disputes between employers and employees arise that require a resolution. This section explores the legal issues in relation to workplace disputes and how those issues are typically dealt with, before explaining how mediation plays a role in resolving a dispute at work – before a formal legal process is initiated.

Legal issues in the workplace

The workplace environment can be unpredictable. People with different backgrounds, ages, ethnicities and interests are thrown together and asked to get along and pursue their employer's objectives, while simultaneously trying to pursue their own ambitions. Workplace issues can occur between an employee and his or her employer, a co-worker or line manager, or similarly with an independent contractor or worker engaged by an employer, on any number of issues. However, some of the most common legal issues that arise out of the employment relationship are unfair dismissal, discrimination, bullying and harassment, and whistleblowing.

Employees who have the relevant qualifying period of service (one year where an employee was employed before 6 April 2012, two years where an employee was employed after 6 April 2012) have the right under the Employment Rights Act 1996 not to be subject to an unfair dismissal. For dismissal of an employee with the relevant qualifying period of service to be fair, an employer has to show that the reason for the dismissal falls into one of the following categories:

1 The employee lacked capability or qualification.

2 The dismissal was a result of the conduct of the employee.

3 There was a genuine redundancy.

4 The continuation of the employee's employment would contravene a statute.

5 Some other substantial reason (any reason that does not fall within the above categories).

Where an employer does prove that a dismissal comes under one of the above categories, it will still be up to an employment tribunal to decide in accordance with equity and the substantial merits of the case whether the dismissal was fair or unfair. However, even if there is a justified reason to dismiss an employee, the dismissal will still be unfair if an employer has not followed a correct process. For dismissals based on misconduct or performance, the process that an employer should follow is largely governed by the ACAS (the Advisory, Conciliation and Arbitration Service) Code of Practice (see further on this below).

Employees also have the statutory right not to be discriminated against at work. Under the Equality Act 2010, it is unlawful to discriminate against people at work because of nine protected characteristics. The nine characteristics codified in the Equality Act are age, disability, gender reassignment, marriage and civil partnership, pregnancy and maternity, race, religion or belief, sex, and sexual orientation. Discrimination at work can be either direct or indirect. Direct discrimination occurs where someone is discriminated against on the grounds of their protected characteristic, for example where an employer dismisses an employee because of his or her race. Indirect discrimination occurs when an organization's policy, practice or procedure has the effect of disadvantaging people who share a protected characteristic, for example an employer's policy of not allowing headwear at work might have the effect of disadvantaging someone who wears a headscarf for religious reasons – and the employer is unable to demonstrate that the relevant policy, practice or procedure is a proportionate means of achieving a legitimate aim.

Similarly, employees have the right not to be bullied or harassed in the workplace. Harassment is defined in the Equality Act as unwanted conduct related to someone's age, disability, gender reassignment, race, religion or belief, sex or sexual orientation. ACAS gives several examples of what may be bullying or harassing behaviour, including spreading malicious rumours or insulting someone, exclusion or victimization, unfair treatment or deliberately undermining a competent co-worker by constant criticism.

The term 'whistleblowing' is used to describe a situation where a worker (including both employees and independent contractors under the control of an employer) makes a 'protected disclosure'. In certain circumstances, whistleblowers are protected from being dismissed under the Public Interest Disclosure Act 1998, and from detrimental treatment under the Employment Rights Act 1996. A worker's disclosure is only a protected disclosure if an employee reasonably believes that the act that is the subject of their disclosure is a criminal offence, a breach of a legal requirement, a miscarriage of justice, is likely to endanger people's health and safety or will cause environmental damage, and is made in the public interest.

A company may also recognize a particular trade union and be subject to a collective consultation agreement. By the terms of this agreement employees may have a right to be consulted in respect of certain topics (possibly such as pay, hours, holiday entitlement and other terms and conditions of employment). Employees may also have a statutory right to take time off to engage in union activities, as well as not be subjected to a detriment because of their trade union membership.

These legal issues carry significant risks for an employer. Employees who pursue such claims in an employment tribunal can seek a variety of remedies to compensate them for breaches of their contractual or statutory rights. These legal issues often overlap with an employee's claim that he or she has been unfairly dismissed, but unlike compensation for unfair dismissal which is capped (currently at 12 months' pay or £80,541 from April 2017, whichever is lower) there is no cap on the amount of compensation an employment tribunal can award in respect of a successful claim of discrimination or whistleblowing. An employer therefore has to be extremely mindful of the way these legal issues are dealt with in the workplace, as the risks to an employer of a successful employment tribunal claim are substantial. However, before the employment relationship is terminated and formal legal action is instigated against an employer, where an employee feels he or she has been discriminated against, has been the subject of harassing behaviour, or is suffering a detriment as a result of making a protected disclosure, he or she has the right to try to resolve the issue in the first instance by raising a grievance with his or her employer.

Dispute resolution at work: the grievance and disciplinary processes

The grievance process is how an employee formally raises a complaint with the employer and the disciplinary process is how employers formally address issues of (alleged) misconduct committed by their employees or poor performance. Although there is no legally binding process an employer must follow in dealing with an employee's grievance or conducting a disciplinary process, the ACAS Code of Practice (the Code) provides guidance on these procedures for both employers and employees. A failure to follow the Code does not, in itself, mean the company has acted unlawfully. However, employment tribunals are obliged to take the Code into account when considering the reasonableness of the parties' conduct and can adjust any awards made in relevant cases by up to 25 per cent for the unreasonable failure to comply with any provision of the Code. It is therefore very important for employers to be aware of this when considering an employee's grievance or conducting a disciplinary process.

In broad terms, the Code requires employers and employees to act reasonably and in a timely manner in respect of raising and dealing with a grievance or disciplinary issue. More specifically, an employer is obliged to conduct an investigation into the employee's grievance or alleged misconduct to establish the facts of the case. The employee should then be given the opportunity to explain his or her grievance or version of events around the act of misconduct before a decision is made, as well as having the right to be accompanied at any formal meeting and given the opportunity to appeal any formal decision.

An employer will either uphold or reject an employee's grievance (including any appeal) or find that an employee has or has not committed an act of misconduct. In practice, this has the impact of promoting positional negotiations where both employee and employer hold extreme positions regarding the ultimate solution to the dispute. As such, the grievance and disciplinary processes tend to be binary in nature and promote an adversarial mentality between employee and employer. The grievance and disciplinary processes therefore naturally inhibit a mature resolution.

This is in contrast to using mediation as a form of workplace dispute resolution, which encourages principled negotiations. The basis of principled negotiations in an employment dispute is to seek a winning outcome for employee and employer by bargaining over the interests of both parties. As a result, and in contrast to the typical grievance process set out above, a whole range of potential outcomes are possible when it is used as a means of resolving an issue in the workplace. However, notwithstanding these substantial differences, there is evidence that the grievance and disciplinary processes and mediation can work together to provide a more holistic outcome to an employment dispute.

Mediation as part of the grievance and disciplinary process: the way forward?

Mediation was given particular attention in the Gibbons review of employment dispute resolution in 2007 and the Employment Act 2008. Following these, ACAS introduced mediation in the foreword of the Code, stating that where it is not possible to resolve disciplinary and grievance issues in the workplace, employers and employees should consider using an independent third party to help resolve the problem. Further, the Code states that the third party need not come from outside the organization but could be an internal mediator (as long as he or she is not involved in the disciplinary or grievance issues), although in some cases an external mediator may be appropriate. In addition to the guidance in the Code, in its response to its 2011 'Resolving Workplace Disputes' consultation, the UK government stated that it was even more convinced about the role that mediation can play as one of the forms of early dispute resolution and that there is much work to be done to embed it as an accepted part of the dispute resolution process.

In recent years, many employers have reacted positively to the greater emphasis on the use of third-party mediation as a means of resolving an employment dispute. According to the ACAS report on the 2011 Workplace Employment Relations Survey published in 2014, mediation has become a significant part of workplace dispute resolution regimes, being used in 17 per cent of workplaces that experienced a formal individual grievance.[1]

The benefits of embracing mediation as part of the grievance or disciplinary processes are significant. Not only are time, money and resources saved on potential litigation where an employee is dissatisfied with a rejected grievance and looks to more formal legal action, but mediation can also promote repaired relationships and empower staff to reach their own solutions to disputes, rebuilding mutual trust and respect between employer and employee in the process. Therefore, using mediation as part of a grievance or disciplinary procedure may provide the template as to how employment law issues should be dealt with by an employer to give itself the best possible chance to avoid everyday workplace issues escalating into substantial legal claims. Indeed, it may be that employers would benefit from replacing their grievance and disciplinary policies with a resolution policy that encompasses these points and encourages a new way to deal with workplace issues.

Mediation and the legal process – navigating through the quagmire

Issuing an employment tribunal claim signals once and for all that open hostilities have commenced. This is, in most cases, a crucial psychological stage for employees to have passed. They have indicated that they are prepared to pursue their employer to an open and formal forum and to press their legal claim.

On average, up to approximately 60 per cent of claims issued in the employment tribunal are settled by way of ACAS conciliated settlements or withdrawn.[2] Of these withdrawn claims, we assume that a substantial number were withdrawn as a result of privately negotiated settlement agreements (though of course the exact figure cannot be known). The prevalence of negotiated settlements even at this late stage shows that genuinely aggrieved litigants consistently opt for an out-of-court method of dispute resolution by an overwhelming majority. These numbers do not take into account the number of privately negotiated settlement agreements that conclude the dispute (between, possibly, just as aggrieved litigants) before a tribunal claim is made. What this statistic shows us is that most parties involved in an employment dispute will ultimately find a preferable method of dispute resolution to the employment tribunal process. There are several reasons why this is the case, ranging from the respective litigants' changing appetites to continue the litigation to simple cost considerations.

Consider the practical downsides presented by open litigation:

- *Litigation is expensive,* with legal fees often running to tens of thousands of pounds. In the employment tribunal there are very limited prospects for recovering costs from the other side.

- *Delay.* The extent of this will obviously depend on how busy the court or tribunal is, but it is nonetheless likely that there will be a period of several months of the prospect of the unresolved case hanging over the organization. These months are likely to be spent complying with tribunal/court orders; preparing witness statements, carrying out extensive searches of document filing systems, including electronic systems, for disclosure (which can be another added expense in terms of cost and management time).

Finally, there is the clear downside of open litigation:

- *Reputation management.* The prospect of defending even an unmeritorious employment-related claim in public is not appealing.

- *Uncertainty of outcome.* Employment tribunal hearings are unpredictable. Even if you are sure of the legal merits of your case, there are any number of potential pitfalls that can trip up your defence in the course of a tribunal hearing (ranging from witnesses performing badly to the judge just disagreeing with your arguments). It is impossible to guarantee the outcome and there is always an element of risk.

- *Stress and lifestyle impacts.* Employment tribunal proceedings are stressful and time-consuming and will (at points) monopolize the attention of management. Lengthy disclosure exercises, witness statements and the preparation for the tribunal hearing can take a toll on individuals and organizations, as well as having to recount the flash points of what may well have been a difficult employment relationship.

All points considered, there are several basic reasons why parties would wish to give serious thought to an alternative form of dispute resolution. This section sets out how mediation can assist in finding a way out of an employment dispute. It is split into three parts:

1 The procedural imperative to consider mediation.

2 The strategic benefits it offers in managing the dispute.

3 The main legal points to consider when approaching mediation.

1 The procedural imperative to consider mediation

Depending on the subject matter of the dispute, parties to employment-related litigation will find themselves in the county or high court or the employment tribunal. Irrespective of which of these will hear their dispute, before commencing full litigation there is a procedural imperative for the parties to have considered mediation. Before commencing litigation in the county court or high court, parties must comply with the Pre-Action Protocols, which require the parties to consider litigation as a last resort or engage in some efforts to settle the dispute possibly including mediation. Civil Procedure Rules Part 1 Rule 1.4 provides that when managing cases the court must encourage the parties to use an alternative dispute resolution procedure.

This procedural imperative to consider mediation also applies in the employment tribunal (ET). Rule 3 of the ET Rules of Procedure requires tribunals to 'wherever practical and appropriate encourage the use by the parties of the services of ACAS, judicial or other mediation, or other means of resolving their disputes by agreement.' Rule 53(1) of the ET Rules of Procedure provides further that the employment tribunal at a preliminary hearing must 'explore the possibility of settlement or alternative dispute resolution (including judicial mediation)'. In accordance with this rule, if the case is deemed suitable, the parties may be offered the opportunity of judicial mediation. While judicial mediation remains a comparatively formal exercise for both parties, it nonetheless offers similar benefits to private mediation. Importantly also (from a procedural perspective) if a judge were to recommend this to parties it should be given due consideration. Similar obligations of the tribunals to consider, and powers to order, mediation are also present in the Employment Appeal Tribunal Rules.

It would be prudent for organizations to be aware – regardless of whether they are facing (or considering) claims in the county or high court or employment tribunal – of their obligations to give consideration to whether the dispute could be settled by mediation or be prepared for the potential for the court or tribunal to order it.

2 Strategic benefits

While any mediation will almost certainly be conducted on a confidential and 'without prejudice' basis (detailed below) and so not able to be referred to by either party at a later hearing, engaging in mediation *even if unsuccessful* can be useful in managing the overall dispute process for several reasons:

- Mediation gives employees the opportunity to be more detailed and structured in their arguments than they have perhaps been required to be up until that point, and an effective mediator will assist them with this. This allows an organization to more accurately assess the legal (and financial) risks posed by the potential claim and can help provide some useful strategic insights even if the mediation is not successful.

- As part of the above, mediation can also be an effective tool for narrowing the issues between the parties. This can be especially useful in the context of an employment dispute in which it is not uncommon to see a wide range of claims alleged by an aggrieved employee. While not all of these may be resolved, mediation may well enable the parties to agree that some elements of the claim can be settled or dropped and effectively define their differences in respect of others. This will not only save time and expense throughout the remainder of the dispute but will enable the parties to more accurately conduct an assessment of the strength of their respective positions going into a hearing (which may, even after the mediation has concluded, yield more fruitful settlement discussions).

- Though subject to the confidentiality considerations discussed below, if it is possible to raise in submissions at a tribunal hearing that the company had participated in mediation, it will go some way to showing the employer's reasonable behaviour in the workplace dispute. Though clearly very fact-sensitive, this can be a persuasive point when a tribunal is later assessing whether a company's actions were within the range of responses. This is also especially applicable should an organization be facing the risk of a constructive unfair dismissal where the alleged repudiatory breach is failure to change a particular working environment. It becomes increasingly difficult for an ex-employee to claim that an employer has repudiated the employment relationship when it has actively taken steps to manage frayed relations between employees through mediation.

- In addition, preparation for the mediation will to an extent duplicate the preparation process for the hearing. While it is, of course, a benefit of the mediation process that preparation is not as onerous in time or cost as for a full hearing, the key consideration is that even if the mediation is unsuccessful not all of the cost and effort will have gone to waste. A party that engages in good faith in mediation will have prepared documents and investigated the issues raised.

There is, therefore, merit in engaging in even a failed mediation. It effectively serves as a 'dummy run' for a later tribunal hearing, disclosure exercise and preparation of witnesses and reduces the costs when having to do this ahead of the full hearing.

3 Confidentiality as a key legal consideration

Confidentiality and whether a mediation is held on a 'without prejudice' basis are key legal considerations for parties to bear in mind. Almost all mediations will be held at least on a confidential basis; meaning that what is discussed within the mediation cannot be discussed with other colleagues or outside the organization. However, in certain circumstances, mediations will be held on a without prejudice basis. The without prejudice rule provides that discussions between parties in a genuine attempt to resolve a dispute will be inadmissible as evidence in any subsequent employment tribunal proceedings or other litigation. The discussions are essentially 'off the record'. This is different to mediations held only a confidential basis as these mediations (and the discussions that occurred during them) can be referred to in subsequent proceedings.

Importantly, however, whether a mediation will be conducted on a without prejudice basis is not necessarily a choice for the employer. It is possible for either party to assert that any discussions that are had in an attempt to resolve a dispute are covered by the without prejudice rule even if this was not expressly noted at the time. To come within the definition of 'dispute' there is no need for formal legal proceedings to have commenced and the dispute does not need to be well defined, but it must exist prior to the settlement discussions. In a workplace scenario, a dispute will most likely have arisen in any situation in which a breach or unlawful act (by either party) has already occurred or is being alleged.

Tactically, however, holding mediations on a without prejudice basis will be broadly beneficial for the employer. Without prejudice discussions allow parties to negotiate more freely without the worry that what they say during the mediation or their willingness to engage in settlement talks implies acceptance of liability. Even though the without prejudice rule may clearly apply, it would be sensible from a practical perspective to make this clear to all parties prior to the mediation (and to label documents and correspondence clearly as being sent on a without prejudice basis).

However, parties should be aware that the without prejudice rule is not without exceptions. It was established in the case of *BNP Paribas v Mezzotero*[3] that the without prejudice rule does not necessarily extend to protect unguarded comments that reveal a clearly unlawful intent to a party's action. Parties should therefore be aware that not all comments made during what would otherwise have been a without prejudice mediation will necessarily be covered by the without prejudice rule and that imprudent remarks, such as discriminatory comments, may well severely damage a party's prospects if the matter proceeds to a full hearing or gives rise to an additional claim.

Conversely, a mediation arising from a situation in which there hasn't been a dispute (such as a mediation following a breakdown of a professional relationship between colleagues) will not be conducted on a without prejudice basis. Such mediations would be covered only by the normal rules of confidentiality (meaning the participants could not immediately discuss it widely) but would not be on a without prejudice basis. Importantly, in these types of 'non-dispute' scenarios, it can improve an employer's ability to defend subsequent potential claims of constructive unfair dismissal and/or discrimination if it is able to show that it has proactively managed a situation and sought to resolve it through encouraging the involved employees to engage in a mediation. Tactically, organizations may wish to avoid discussing topics over which there is a clear dispute in that mediation to avoid the risk that they would be barred from including it in the defence of a future possible claim.

In addition, prior to the mediation the parties and the mediator should enter into a mediation agreement. This provides an additional layer of contractual confidentiality between the parties that enables a party to protect itself further by seeking (in the event of a breach) injunctive relief. This will also provide a direct contractual relationship of confidentiality between the mediator and each party separately.[4] This direct contractual confidentiality between the parties and the mediator is what allows the parties to share information more freely with the mediator in private sessions. Covered by this direct relationship of contractual confidentiality the mediator can gain an insight into the relative importance of different points and will be able to see the areas for negotiation and agreement. Importantly, the parties are given a method by which to share information with the other side through the conduit of the mediator, knowing that the mediator is bound by the respective duties of confidentiality. Therefore, these legal protections of confidentiality and/or 'without prejudice' that underpin the mediation process are often important factors enabling the parties to resolve their dispute and should be given due consideration when approaching a mediation exercise.

Practical considerations

Having considered mediation as a means of resolving disputes during employment and assessing the benefits of using mediation as a formal dispute resolution procedure, we now turn to looking at some practical considerations and guidance for organizations that want to be proactive in seeking alternatives to litigation. This section will look at mediation clauses in contracts of employment, highlighting the key points to be aware of when drafting an ADR clause, and then moving on to discuss the various guises of early neutral evaluation – a practice that has gained much popularity in recent years.

Mediation clauses in contracts of employment

Having recognized the benefits of mediation, organizations may wish to incorporate references to mediation in their key documentation. This will enable (or at least strongly encourage) both the company and the aggrieved employee to participate in a form of alternative dispute resolution before commencing an open dispute. In doing so, employers can manage conflict proactively and control risk factors in litigation.

The key pieces of documentation into which organizations should consider incorporating references to mediation are primarily their standard form employment contract and grievance and disciplinary policy within the staff handbook. These clauses should provide that if any dispute arises in respect of matters governed by those documents themselves, both parties should first participate in mediation with a view to resolving that dispute without the need for recourse to a tribunal or court. These clauses should refer to a separate mediation policy that sets out the main provisions for and basic terms of how the mediation will be conducted. A standard mediation clause in an employment contract may be as simple as:

> *Mediation and Alternative Dispute Resolution.* If any disputes arise from this Agreement or employment relationship the parties will attempt to resolve such disputes in accordance with the mediation policy contained within the staff handbook prior to commencing any formal legal action in any court of England and Wales.

The mediation policy itself should address three key areas: confidentiality (as discussed above); the circumstances in which the parties will be bound by any outcomes (usually to require a further formal document setting out the terms of the agreement between the parties); and costs (in respect of which the company should be careful not to agree to paying for the employee's own advice, but may be willing to cover the cost of any external mediator). It may also wish to provide for the mediation to be covered by a further mediation agreement that would set out the terms that expressly govern that specific mediation (and would incorporate more detailed terms on the above issues). This would be especially appropriate for mediations of more serious disputes that present a higher legal risk.

The role of early neutral evaluation

While mediation may be the best approach to resolving a workplace dispute, the statistics tell us that a substantial number of claims still reach the employment tribunal and court system. As we noted above, the employment relationship can be complex and can sometimes prove to be a barrier to reaching a resolution. For example, even where there is a well-drafted and comprehensive mediation clause in an employment agreement, sometimes an employer and employee have such contrasting understandings or perceptions about the legal issues or the facts affecting their dispute that a resolution seems impossible. In such a case, where a commercial resolution is sought but the parties' contrasting views of the issues in the case are proving problematic, early neutral evaluation is a practice that has gained popularity in recent years.

In early neutral evaluation, a neutral person with specialist knowledge and skills is invited to evaluate the case or any particular issues in it. That evaluation is not binding, but it is made available to both parties to consider and will inevitably inform the discussions that follow. Indeed, an independent view of the case or issues can sometimes clear the way for more constructive negotiations to take place, and as such is often seen as beneficial for both parties to a dispute.

One form of early neutral evaluation that is of particular relevance to employment disputes is judicial assessment in the employment tribunal. Judicial assessment requires both claimant and respondent to agree to a free appraisal of the claim or response by an employment tribunal judge. The intended outcome of judicial assessment is that the judge will indicate the merits of each party's case and then offer an assessment of each party's prospects of success. While it is important to emphasize that judicial assessment is a strictly provisional view of a case without any regard to the relevant evidence, the impact of a judge's view on litigants cannot be underestimated. For example, where a claimant and a respondent both think they have an iron-clad case against the other prior to judicial assessment, if a judge indicates that each party's prospects of success is finely balanced, that may well be enough to encourage settlement negotiations to take place at an earlier stage than where an independent view of the case had not been sought.

Judicial guidance on the value of early neutral evaluation has been clear. In the recent case of *Seals & Anor v Williams*,[5] Norris J noted that early neutral evaluation is particularly useful where the parties have very differing views of the prospect of success and perhaps an inadequate understanding of the risks of litigation itself. The various guises early neutral evaluation can take, and the merits of doing so, are therefore important to bear in mind when a dispute between two parties has reached formal litigation, as it may provide a platform for resolving a conflict, where other methods, including mediation, have been unsuccessful.

Conclusion

Conflict is an inevitable reality of the employment relationship. The legal issues that arise have their root in statute and contract, and carry significant consequences. However, the way in which disputes are resolved in the workplace can have a substantial impact on whether open litigation is unavoidable.

Treating an employee's grievance as a management problem that requires a swift and decisive (if not adversarial) response may not be in the organization's strategic or legal best interests. Rather, incorporating a requirement to engage in principled negotiations to resolve a dispute before the commencement of formal legal proceedings has been shown to be a more effective approach. In this regard, the way forward may be to replace an employer's grievance and disciplinary policies with one resolution policy that incorporates a more holistic approach to dispute resolution.

However, when litigation is unavoidable, it is important for employers to have due regard to the options available to them to resolve the dispute outside the courts. Not only have these methods been shown to be effective in their own right, but also the parties may well be under a procedural obligation to consider them. While imperfect, mediation and early neutral evaluation have considerable benefits and can enable settlement discussions to occur more organically. It must be remembered that litigation is a last resort, and the parties should openly look to explore the available alternative means of dispute resolution at their disposal.

Notes

1 http://www.acas.org.uk/media/pdf/2/d/1014-WERS2011-analysis-D-and-G-procedures-workplace-mediation.pdf

2 https://www.gov.uk/government/collections/tribunals-statistics

3 *BNP Paribas v Mezzotero* [2004] IRLR 58 (EAT).

4 https://www.cedr.com/articles/?item=Confidentiality-a-guide-for-mediators

5 *Seals & Anor v Williams* [2015] EWHC 1829 (Ch).

PART TWO
A practical guide to managing conflict

PART TWO
A practical guide
to managing
conflict

Measuring the costs of conflict 05

The conflict at work made me feel like I had bricks in my belly. I couldn't sleep, I couldn't eat. It was all I thought about. It affected my relationship with my kids and my partner. It was probably one of the most difficult periods of my life next to losing my father. (Anonymous)

KEY LEARNING POINTS IN THIS CHAPTER

- There are significant costs of conflict to organizations. These may be visible or hidden costs.
- Unresolved conflict can have a direct impact on 10 areas of the modern organization:
  1 Time spent.
  2 Absence levels (stress and wellbeing).
  3 Employee attrition (turnover) levels.
  4 Employee engagement levels and reduced motivation at work.
  5 Productivity levels.
  6 Reputational damage.
  7 Impact on customer experience.
  8 Legal costs.
  9 Settlement agreements, compensation awards or costs.
  10 Overall financial impact.
- Organizations benefit by evaluating the costs and impact of conflict as a precursor to developing a conflict management strategy.
- The method for undertaking a conflict analysis is based on a participatory action research model. This model utilizes quantitative and qualitative data techniques in order to understand the nature of conflict management within your organization.

- Using the TCM Conflict Calculator™ can be a valuable way of gathering data about the costs and the impact of conflict in your organization.
- The costs of conflict are a valuable source of baseline data for use in evaluating the cost-benefit and return on investment of a future conflict management strategy.

Introduction

So far in this book, I have explained that conflict can be either 'functional' – constructive and healthy, or 'dysfunctional' – destructive and harmful. I have also described numerous causes of conflict and I have highlighted five potential reactions to conflict: fight, flight, freeze, fall and a new f, flow, which happens at times of functional conflict and during adult-to-adult dialogue. I have asserted that most conflicts follow a distinct and broadly predictable lifecycle and the earlier the resolution process can happen, the less of a negative impact the conflict will have. It won't have passed you by, I'm sure, that I have also made some critical assessments of the traditional approaches for managing conflict, in particular the discipline, grievance and bullying policies.

In previous chapters, I have explored some of the common causes of conflict and I have set out some of the broad costs of conflict to people, to teams and to the organization as a whole. The costs of conflict to any business can be great. There is a growing body of evidence that supports this view but, a lot more work needs to be undertaken to understand the true cost of conflict. The challenges that we face in gathering data include:

- Organizations are often resistant to sharing sensitive data they perceive may paint them in a bad light. For example, for every case study that I got consent to use in this book, I had at least 20 organizations that felt uncomfortable contributing.
- Conflict is complex (academics call it multi-modal) and it is sometimes hard to pin down its exact impact as opposed to other factors at play.
- Many organizations do not gather specific data relating to conflict and, thus, many of the costs of conflict are below the horizon, hidden and invisible.

However, more research is being carried out in this area and more and more data is beginning to emerge relating to the costs of conflict. For instance, in a report published jointly by the CIPD and OPP in 2008, it was found that the majority of employees (85 per cent) have to deal with conflict to some degree. The report goes on to suggest that 'The average employee spends 2.1 hours a week dealing with conflict. For the UK alone, that translates to 370 million working days lost every year as a result of conflict in the workplace.' According to the joint CIPD/OPP (2008) report:

- 16 per cent say a recent dispute escalated in duration and/or intensity.
- 27 per cent of employees have seen conflict lead to personal attacks.
- 25 per cent have seen a workplace conflict result in sickness or absence.
- 9 per cent saw it lead to a project failure.

The financial cost of conflict

In 2006, the Centre for Dispute Resolution (CEDR) announced at a conference that conflict costs United Kingdom organizations an eye-watering £33 billion each year.[1] Whether this data is a true or accurate reflection of the real cost is hard to say, but it certainly does bring the issue into perspective.

The CIPD has produced a number of reports examining conflict and the role of conflict management programmes such as mediation. Most recently, a report published by the CIPD suggested that almost 4 out of 10 (38 per cent) of UK employees had experienced some form of interpersonal conflict in the workplace in the previous year (CIPD, 2015).

The organizational cost of conflict

A report published by ACAS in 2015 presented findings from one of the most in-depth examinations of conflict management ever undertaken in the United Kingdom. The research was undertaken by two prominent academics at a large hospital – Northumbria Healthcare NHS Foundation Trust. Coincidentally, I had been working with the Trust for several years to establish their conflict management programme. According to the report, managers within the Trust identified wasted time (staff and management) as the greatest perceived cost of conflict.

The report revealed that 29 per cent of the conflicts experienced by managers lasted for more than 12 months. The report also provided evidence suggesting that workplace conflict had a more direct impact on both performance and wellbeing:

- Over a third of managers felt that conflict reduced motivation and productivity.
- 28 per cent reported that it had a negative impact on decision making.
- Almost a third felt that it led to increased health costs or staff absence.

- Almost one in five respondents mentioned conflict as having compromised the quality of patient care/experience.

Unresolved conflict as a driver of disengagement

I am particularly interested in the impact of conflict on motivation and employee engagement. During an in-depth interview with Cathy Brown, Chief Executive of Engage for Success, she summed up the impact of conflict:

> When it is ignored or it is handled badly, conflict can have the most significant impact on employee engagement within an organization. Unresolved conflicts also have an aggregated impact throughout an organization. I think it's because conflict sits in that bucket of things which people find incredibly hard to deal with. It's about people and emotions, and we find that difficult to deal with in our personal lives and at an organizational level. Dealing with conflict is hard because it's messy, its untidy and because there isn't necessarily a right answer or a mathematical way of doing it that will result in a particular outcome. It makes us feel hugely uncomfortable and so, as a result, we avoid tackling it, we avoid learning about it, and by doing so we make situations very much worse.

How to measure the cost and impact of conflict in your organization

Effective research into the nature and extent of organizational conflict will:

- Help organizations to understand the causes and the costs of conflict.
- Enable organizations to develop meaningful conflict management strategies.
- Help organizations to measure the impact of their conflict management activities.
- Support the government and policy makers in developing effective conflict management policies and strategies.
- Facilitate benchmarking exercises and the dissemination of best practice.

Building a business case for managing conflict

One way to build a business case to evidence the need for change and to demonstrate the potential value of a new approach for managing conflict is to gather evidence that is specific to your own organization. Many organizations tell me that data and evidence that is collected by the organization itself is:

- More relevant to them and is therefore more meaningful.
- More closely aligned to their own situation and context.
- A valuable way to secure engagement from a wide and diverse range of organizational stakeholders.
- Likely to be taken more seriously by senior decision makers.
- A precursor to the development of an integrated conflict management system.
- A useful baseline measure for evaluating the impact of any subsequent conflict management strategy or mediation scheme.

Gathering data can be fun and can have unintended consequences

Gathering data and evidence about the impact of conflict on your organizations need not be a harrowing or all-consuming task. It can be a fun, challenging and enjoyable piece of work. Many times, I have come up against challenges from people who see data gathering as too time-consuming, too complex or too confusing. It really does not need to be any of those things. In reality, gathering data and listening to people's experiences of conflict can begin to engage them in the process of developing a conflict management strategy or an internal mediation scheme.

Data that can support the business case

Visible costs

These are generally easier to measure and deliver quantitative data. Most of the data will be available already as part of other monitoring processes and the data will need to be consolidated and triangulated.[2] In some cases, systems for gathering the data may need to be designed. This chapter supplies everything that you need to do this:

- Time spent – how much time was spent by each person involved.
- Opportunity costs – what could they have been doing instead of dealing with the conflict.
- Sickness absence.
- Turnover – costs of losing good staff.

- Cover and hiring costs – costs of covering posts or hiring new staff.
- Legal fees – the inevitable legal bills that follow a conflict.
- Compensation awards – these are applied by the tribunal. Where there is proven discrimination, the awards at an employment tribunal are uncapped.
- Delays on project delivery and associated fines and litigation.
- Regulator fines and costs – costs applied in cases of conflict that result in regulatory or compliance issues.

Hidden costs

These costs are often harder to measure and may require quantitative data to be gathered via focus groups, interviews and surveys:

- Settlement agreements (out of court payments) – these are often confidential but can run into tens if not hundreds of thousands of pounds.
- Reduced productivity.
- Impact on employee engagement/staff satisfaction.
- Impact on customer experience – measured by increased volumes of complaints and reductions in repeat business.

Intangible costs

These are hard to quantify but qualitative data (stories and narratives) can be a useful way of demonstrating the intangible impact of conflict in the workplace:

- Increased stress, anxiety, depression and other issues relating to mental health.
- Reduced morale.
- Presenteeism.
- Insomnia.
- Damage to branding and reputation.
- Damage to employee brand.

I recall setting up a mediation scheme in a large public transport organization and one of the people who attended a focus group was extremely cynical at the outset. However, he had some great stories to tell about conflicts that he had been involved in and he contributed enormously to the data gathering exercise. He then went on to train as an internal mediator and become a champion of mediation across the organization. Had he not been at the focus group, he may never have got involved and his voice would not have been heard.

The method of gathering data can help you to develop a multidisciplinary working group to assist you as you develop and deliver your conflict management strategy.

Resolution recommendations

Undertaking a conflict analysis is not an academic exercise and it does not require a PhD. The evidence and data do not need to be validated in the same way as a doctoral thesis needs to be. Good enough is good enough. As long as the data you gather is accurate and reflects the current reality of your organization, it will be more than adequate for you to use in your conflict management strategy and as a baseline measure for future evaluation and return on investment (ROI) purposes.

It is right that conflict management becomes an evidence-based activity. Just because it is morally a good thing to do does not give mediation and the associated resolution activities a special dispensation not to be held to account in the same way that every other pound spent is. For those gathering the data it can have a positive impact on their CV. Demonstrating to a future employer or during a promotion that you have developed an evidence-based project and have generated data that is used as baseline for an ROI measure is a sure-fire way to jump the queue when it comes to applying for that next promotion.

Many organizations are now submitting their conflict management approaches for awards and accolades. Any half-decent award process will put gathering of baseline data and evidence at the top of the criteria to be used to choose the winners.

Undertaking your conflict analysis: a practical guide

The quick conflict health check in Part Three of this book provides a valuable insight into how conflicts are managed within your organization. The following sections provide a more in-depth analysis. They draw on various diagnostic processes that I have developed for use in organizations to help them to secure a better understanding of the cost to them of conflict. The diagnostic tools will enable you to gather data relating to the impact of conflict on the following 10 areas of your organization:

1 Time spent (including time spent by managers, HR and unions, etc).

2 Impact on wellbeing – including stress and absence levels.

3 Attrition levels – losing valued and skilled employees.

4 Reduced employee engagement levels and trust in the workplace.

5 Reduced productivity levels including innovation and motivation.

6 Reputational damage.

7 Impact on customer experience.

8 Legal costs – including the cost of lawyers, legal advice and legal representation at proceedings.

9 Settlement agreements, compensation awards, tribunal claims, etc.

10 Overall financial impact on the organization.

The methodology that I recommend to gather quantitative and qualitative data is based on a research model called Participatory Action Research (PAR). The conflict analysis is a participatory and active means of gathering quantitative and qualitative data.

Quantitative data is information about quantities; that is, information that can be measured and written down with numbers. As part of a conflict analysis, quantitative data will include measures such as how many grievances were received in the last year; how much time was spent handling conflict; how many cases ended up in a formal process; how much money was spent on legal advice, etc. *Qualitative data* is descriptive and draws on people's personal experiences, feelings, interactions and concerns. It is, by nature, subjective, but the stories that are gathered can be profoundly powerful and can provide valuable insights into the reality of managing conflict in a way that statistics, numbers and percentages fail to do. When combined as part of a conflict analysis, quantitative and qualitative data provide a valuable and often challenging picture of conflict within the organization.

The conflict analysis that I recommend includes five distinct data gathering methods:

1 Desktop review.

2 Surveys.

3 In-depth interviews.

4 Focus groups.

5 Conflict Calculator™.

1 Desktop review

This is an opportunity to draw together historical data gathered from existing sources and processes within your organization. The data may be collected from the past 12, 24 or 36 months. For purposes of expediency, I don't generally recommend going back further than three years. However, my experience has led me to believe that the further back in time that you can go, the more detailed and valuable the subsequent trend analysis will be.

Resolution recommendations

Data that is collected as part of the desktop review may include any of the following:

- Grievance levels, including action taken and outcomes.
- Bullying and harassment allegations, including action taken and outcomes.
- Disciplinary action taken relating to workplace grievances or bullying and harassment allegations.
- Data from stress audits or other audits into workplace wellbeing.
- Allegations and findings of discrimination, including action taken and outcomes.
- Employment tribunal levels and outcomes.
- Volume and value of settlement agreements or COT3s arising from unresolved conflicts (COT3 forms are used to record the settlement of a dispute at an employment tribunal or through early conciliation provided by a conciliation officer from ACAS).
- Absence data, particularly any data that relates to stress absence or suspensions due to workplace conflicts or allegations of bullying.
- Employee engagement survey data.

- Data gathered from exit interviews.
- Data gathered from analysis of whistleblowing cases.
- Data gathered from appraisals.
- Customer complaints or serious incidents that have arisen as a result of a conflict at work.
- Levels of public awareness of conflict in your organization such as press clippings, comments on social media or in the news media.

Making sense of the data that you have gathered

It is unlikely that all of the above data will be available; that is ok. It is possible to work with a limited amount of data to develop an understanding of the organizational needs and context. Some organizations, recognizing that the data may be a bit sparse, design conflict analysis data gathering processes to help them collect data for the future. For example, they may ask a question about conflict in future employee engagement surveys or they may start to develop more effective grievance and dispute resolution case management systems. In any event, once you have identified and gathered the data, it is important to prepare a series of questions ready to answer as part of your desktop analysis:

- Is the data current and accurate? In other words, can you trust it?
- What does this data tell us about conflict and the management of conflict in our organization?
- How does the data triangulate with other data, ie does it compare with or match any other data that you have gathered?
- Are there any trends or patterns that are discernible?
- What conclusions can we begin to draw from the data?
- Are there any gaps in the data?
- What research is needed as part of the conflict analysis to fill the gaps?

2 Surveys

A survey can be a useful way of gathering data from a selection of your employees. There are no hard and fast rules on how the survey should be set up. However, it needs to generate data that will stand up to scrutiny and from that point of view it is generally better that the respondents can supply their responses anonymously.

In the past, I have run surveys as part of organizational conflict analysis as follows: 1) a survey of people who have been part of a grievance, bullying, discrimination process to ask for feedback about their experiences; and 2) a survey to a random sample of the workforce. In smaller organizations (500 employees or fewer) it may be feasible to send the survey to all employees. There are numerous online survey systems that are available to help you design and evaluate the data gathered; one such is Survey Monkey. The three types of questions that I use most commonly in surveys are:

1 Open-ended questions where the respondents can enter their response into a text box.

2 A Likert question where the respondents rate their experience on a scale. This is generally followed up by a free-text box so that the respondents can enter more detail if required.

3 Multiple choice – where the respondents choose one or more answers from a range of possible responses.

Below is a series of questions that I use in surveys as part of a wider conflict analysis.

Survey questions

Survey to individuals who have experienced a grievance, bullying or harassment procedure

Introduction

We are gathering data as part of a conflict analysis and to help us to develop a conflict management strategy. You have been sent this questionnaire as you have participated in a conflict management exercise in the past one, two or three years.

This is an anonymous questionnaire, which means that you are not required to provide your details and we will not be able to identify you. Please complete the questionnaire as honestly and as thoroughly as you can. The information that you supply will be used as part of our review of how we handle conflict and also to help us decide how we should handle conflict in the future.

Table 5.1 Conflict analysis survey

Main question	Question type	Supplementary 1	Supplementary 2
1 Which process did you experience?	Multiple choice: **1** Grievance **2** Bullying and harassment **3** Fair treatment		
2 Please use up to 5 words or phrases to describe your experience of the process	Free text		
3 In your view, what was the process trying to achieve?	Free text		
4 If you initiated the process, what did you expect would happen?	Multiple choice or free text	Did the process meet your expectations?	
5 If the process was initiated against you, what did you expect would happen?	Multiple choice or free text	Did the process meet your expectations?	
6 What, if any, impact did the process have on you?	Free text	What, if any, impact did the process have on your relationship with your colleagues?	What, if any, impact did the process have on your relationship with your family?

(continued)

Table 5.1 (Continued)

Main question	Question type	Supplementary 1	Supplementary 2
7 What changes would you like to make to the process to make it more effective?	Free text		
8 Were you provided with adequate opportunities to resolve the issues informally?	Free text	How effective were these?	
9 Were you offered mediation as part of the process?	Multiple choice	If not why not?	If so what was the outcome of mediation?
10 Roughly, how long did the process take: from start to finish?	Multiple choice	Was this.... • About right? • Too long? • Too short?	
11 On a scale of 1 to 10 (10 being excellent and 1 being very poor) how satisfied were you with the process?	Likert	Please describe your reason for your response	
12 Please provide further details here about the process.	Free text		

Employee survey

Introduction

We are gathering data as part of a conflict analysis and to help us to develop a conflict management strategy. We are sending this questionnaire to a sample of employees within xyz to give you the chance to let us know what we are getting right and where we need to improve.

This is an anonymous questionnaire, which means that you are not required to provide your details and we will not be able to identify you. Please complete the questionnaire as honestly and as thoroughly as you can. The information that you supply will be used as part of our review of how we handle conflict and also to help us decide how we should handle conflict in the future.

Table 5.2   Employee survey as part of developing a conflict management strategy

Main question	Question type	Supplementary question
1 Please use up to 5 words or phrases to describe your experience of the process	Free text	
2 Have you ever experienced conflict at work?	YES/NO	When was the conflict?
3 What was the conflict about?	Free text	What impact did it have?
4 Have you ever witnessed other people in conflict?	YES/NO	When was the conflict?
5 What was the conflict about?	Free text	What impact did it have?
6 On a scale of 1 to 10 (10 being excellent and 1 being very poor) how effective is your manager at handling conflict?	Likert scale plus free text	
7 On a scale of 1 to 10 (10 being excellent and 1 being very poor) how effective is our current grievance and bullying procedure at resolving conflict?	Likert scale plus free text	

(*continued*)

Table 5.2 *(Continued)*

Main question	Question type	Supplementary question
8 On a scale of 1 to 10 (10 being excellent and 1 being very poor) overall, how effective is our organization at handling conflict?	Likert scale plus free text	
9 What would you change to make our organization better at handling conflict?	Free text	

3 In-depth interviews

Interviews can be an effective way of gathering qualitative data. In the past, I have interviewed the following people or representatives of a particular function as part of undertaking a conflict analysis (it is generally helpful to interview a senior leader from many of the functions as well as a front-line role):

- members of the senior leadership team;
- line management;
- organizational development;
- human resources;
- learning and development;
- union or works council reps;
- industrial relations;
- employee relations;
- occupational health;
- equality or diversity groups;
- customer experience;
- supply chain management.

In-depth interviews tend to last for about an hour and can be carried out face-to-face, by phone or via a video conference. See over for some typical questions that I would ask during an in-depth interview. For each question, ask the interviewee to provide supporting evidence or as much detail as possible. Allow the interview to flow naturally and avoid making it sound scripted. Phone or video calls may be able to be recorded. If the interview is face-to-face, most mobile phones now have memo recording. In any case, it is advisable to check with the interviewee if they are happy for you to record the interview so that you can refer to it later.

Resolution recommendations

How to set up and run an in-depth interview

Here are some typical conflict analysis in-depth interview questions:

- Please describe your role in relation to managing conflict.
- What are some of the common causes of conflict in xyz organization?
- What is the organizational impact of unresolved conflict?
- What is the human impact of unresolved conflict?
- How effective is xyz at managing conflict?
- Does xyz do enough to measure the impact of conflict? If not, what more can be done?
- What stands out as best practice within xyz?
- What is xyz organization getting wrong?
- What needs to change in order to improve conflict management in xyz organization?
- How effective are our leaders and managers at handling conflict?
- Do we do enough to support our leaders and managers to manage conflict?
- What role do unions play in managing conflict?
- What role does HR play?
- What role do others play?
- What is your attitude to mediation?
- What are your constituents' or colleagues' attitudes to mediation?
- If you could describe the kind of culture you'd like to see in three years' time, what would it be?

4 Focus groups

Focus groups bring people together to discuss a particular topic or issue. Used as part of a conflict analysis, focus groups are a highly effective way of getting people talking about conflict and generating valuable qualitative data. Invite a wide cross-section of stakeholders to attend the focus groups. Such multidisciplinary focus groups are an effective way of generating debate and therefore yield more valuable data for use as part of the conflict analysis. By conducting a focus group, you are also sending a powerful message to your stakeholders about your commitment to listening to them and valuing their views and experiences.

Resolution recommendations

How to set up and run an effective focus group

Focus groups tend to include group sizes of between five and 20 individuals. It is advisable to have two people present to facilitate the focus group. The format of the focus group is highly participatory. One person takes the lead, managing the questions and the follow-up discussions; another takes notes and provides support where required during discussions.

Note. Avoid entering into the debate yourself. Your role is to facilitate the debate by asking questions, listening to the group's responses, reflecting back what you have heard and gathering information for use as part of the conflict analysis.

Focus groups tend to last for two to three hours (depending on size) and are split into roughly four parts:

1 Welcome, introductions and objectives (10 minutes).

2 Conflict: context and analysis (60–90 minutes).

3 Testing potential conflict management solutions (40–60 minutes)

4 Wrap up, next steps and close (10 minutes).

What resources do you require to run a successful focus group?

- A large enough room, booked for at least two hours. Ensure that the room is fully accessible.

- Suitable resources for any attendees who may be visually impaired, have mobility problems or have hearing problems.
- Two facilitators.
- Name badges for attendees (sticky labels work well).
- Pens.
- Paper/flipchart.
- Enough chairs and, if possible, tables.

In some cases, the focus group evolves into a managing conflict working group. In these cases, ask participants if they are happy for you to contact them again to discuss next steps and to agree actions.

5 The TCM Conflict Calculator

I have designed the TCM Conflict Calculator for organizations to use when they first start setting up and embedding internal mediation schemes. The data that it collects helps them to make rational and strategic decisions about the most effective way to reduce the costs and the overall burden of conflict. Using the calculator to measure the real cost of conflict will help you to understand the cost to your organization and act as a valuable baseline measure for the development and subsequent evaluation of your conflict management strategy and mediation scheme.

Resolution recommendations

The TCM Conflict Calculator

The TCM Conflict Calculator has been designed to help you to capture quantitative data during your conflict analysis. The headings in each column can be modified to suit your own needs, circumstances and context (see Table 5.3 Internal costs, and Table 5.4 External costs, settlement agreements and awards; adding the two together gives the total cost of conflict).

How to use the Conflict Calculator

Step 1. Identify a sample population of complaints, grievances, bullying cases, discrimination cases or team conflicts that have concluded in the past 48 months. It is important that you have detailed records for each conflict that can be analysed and tracked throughout the lifecycle of the conflict.

Step 2. Identify each of the key players (stakeholders) involved at each stage of the conflict. You will also need their gross annual salary details so that you can calculate the cost of one day of their time. You can now allocate a cost per day to each stakeholder.

To calculate the day rate, divide the gross annual salary by 260 (the number of working days in the year assuming that the employee is full time):

Gross salary/260 = day rate (£)

Step 3. Identify any additional costs such as:

- Legal fees.
- Temp cover costs.
- Recruitment costs.
- Settlement or out of court agreements.
- Litigation costs.

Step 4. Run the Conflict Calculator on as many cases as you are able. Generally, I recommend a minimum of three cases with no upper limit. To calculate the mean cost of conflict to your organization: divide your total figure by the number of conflicts that you have analysed. If you wish to isolate particular types of conflicts, it is possible to calculate the costs of team conflicts, bullying allegations, discrimination allegations and performance management cases in this way too.

Table 5.3 Internal costs

Stakeholder	Informal resolution	Investigation	Determination	Appeals	Legal fees	Tribunal	Suspension and sickness	Temp cover	Total
Cost per day	no. of days	no. of days	no. of days	no. of days	no. of days	no. of days	no. of days	no. of days	TOTAL Days × cost per day
Party 1 (aggrieved)									
Party 2									
Party 3									
Parties rep A									
Parties rep B									
HR person 1									
HR person 2									
HR person 3									
Manager a									
Manager b									
Manager c									
Witness x									
Witness y									
Witness z									

(continued)

Table 5.3 (Continued)

Stakeholder	Informal resolution	Investigation	Determination	Appeals	Legal fees	Tribunal	Suspension and sickness	Temp cover	Total
Cost per day	no. of days	no. of days	no. of days	no. of days	no. of days	no. of days	no. of days	no. of days	TOTAL Days x cost per day
Investigator									
Temp/locum a									
Temp/locum b									
Determination panel									
Legal representative									
Barrister/ counsel									
Other									
TOTAL									

Total of Table 5.3	£

Table 5.4 External costs, settlement agreements and awards

Stakeholder		Informal resolution	Investigation	Determination	Appeals	Legal fees	Tribunal	Suspension and sickness	Temp cover	Total
	Cost per day	no. of days	no. of days	no. of days	no. of days	no. of days	no. of days	no. of days	no. of days	TOTAL Days x cost per day
Other costs										
Specialist advice										
Settlement agreements										
Awards at tribunal										
Other costs										

Total of Table 5.4	£

TOTAL cost of conflict (sum of Tables 5.3 and 5.4) = £

Notes

1 www.cedr.com/news/?item=Conflict-is-costing-business-GBP-33-billion-every-year

2 See https://en.wikipedia.org/wiki/Triangulation_(social_science) for more details on data triangulation

References

ACAS (2015) *Towards a System of Conflict Management? An evaluation of the impact of workplace mediation at Northumbria Healthcare NHS Foundation Trust*, ACAS, London

CIPD (2015) *Getting Under the Skin of Workplace Conflict: Tracing the experiences of employees*, CIPD, London

CIPD/OPP (2008) *Fight, Flight or Face it? Celebrating the effective management of conflict at work*, CIPD/OPP, London

The psychology   06
of conflict
and conflict
management

Contrary to what we usually believe, the best moments in our lives are not the passive, receptive, relaxing times... The best moments usually occur when a person's body or mind is stretched to its limits in a voluntary effort to accomplish something difficult and worthwhile. (Mihaly Csikszentmihalyi, 2008)

KEY LEARNING POINTS IN THIS CHAPTER

- Conflict can be a major cause of work-related stress, anxiety, depression and absence. By understanding how and why conflicts occur, and by developing the necessary skills to manage conflict, organizations can significantly reduce these levels.

- Most, if not all, workplace conflicts are caused by powerful emotional and psychological triggers, of which loss is a major factor. By better understanding these emotional and psychological triggers, it becomes easier to understand, manage and subsequently resolve a conflict.

- Emotional intelligence is a powerful approach for creating a space where conflicts can be discussed and resolved constructively and empathetically.

- Positive psychology is a relatively new branch of psychology that creates new opportunities and possibilities for the effective management of workplace conflict. Positive psychology is about understanding and building on our strengths and positive attributes. It is also about generating flow as an alternative to the automatic and innate 'fight or flight' response.

- Many conflicts arise due to dissonance between the impact of a behaviour and the recipient's often incorrect perception of the intention behind the behaviour.

- Positive psychology and emotional intelligence (EQ) offer valuable methodologies that underpin many of the emerging alternative dispute resolution systems. By using mediation or by developing integrated conflict management systems, more and more organizations are adopting positive psychology and EQ for managing conflict in favour of the traditionally procedural, divisive and litigation based systems.

- People are not mind-readers. Unless the parties in a dispute can describe what is going on inside their minds and bodies to each other, the chance of misperceptions and unconscious biases impeding the resolution of the conflict increases.

Introduction

Although not a psychologist, I do know this: conflict is not logical; it is irrational. Conflict is not black and white; it is grey. Conflict can be overt or it can be subtle, it can be simple or it can be incredibly complex. Conflict is deeply human and it can't be resolved by reducing it to right/wrong, good/bad, defend/attack or win/lose.

I realized early in my career that having at least a rudimentary understanding of human behaviour and psychology would assist me in my work. Understanding how and why people behave the way they do at times of conflict is deeply fascinating and rewarding. After all, managing conflict is all about human nature and human relationships. Mediation is of particular interest because it is so transformational. In just one day, the parties in a seemingly intractable conflict make the decision to act, interact and react differently in the future. The question I often ask myself is: how and why do they do it during mediation rather than at any other time in the conflict?

One answer may be that traditional conflict management paradigms often ignore the emotional and psychological impact of conflict. Unconsciously, they perpetuate parent-child relationships in the workplace, which, as I alluded to earlier, infantilize the workforce and undermine, rather than promote, empowerment and engagement. Processes such as early resolution, mediation, roundtable facilitation and conflict coaching promote adult-to-adult conversations, they assist with the development of empathy, they allow strong feelings to be communicated openly and they create a safe space for the parties to craft a solution to their conflict. These seemingly informal approaches for managing conflict are aligned to the emotional and psychological needs of the parties far more closely than their formal cousins.

Resolution reflection

A conflict with your manager

Imagine that you are sat in a weekly briefing meeting with a group of your colleagues and your manager. Your relationship with your manager has been getting increasingly fraught and you find it hard being in the same room as him or her. Your manager says something during the meeting that you find demeaning and overtly critical.

- What impact does this have on you?
- How do you feel about it?
- What happens to your body?
- What did you perceive were your manager's intentions?
- How will you respond?
- What happens next?

Conflict and loss

For many of us, conflict can create a profound sense of loss: loss of face, of esteem, of confidence, of trust, of status and of control. To manage conflict effectively, organizations need to become much better at recognizing the root causes and the impact of this loss and to give the parties the space and the time to discuss these and to learn from them – to develop insights. The ultimate conflict management systems transform a loss into a gain.

Dr Elisabeth Kübler-Ross identified five stages of grief that people may experience. These have been adapted to form a grief curve. Not everyone will respond to loss or grief in the same way but these five stages are a good rule of thumb to help us understand how people will react to loss. The stages of grief that Kübler-Ross (1969) described are:

1 Denial and isolation – a temporary refusal to accept the situation.

2 Anger – with themselves or with others.

3 Bargaining – trying to negotiate a different outcome.

4 Depression – deep feelings of sadness, regret and uncertainty about the future.

5 Acceptance – the beginning of coming to terms with the loss.

In recent years, the grief curve has been adapted to become the change curve, used to describe people's reaction to change. However, in conflict, the grief curve is even more pronounced than during periods of change. I have worked with parties in a dispute who can exhibit all five stages of the grief curve within a few hours.

Mediation and facilitation are powerful ways of helping the disputing parties move into the acceptance stage. Without dialogue, the parties often get stuck in the depression stage and they find it hard to move into acceptance as there appears to be no end to the conflict and no meaningful remedy to it. I have often speculated that this inability to move into the acceptance stage is a major factor in the stress and anxiety that so many people experience, which can lead to more serious underlying mental health concerns with all the associated costs of absence and sickness.

By creating a safe space and by giving parties control of the resolution process, organizations can reduce significantly the incidence and the levels of stress. This can deliver a net benefit in terms of reducing short-, medium- and long-term absence. By adopting a more positive approach to conflict, organizations can also help to generate happier, healthier and more harmonious workplaces.

Figure 6.1 is a diagram of a volcano. I use this to demonstrate to my students how unmet needs, and the associated loss from those needs not being met, are buried deep within the volcano. The lava and the magma pouring out represent the outward, visible behaviours. It is these behaviours that the organization often reacts to and tries to manage and control. To manage conflict effectively, we need to look inside the volcano. Within it, we will find a wide range of feelings and emotions that are driving the behaviours: frustration, upset, anger, sadness, fear, anxiety, guilt, etc. Below these feelings are the unmet needs that are creating the loss. To identify the root cause of a conflict – the unmet needs – we need to walk towards the heat rather than walking away from it. Once we identify the unmet needs and the

Figure 6.1   The conflict volcano

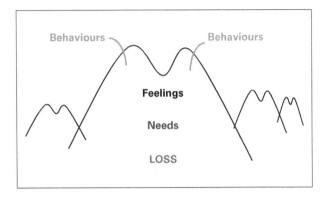

associated loss, we can begin a far more effective conversation about what needs to happen next. Somewhat miraculously, as we dig deeper into the volcano what one party says he or she needs is often very similar to what the other party says he or she needs: to be respected, to be valued, to be heard, to feel safe, to be treated with dignity, to find a resolution, etc. This is a step towards the ZOPA – the zone of possible agreement.

The role of the amygdala during conflict

The amygdala is a small, almond-shaped section of nervous tissue located in the temporal lobe of the brain; see Figure 6.2. The amygdala is responsible for detecting fear and preparing for emergencies. The amygdala is part of our limbic system: we have two amygdalae and they are responsible for driving our emotions, survival instincts and emotional memory.

The amygdala is our brain's early warning system and it is responsible for detecting and responding to threats. It communicates these threats to glands in our body such as the adrenal gland, which is situated just above our kidneys. These glands then secrete a variety of hormones that travel around our body, such as adrenalin and cortisol. The amygdala is also thought to be responsible for the release of neurotransmitters (chemical communicators in the brain) such as dopamine and serotonin. This mix of chemicals and hormones is responsible for the classic fight or flight response.

The amygdala is responsible for the perception of emotions such as anger, fear, and sadness, as well as the controlling of aggression. The amygdala may help to store memories of events and emotions so that an individual may be able to recognize similar events in the future. For example, if you

Figure 6.2   The structure of the brain showing the location of the amygdala

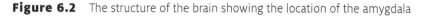

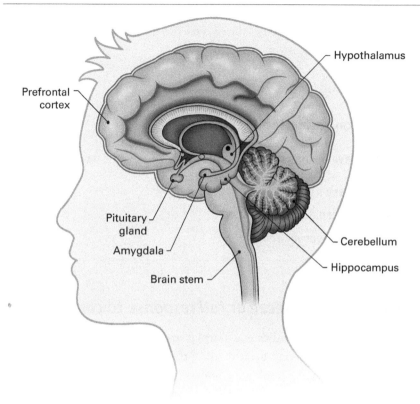

SOURCE iStock

have ever burnt your hand in a fire, then the amygdalae may help in processing that event so you are less likely to put your hand near a fire in the future.

Where the 'stressor hormones' such as cortisol build up over time, it presents a real risk of physical and emotional issues manifesting: irritable bowel syndrome, insomnia, bad backs, stomach ulcers or mental health issues such as depression, anxiety, post-traumatic stress disorder and even suicide. The impact on the individual can be acute and the cost to the organization can be significant. Research is pointing towards unresolved dysfunctional conflict as a cause of stress, anxiety and harm to organizations and employees. 'Interpersonal conflict at work is regarded as a leading source of stress and has been conceptualized as a social stressor linked to psychological, behavioural and physical strains' (Bruk-Lee *et al,* 2013).

In some cases of conflict, the impact is so sudden and so profound, psychologists refer to this as an 'amygdala hijack'. Once the 'red mist' has worn off, we realize it was often an overreaction to the stimulus that caused it. Nonetheless, the amygdala can take people into what I refer to as the zone of negative conflict (ZONC) and it is precisely at this stage of the conflict that action must be taken to get the two parties into a room to discuss what happened and to agree a way forward.

Resolution reflection

If you have ever experienced an 'amygdala hijack' or a 'red mist' moment:

- What caused it?
- What impact did it have?
- How did you recover from it?

The fight, flight, freeze or fall response to conflict

As previously stated, conflict is a normal and indeed a necessary part of being a human and having healthy and productive relationships. Humans have a huge capacity for resolving conflicts; however, we are constrained by our four instinctive responses. Our body's primitive, automatic and innate response to a threat or harm, which prepares the body to do one, some or all the responses, is shown in Figure 6.3.

Figure 6.3   Responses to conflict

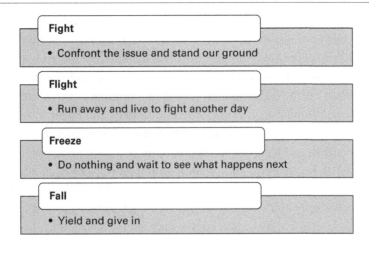

Fight
- Confront the issue and stand our ground

Flight
- Run away and live to fight another day

Freeze
- Do nothing and wait to see what happens next

Fall
- Yield and give in

There is a fifth f, which is not instinctive but which is more effective at resolving conflict than the other four f's put together. This fifth f is flow, which I will explore shortly. However, before I do so, I would like to introduce you to a wonderful and relatively new branch of psychology called positive psychology. Positive psychology has inspired me and it has completely changed the way that I think about conflict.

Introducing positive psychology

Positive psychology is a study of positive aspects of human life, such as happiness, meaning, wellbeing, strength and flourishing. It can be summarized in the words of its founder, Martin Seligman, as the: 'scientific study of optimal human functioning [that] aims to discover and promote the factors that allow individuals and communities to thrive' (Seligman and Csikszentmihalyi, 2000). Seligman argues that traditional psychology often emphasizes the shortcomings of individuals rather than their potentials. Positive psychology focuses on human potential. It is focused on identifying things that make life worth living; in short, positive psychology is concerned with making us feel good and driving positive changes in our lives and in our relationships.

This new focus in psychology was established about 10 years ago and it is a rapidly developing field. Its aspiration is to bring solid empirical research into areas such as wellbeing, flow, personal strengths, wisdom, creativity, psychological health and characteristics of positive groups and institutions. As Ilona Boniwell explains in her accessible and informative book: *Positive Psychology in a Nutshell:* 'it [positive psychology] simply studies different (and often far more interesting) topics and asks slightly different questions such as "what works?" rather than "what doesn't?" or "what is right with this person?" rather than "what is wrong?"' (Boniwell, 2012). This is in stark contrast to traditional approaches for managing conflict yet it is very closely aligned to the mediation process and the underlying principles of mediation.

Introducing flow – the fifth f

As seen earlier, traditionally, psychologists have talked about the fight or flight responses to conflict and most conflict management strategies are designed to deal with these reactions. However, an additional response, which draws from positive psychology, can lead to a much more effective resolution of conflict – flow. Unlike fight or flight responses, flow is not generally a natural or instinctive response to conflict. Flow can be achieved by possessing an enhanced level of self-awareness and empathy. The more that organizations can do to promote self-awareness and empathy at times of conflict, the greater the chance for flow to occur. Mediation is a powerful way of generating flow at times of conflict.

What is flow?

Flow is a state of mind that allows us to accept a new meaning, a surprise or an unexpected change in our lives. It is similar to mindfulness in as much as it enables us to build confidence and to take control in the present moment. In so doing, during flow, we became consciously aware of how our body and mind are reacting to the threat and we reject our innate reactions, ie we consciously reject the fight or flight response in favour of flow. In other words, flow means changing oneself to adapt to the new reality. Flow becomes the optimal choice to cope with a range of workplace challenges, large and small, and represents a real choice that individuals have. Once chosen, it offers an extremely useful path to start to appreciate the positives in the new reality being faced. Mihaly Csikszentmihalyi is a leading figure in the world of positive psychology and he has written widely about the power of flow:

> There are many reasons why experiencing flow is beneficial. Perhaps the most important is also the most obvious: the quality of life depends on it. People are happier after having had a chance to experience flow, and as we have known ever since Aristotle, happiness is the true foundation of existence.
> (Csikszentmihalyi, 1993: 192)

He describes eight characteristics of flow:

1 Complete *concentration* on the task.

2 *Clarity of goals* and reward in mind and immediate feedback.

3 Transformation of *time* (speeding up/slowing down of time).

4 The experience is intrinsically *rewarding*, has an end itself.

5 *Effortlessness* and ease.

6 There is a balance between *challenge and skills*.

7 Actions and awareness are merged, *losing self-conscious rumination*.

8 There is a feeling of *control* over the task. (pp 179–80)

During mediation, the parties are given the chance to listen to each other and they are able to draw insight and understanding from the situation, which they were unable to do during the dysfunctional conflict stage. Mediation shifts the paradigm from fight or flight to flow. This may not be quite the same meaning of flow that Csikszentmihalyi describes, but it is the best way for me to illustrate the power and the transformation that occurs during dialogue:

A flow of emotions.

A flow of empathy.

A flow of insight.

A flow of understanding.

A flow of recognition.

A flow of ideas.

A flow of transformation.

A flow of forgiveness.

Positive psychology, when applied during a facilitated roundtable conversation or a mediation process, shifts the focus from process to people. The role of the facilitator, or the mediator, is to give the disputing parties the time and space to identify and communicate the root causes of the conflict, to seek out shared interests, to identify common ground, and to create mutually acceptable working relationships. The mediator's or facilitator's role is to help the parties to generate and engage in flow. That is achieved by:

1 Giving the parties the time and the space to focus entirely on resolving their conflict. Reduce distractions to a minimum and create a set of boundaries that all parties subscribe to: privacy and confidentiality, talk and listen with respect, be open and honest, put yourself in the other person's shoes, consider what you want to say before you speak, and have an open mind.

2 Listening to all sides without blaming or judging them.

3 Encouraging the parties to describe clearly their needs, goals, hopes and fears, and engage them in dialogue about those.

4 Speeding up the process or slowing it down based on the topic being discussed and the needs of the parties. The mediator also holds the space during periods of silence that allow the parties to engage in deep reflection.

5 Challenging the parties but always remembering that this is their conflict and the resolution needs to be theirs too. However, from time to time, the mediator will apply a set of skills that can unblock a particular impasse such as reframing, which helps the parties to examine the positives of a situation and to reframe their language and their mindset.

6 Engaging the parties actively in the process and encouraging them to develop future solutions by drawing on understanding and insights from the past. Mediators challenge them to think more deeply but without patronizing them or undermining them.

7 Treating the parties with absolute respect and allowing the parties to express themselves in the way that is most natural and comfortable to them – to tell their stories.

8 The parties control the content of the mediation process at all times. The outcome from mediation is theirs and theirs alone.

Conflict resolution processes such as mediation are hard work; they require courage and a desire to change the situation and to make it better. For the parties in a seemingly intractable conflict, who have the courage to engage into mediation, there is no greater sense of achievement than knowing that they have worked hard and overcome insurmountable obstacles to reach a resolution. The hugs, the handshakes, the smiles, the tears and the joy – the outcomes from mediation are incredible. Compare those with the outcomes of an investigation process, a determination panel or litigation.

To recap, the application of positive psychology to managing conflict results in a positive chain reaction – flow:

- the parties focus on the positives and the strengths of the relationship, not just the negative elements, *therefore*

- people feel affirmed and valued; they are less fearful of each other; they are less likely to attack each other and the instinctive 'fight or flight' responses are diminished, *therefore*

- the parties respond less defensively and are willing to engage with each other in a dialogue, *therefore*

- they are more likely to be open and honest (authentic) with themselves and with each other, *therefore*

- they listen to each other and, in so doing, they gain a heightened level of personal and shared awareness of the conflict, its causes and potential remedies, *therefore*

- they are more likely to share knowledge and make requests rather than make demands or issue ultimatums, *therefore*
- they become more resilient and can begin to develop insights about the necessary changes to help resolve the situation, *therefore*
- they use those insights to drive behavioural changes that transform the conflict from dysfunctional to functional.

How emotional intelligence is changing the way we handle conflict at work

By focusing on what is working and what positive changes the parties can make, the parties in conflict will feel less threatened and, thus, are less defensive. This allows them to engage in flow, which ultimately leads to a less confrontational dialogue. The net result is that the parties are more open, they become more authentic and they benefit from a greater level of personal and shared awareness.

The different forms of intelligence

In her book, *Managing and Leading People Through Organizational Change* (2016), Julie Hodges identifies the following areas of intelligence that relate to the management of change. These are equally important in terms of the management of conflict:

- Cognitive intelligence (IQ) – the ability to manage abstract concepts and complex problem solving.
- Contextual intelligence – the ability to adapt quickly to a specific set of circumstances, environment or situation.
- Emotional intelligence (EQ) – a term first created by two researchers, Peter Salovey and John Mayer (1997) and popularized by Dan Goleman in his 1996 book of the same name. From my experience of working with conflict, I define EQ as the ability to:
  - be self-aware, ie possessing the capacity to recognize, understand and manage one's own emotions and emotional reactions to situations;
  - recognize, understand and influence the emotions of others with integrity and compassion;

- learn from previous emotionally charged situations/conflicts and to assimilate that learning into positive behavioural change;
- engage with others constructively and calmly during difficult conversations and during times of change, conflict and crisis;
- be empathetic (to see the world through another person's eyes) and able to respond to others in a compassionate and supportive manner;
- receive difficult feedback and to respond non-defensively;
- anticipate factors or situations that may create an emotional response in others and to reduce stress and anxiety if, or when, it occurs;
- create the conditions for flow and engaging others in adult-to-adult dialogue;
- recognize dysfunctional conflict and to transform it into functional conflict, moving parties from ZONC to ZOPA;
- role model emotional intelligence and develop and value EQ in others.

This book is all about emotional intelligence. One of the main theses of this book is the need for organizations to value, adopt and integrate EQ across all levels of the organization:

- Social intelligence – the ability to read and adapt to a variety of social situations. Includes strong communication skills, self-confidence and understanding of social dynamics.
- Cultural intelligence – the ability to connect and interact with people across a variety of cultures.
- Moral/ethical intelligence – the ability to act with integrity, to take responsibility, to act with compassion and to be willing to forgive others when mistakes are made.
- Spiritual intelligence – to be aware of the greater cause, to be able to act spontaneously to a situation and to be able to step back to see the bigger picture.
- Behavioural intelligence – the ability to behave appropriately and the ability to modify those behaviours according to the situation.
- Relational intelligence – the ability to understand other people, to relate to them and to collaborate where required. The ability to facilitate the development of relationships between people.

These different forms of intelligence, when applied in a conflict situation, are incredibly powerful. Organizations benefit from greater levels of engagement, wellbeing, collaboration and motivation when these forms of intelligence are institutionalized through the hiring, training and support for managers and through the systems, structures and policies of the organization. Conversely, where cognitive intelligence (technical ability) is perceived to be the core level of intelligence within an organization, dysfunctional conflicts can, and do, arise.

Resolution recommendations

Applying positive psychology and EQ to conflict management

Here are some questions that I ask when I am working with a conflict, which draw on positive psychology and EQ:

- Can you describe a time when the relationship was working well?
- What elements of your working relationship make you feel proud?
- What elements of your working relationship have you enjoyed?
- If the other person were sat here now, what would you like to say to them to help them understand how you feel?
- How do you think the other person is feeling right now?
- Are you ready to hear the other person's side of the story? If not, what needs to happen to help you to prepare to do so?
- What do you need to resolve this conflict?
- What changes are you willing to make to bring about a resolution to the conflict?
- What strengths do you have that the other person hasn't seen or isn't aware of yet?
- What strengths has the other person got that you value and respect?
- If you had a magic wand, what changes would you make to get your relationship back on track?
- What have you learnt from this situation that will make your relationship stronger in the future?
- If you could go back in time, what changes would you make to your relationship to avoid this situation occurring? (Follow-up: how could you make those changes a reality now?)
- What has made you feel happy or satisfied when you have been working with the other person?

Positive psychology and EQ in practice

Owen Bubbers is a highly-accomplished mediator and mediation trainer. He has worked with numerous disputing parties to help them secure a solution and he has embedded mediation programmes in a wide array of organizations, from large international banks to hospitals and transport businesses. Owen is fascinated by the journey that the parties experience in mediation and how that feeds into the culture of the organization:

> There is something indescribable about mediation. For all the theory, models and techniques involved, one cannot always tell what combination of verbal and non-verbal cues, beats of silence, mood and topic, open the door, bit by bit, to resolution. Regardless of the 'how', mediation can most definitely help people to develop happier working relationships, to build resilience and to create a more harmonious workplace culture.
>
> Time and again, I see parties enter mediation, convinced that things will never change: the other party is out to get them; they feel isolated in the workplace; the conflict feels as though it is consuming their every waking moment. The impact invariably is great and the sense of unmet need often crushing. For organizations, conflict is akin to dry rot that attacks the foundations of a strong home.
>
> And yet, via careful facilitation, parties increase their understanding of one another and what's really going on beneath their respective positions. This in turn creates new insights and tools to deal with the conflict at hand. Gradually, what felt overwhelming now begins to feel manageable; a light at the end of the tunnel.
>
> Developing happier working relationships not only enables people to get along better day-to-day, it leads to higher productivity, lower sickness absence rates and better business outcomes. Make no mistake, there is a golden thread connecting workplace conflicts (even if it's just between two employees) with a collaborative work culture and, finally, the end-customer experience.

Transactional Analysis

Dr Eric Berne designed transactional analysis (TA), as a system that can be used to understand how people act, interact and react. Berne's work has been used extensively in the workplace and conflict management professionals utilize TA heavily. TA is valuable for use as part of managing conflict and as a way of helping us to better understand people's learnt behaviours and their interactions.

Berne recognized that people can interact from one of three 'ego states' – Parent (P), Adult (A) or Child (C) – see Table 6.1 – and that these interactions can occur at a conscious or unconscious level. The interactions between people are described as 'transactions' hence the term 'transactional analysis'. It is worth stating that these ego states have nothing to do with our age or whether we are parents, adults or children.

TA and conflict management

TA is a valuable tool that can help us to understand the dynamics of a conflict in the workplace. It also helps us to understand the relationship between HR, managers and employees. Many policies and processes of the modern workplace represent the controlling parent ego state and, as a result, employees adopt the adaptive child ego state. This creates the classic parent-child transactions that are such a common symptom of dysfunctional conflict. An understanding of TA enables organizations, managers, HR and employees to adopt the preferred state: adult-to-adult dialogue.

Table 6.1 Ego states

P	**Parent ego state**
	This includes behaviours, thoughts and feelings that are copied from our parents. This state is often divided into two parts:
	1 *nurturing parent:* caring, loving, helping, and
	2 *controlling parent:* criticizing, punishing.
A	**Adult ego state**
	Includes behaviours, thoughts and feelings that deal with the here and now and tend to be more rational. It contains those behaviours concerned with collecting information, organizing and analysing. The adult ego state operates dispassionately and without emotion.
C	**Child ego state**
	Includes behaviours, thoughts and feelings that are replayed from our childhood. As with the adult ego state, the child ego state is divided into two:
	1 the natural or free child is spontaneous, energetic, curious, loving and uninhibited, the part of us that feels free and loves pleasure;
	2 the adapted child develops when we learn to change (adapt) our feelings and behaviour in response to the world around us. Feelings of guilt, fear, depression, anxiety, envy and pride are all learnt characteristics of the adapted child. The adapted child can become the most troublesome part of our personality, particularly at times of conflict.

Karpman's drama triangle

Drawing on TA is Karpman's drama triangle (1968). In conflict situations we can often adopt one of the following roles: persecutor (arguably the 'bully'), victim or rescuer; see Figure 6.4. If one person is leaning in one direction (for example, becoming a victim), that can often make others appear as if they are adopting one of the other roles (becoming the persecutor or the rescuer). By adopting one role, it may be that the individual is deliberately trying to manipulate another person to adopt a different role. For instance, someone may adopt a victim role to manipulate someone else to be viewed as the persecutor and someone else the rescuer. As a result, we often perceive each other in terms of these contrasting roles, without recognizing that we have elements of each in all of us. The drama triangle can be useful to help us understand how people are reacting to a conflict situation and also to help them consider other approaches. The triangle may present itself during a dysfunctional workplace conflict as follows:

- *Victims* may deny responsibility for their circumstances and won't take responsibility for resolving the situation. They will often refuse to confront their persecutor and are often extremely sensitive and fragile.

- *Rescuers* may apply short-term repairs to a victim's problems, while neglecting their own needs. As a result, they may resent their role and carry with them a high level of underlying frustration.

Figure 6.4   Karpman's drama triangle

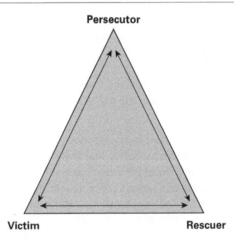

SOURCE Adapted from Karpman, 1968

- *Persecutors* blame the victims and criticize the behaviour of meddling rescuers. They may be critical, unpleasant and good at finding fault in others but not in themselves. They often hide feelings of inadequacy. Persecutors are often referred to as bullies.

The mediator or the facilitator's role is to help the parties move out of the victim/persecutor dynamic. It must be stressed that the mediator or the facilitator is not a rescuer. By acting impartially and dispassionately, they can avoid the perpetuation of the damaging drama triangle. Mediators and facilitators should be trained to recognize the hooks, triggers and buttons that may be used by the parties to manipulate them into adopting the rescuer's role.

CASE STUDY Perception and unconscious bias

Julia and Sandeep were in a worsening conflict that had been rumbling on for many months. The business was growing and Julia, the office manager, decided that the office needed to be reconfigured. Julia proposed that Sandeep's desk would be moved next to Chris – Chris and Sandeep had never got along that well but Julia was not aware of that. Sandeep went home that night frustrated. This is what Sandeep perceived:

- That there was no need to reconfigure the office. Julia was only doing so to make his life miserable.
- That Julia was moving his desk on purpose to cause a deliberate disruption.
- Julia was acting out of malice due to the conflict that they were involved in.
- That Julia somehow knew that Chris and he didn't get along and was putting him next to Chris in an attempt to punish him.

Sandeep had joined the dots but he had, as many of us would, fallen foul of the power of misperception and his own unconscious biases. He could be right of course, but equally he could be wrong. However, without sitting down with Julia and testing his perceptions they remain just that – perceptions. Nonetheless, Sandeep can't stop them going round and round in his head. The more he thinks these thoughts, the more he begins to believe them.

In my definition of conflict in Chapters 1 and 2, I explained that conflict occurs when one person (or a group) perceives that another person (or a group) is preventing them achieving their needs or is blocking them from expressing their values and beliefs in a way that they think is reasonable.

The terms 'perceive' and 'perception' are vital here. Our perception is central to how we will react to a conflict and the most common perception that I hear when I am mediating is that party A perceived that party B set out to cause intentional harm. In over 90 per cent of the cases that I mediate the parties realize that their perceptions, while valid, were incorrect – they had wrongly assumed malintent by the other. Interestingly, my team and I secure a resolution in 90 per cent of cases that we mediate. This is not a coincidence. Why isn't this being picked up earlier?

Our brains are hardwired to rapidly and instinctively categorize people and situations. We use a range of visible (eg, age or height) and invisible (eg, accent or seniority) categories to do this. These categories assign a whole suite of unconscious characteristics: good or bad, friend or foe, etc. These are automatic and unconscious biases over which we have little control, and which influence everyone, no matter how unbiased we think we may be. In the modern world of work and the emergence of a policy framework for virtually everything, having an unconscious bias is bound to contravene one of them. Thus, we don't admit to having a bias, so we suppress them – often deep down.

In conflict, our biases come to the surface very quickly but most people are smart enough to know that being prejudicial or discriminatory may result in dismissal. What we do is we put them in a box and try to stop them 'leaking out'. It's exhausting and it's very hard to stop them leaking out, however hard we may try. Buried deep down, these unconscious biases can then become prejudices. If we add power or authority to those prejudices – we get discrimination. Discrimination is unlawful; having an unconscious bias is not. We must not get the two mixed up.

Mediation, facilitation and coaching are powerful ways of allowing the parties to test their assumptions and to explore their unconscious biases in a safe and controlled environment. Mediation is powerful as it gives the parties an opportunity to listen and to learn from each other. They can then make one of two choices: 1) carry on thinking and acting in the same way, or 2) modify how they think and act.

It's hard to make a sound effect in a book but there is a great sound that I often hear in mediation – 'ahhhhhhhh'. That is the sound that many of us make when our unconscious biases are challenged and we start to see the world for what it is, rather than how we have chosen to perceive it. Let's go back to Julia and Sandeep:

ahhhhhhhh, I didn't realize that when I suggested that I move you next to Chris it made you feel frustrated and upset. I can understand now why you would assume that I had intended to do that. My intention wasn't to make you feel either frustrated or upset, Sandeep. My intention was to create the right office environment for all of us. If you and I could communicate better and resolve our differences, we could work together on the office reconfiguration – I would value your input. I am sorry that my proposal made you feel that way; I can assure you that was genuinely not my intention.

Feelings and conflict

Feelings are the 'f word' of the modern business. During a conflict, feelings come to the surface more readily and have an even more significant impact than they may do when we are not in conflict. It is a surprise to me, therefore, that at times of conflict we often ignore feelings – they are rarely talked about and they are not seen as being useful. In fact, the opposite is often the case: feelings and the emotional person may be viewed as a risk and as potentially harmful and destructive.

We have become afraid of feelings and it is easier to dehumanize the other person than to accept him or her as a real human being with real feelings. Our organizations are culpable in so much as the rules and the policies used to manage conflict make very little room for people's underlying feelings. Reference to emotions or empathy in most grievance and associated people policy frameworks is notable by its absence.

As a manager once told me during a conflict coaching session: 'David, when I deal with a conflict at work I ask the parties to leave their emotions at the door.' You can imagine that we spent a bit of time working on the ways that he could open the door to the feelings and use those feelings to generate greater empathy, awareness, understanding and insight. That manager e-mailed me the next day saying that this conversation had a profound impact on him and it would change the way that he would manage people forever.

A want is not a need!

We all have needs. Maslow (1943) identified a hierarchy of needs which, once met, allow us to move onto the next level of need; see Figure 6.5. When I am training people to manage conflict effectively, I always ask them what they currently do to manage conflict, particularly at the informal stage of a procedure. Initially, I am told that they ask the parties what they want to

Figure 6.5   Maslow's hierarchy of needs

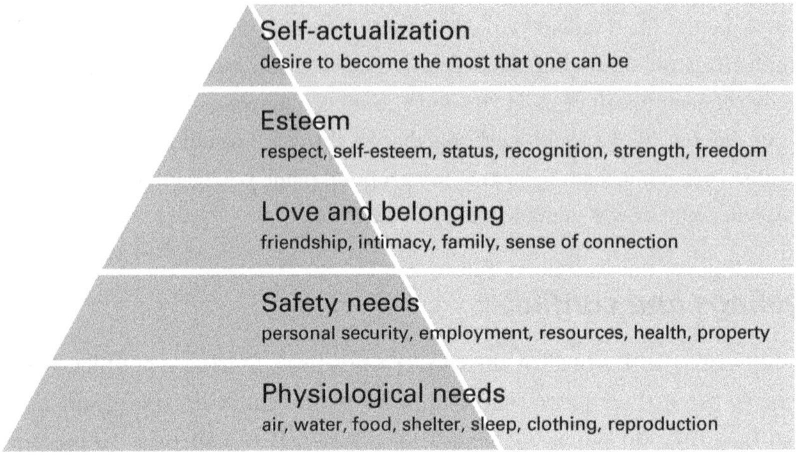

Self-actualization
desire to become the most that one can be

Esteem
respect, self-esteem, status, recognition, strength, freedom

Love and belonging
friendship, intimacy, family, sense of connection

Safety needs
personal security, employment, resources, health, property

Physiological needs
air, water, food, shelter, sleep, clothing, reproduction

SOURCE Shutterstock

achieve. 'Great,' I say. 'How does that go?' They tell me that it doesn't really help as the parties often have unrealistic expectations of what can be done.

In that regard, asking the 'What do you want?' question can make the conflict appear even more intractable and entrenched than it already was – wants are often framed as demands whereas needs are often framed as requests. This is what we may be told when we ask the parties 'What do you want?':

I want (demand) that the other person is fired.

I want (demand) you to resolve it for me.

I want (demand) an apology.

When I am mediating a conflict, I don't hear much of this demanding language. What is different between what I do as a mediator and what others tend to do? One thing that a mediator will always do is ask the parties to describe to him or her (and then to each other) what they need. This is what they often describe:

I need to be heard.

I need to be respected.

I need to feel valued.

I need to be treated with dignity.

I need to be affirmed, acknowledged and appreciated.

I need to feel safe.

I need to understand the intention behind the behaviour.

I need them to be open and honest with me.

I need to receive an explanation.

I need to be trusted and to be able to trust the other person.

I need the conflict to end and the harm to stop.

Shared interests and convergent needs – the holy grail of conflict management

In terms of managing conflict at work, unmet needs are the catalyst for dysfunctional conflict. They are also the catalyst of the resolution of the conflict. During mediation, the parties often explain that they need the same thing – that they have shared interests and convergent (common) needs. However, this insight is inhibited by the conflict and, in many cases, the organization's own dispute resolution policy framework. As such, the more that can be done to allow the parties to express their needs and listen to each other, the greater potential they have of agreeing a solution that is mutually acceptable and meets their shared needs and interests. Remember: a want is not a need.

Resolution reflection

Bearing in mind what you have read in this chapter, spend a few minutes reflecting on the following questions:

- What changes will I make to the way that I manage conflict at work?
- How will I apply the principles of positive psychology and EQ in my work?
- How will I generate flow when I am handling conflict?
- How will I ensure that the parties can express their feelings openly?
- What will I do to promote adult-to-adult dialogue?
- How will I identify and work with the parties' needs?

Conclusion

Positive psychology and emotional intelligence provide a valuable backdrop for workplace conflict management. The traditional systems for tackling conflict at work are based on a reward and punish paradigm. The newer approaches are about helping people to examine what is happening in their lives, to reflect on those things, to give them meaning, and to deliver positive changes in their working relationships.

Having a basic understanding of human psychology is helpful for managing conflict. The main reason is that the outward, observable behaviours are a symptom and simply treating the symptom will not address the underlying issues in a conflict. If we do not have an appreciation of what is going on under the surface, it is much harder to understand the situation and to help the parties to achieve a lasting resolution.

As a conflict management professional, I use my insights from psychology to appreciate and act on the following:

- Conflict is normal, it is healthy and it is predictable. Conflict can make us stronger and it can enrich our lives – if is handled effectively.

- Applying positive psychology enables the parties to explore the positives in their relationship and build on these rather than focusing on the negatives.

- The fight or flight response to conflict is powerful but, with courage and willingness, the parties can reject those innate responses in favour of flow.

- Flow is a powerful state and it can create meaning and deliver positive change in our lives. Ultimately, resolving a conflict can make us much happier and engaged at work.

- Adult-to-adult dialogue is the preferred state and is more effective at resolving disputes than parent-to-child dialogue.

- Loss is a powerful driver of negative behaviour during conflict – a loss of control, of face, of esteem. If we can help the parties to make sense of the loss, they can begin to focus on things they can do to transform a loss to a gain.

- Putting people in a victim, a rescuer or a persecutor box is restrictive and unhelpful. Organizations need to reject the drama triangle paradigm that is so explicitly and implicitly embedded within traditional approaches for managing conflict.

- The 'f word' of modern workplaces is feelings. Inviting parties to talk about their feelings and encouraging them to hear one another in an empathetic way can be transformational as well as being cathartic and healthy.

- A want is not a need. As the parties explore and describe their underlying needs, it becomes apparent that we often have more in common than we expected.

- Giving the parties control of the resolution process is empowering; it also reduces the stress and anxiety associated with feeling out of control.

References

Boniwell, I (2012) *Positive Psychology in Nutshell: The science of happiness*, 3rd edn, Oxford University Press, Oxford

Bruk-Lee, V, Ashley E, Nixon, A E and Spector, P E (2013) An expanded typology of conflict at work: Task, relationship and non-task organizational conflict as social stressors, *Work & Stress*, **27** (4) pp 339–50

Csikszentmihalyi, M (1993) *The Evolving Self: A psychology for the third millennium*, Harper Perennial, New York

Csikszentmihalyi, M (2008) *Flow: The psychology of optimal experience*, Harper Perennial Modern Classic, New York

Goleman, G (1996) *Emotional Intelligence: Why it can matter more than IQ*, Bloomsbury, London

Hodges, J (2016) *Managing and Leading People through Organizational Change: The theory and practice of sustaining change through people*, Kogan Page, London

Karpman, S (1968) Fairy tales and script drama analysis, *Transactional Analysis Bulletin*, **26** (7) pp 39–43

Kübler-Ross, E (1969) *On Death and Dying*, Scribner, New York

Maslow, A H (1943) A Theory of Human Motivation, *Psychological Review*, **50** (4)

Salovey, P and Mayer, J (1997) *Emotional Development and Emotional Intelligence*, Basic Books, New York

Seligman, M E P and Csikszentmihalyi, M (2000) Positive psychology: an introduction, *American Psychologist*, **55**, pp 5–14

The resolution   07
spectrum

*The HR profession is facing a paradigm shift. We are moving away from
the past models which were very deterministic, very command and control
and very process-centric where we bind people up with lots of rules and
policies. We are moving the HR professional, and business, to think more
about the principles that drive us.* (Peter Cheese, CIPD, CEO)[1]

KEY LEARNING POINTS IN THIS CHAPTER

- The traditional systems for managing conflict are based on a parent-
  child, rights-based and quasi-litigation paradigm. They inflict and
  perpetuate greater levels of dysfunctional conflict and often over-
  look the most basic remedies for resolving it.

- The resolution spectrum outlined in this chapter provides a wide
  range of interventions for organizations, many of which are underpinned by the core principles of dialogue – talking and listening.

- The resolution spectrum is most effective when it is implemented as
  a partnership between HR, management and unions.

- It is important that employers make it clear to employees, at all
  stages of the employment lifecycle, that they expect all of them
  to engage in constructive, collaborative and meaningful dialogue
  when a conflict occurs. This includes, but is not limited to, issues
  pertaining to complex and often serious grievances, and allegations
  of bullying and harassment.

- To accommodate these changes, HR needs to modify its role: from
  the custodian of formal processes to facilitator of dialogue, champion of resolution and advocate of risk-taking.

- The resolution spectrum comprises a wide variety of resolution
  approaches for use by organizations, including resolution triage
  assessment, early resolution meetings, facilitated roundtable conversations, mediation, conflict coaching, early neutral evaluation and
  team conferencing.

Introducing the resolution spectrum

As seen in previous chapters, many organizations rely on an adversarial model of dispute resolution that is enshrined within the traditional grievance, disciplinary, performance, absence, capability or bullying and harassment procedures. Many organizations, including the CIPD, are now rejecting this model for managing conflict and are advocating a shift towards a more person-centred, values-based approach to managing conflict.

This chapter sets out a wide range of conflict management processes that can facilitate the resolution of a conflict or a dispute. These approaches form what I refer to as 'the resolution spectrum'. In and of themselves, each approach is powerful; however, as can be seen in Chapters 9 and 12, when these approaches are combined as part of an organization-wide, holistic and integrated conflict management system, they amalgamate to become a highly effective remedy to dysfunctional conflict.

The resolution spectrum provides organizations with a new approach for managing conflict. The resolution spectrum can form a vital part of the organization's conflict management strategy and is also a powerful way for organizations to express their intentions to promote a culture of resolution and collaborative decision making and constructive problem solving to their workforce. Employees should be made aware of the range of interventions available on the resolution spectrum throughout the employment lifecycle.

The resolution spectrum is defined along the following lines (see also Figure 7.1):

- Formal versus informal resolution.
- Win/win versus win/lose.
- Potential for confrontation versus potential for collaboration.
- Aligned to corporate values versus dissonant with corporate values.
- Early versus late response to the conflict.
- Personal power (agency) to affect a resolution versus organizational power to affect the resolution.
- Accountable to self and peers versus accountable to the organization.
- Private versus public.

Figure 7.1 The resolution spectrum

Resolution triage assessment (RTA)	Early resolution meeting	Facilitated roundtable conversation	Mediation	Conflict coaching	Team conferencing	Early neutral evaluation	Investigation	Formal resolution meeting	Settlement agreements	Litigation

Informal	←→	Formal
Win/win		Win/lose
Increased chance of collaboration		Increased chance of confrontation
Aligned to core values		Dissonant with core values
Early resolution		Late resolution
Greater personal influence to affect the resolution		Greater organizational influence to affect the resolution
Enhanced self-determination		Reduced self-determination
Increased likelihood of a win/win outcome		Increased likelihood of a win/lose outcome
Greater accountability to self and peers		Greater accountability to organization
Low use of resources (money and time)		Greater use of resources (money and time)
Private		Increasingly public

Applying the resolution spectrum to the world of work

In this chapter, I focus on the informal and non-legal elements of the resolution spectrum, which aim to promote dialogue and generate win-win outcomes.

Resolution triage assessment

How to identify the most appropriate route to resolution

Employees and their representatives should have access to a resolution policy and there should be a clear process for 'requesting resolution'. Note that this new term replaces the old one of 'raising a grievance'. Once a 'request for resolution' has been received and prior to identifying the most appropriate method for resolving a conflict or dispute, many HR departments (or in the case of a small business, the office manager, the CEO or COO) are developing resolution triage assessment processes to identify the most appropriate route to resolution.

The resolution triage assessment (RTA) process may also include a meeting with the aggrieved employee(s) and the person being complained about to listen to their underlying needs, goals, hopes and fears. Some examples of criteria for the RTA include:

- The seriousness of the issues being raised.
- The impact of the situation.
- The parties' willingness to engage in a face-to-face meeting with each other as part of an early resolution meeting, a facilitated roundtable conversation, a resolution meeting or a mediation process.
- Previous attempts to resolve the situation.
- The number or frequency of previous complaints.

Potential outcomes of the RTA stage include:

- The aggrieved parties will engage in direct talks – the early resolution meeting.
- A facilitator(s) will be identified and designated to chair a facilitated roundtable conversation.
- The case will proceed to internal or external mediation. HR or a manager will contact all parties and will allocate a mediator.
- The case will be subject to a more detailed assessment (early neutral evaluation) to identify the underlying issues and to assess the most appropriate route to resolution. This is particularly important in more serious allegations that could result in disciplinary action being taken.

- The case will be allocated to an investigator to commence a formal investigation into the allegations.

- A formal resolution meeting (which replaces the old grievance meeting) may be convened at which time the employee will meet with the employer (or the employer's representative such as HR) to discuss the situation and to agree a way forward. In these cases, the employee is advised to put his or her concerns in writing and that he or she has the right to be accompanied to the formal resolution meeting. The formal resolution meeting is an opportunity to explore the concerns, agree a way forward and to establish a suitable course of action. This may include any of the previous stages of the resolution spectrum.

CASE STUDY   Early resolution meeting

Securing an early resolution to conflict

Anita and Joanne found it hard to resolve an issue relating to holiday scheduling. Anita had rejected two requests from Joanna for leave and Joanne was becoming clearly frustrated and upset. She approached her union to discuss her concerns and, as per the resolution policy, the union advised Joanne to meet with Anita to discuss the issues and to try and resolve them face-to-face.

How does early resolution work?

The simplest, quickest and most effective way to prevent a harmful and costly conflict from escalating is to have a direct conversation with the other person as early as possible. Adult-to-adult conversations encourage a calmer, more collaborative, more rational and more empowering mindset and behaviour in the parties. The resolution meeting should be a set stage in the organization's efforts to promote the early and effective resolution of conflicts and disputes.

It goes without saying that this kind of conversation has always happened and is nothing new. Experienced managers and leaders know that sitting down and discussing an issue is generally the best way to resolve it. However, over recent years, I have observed fear creeping in that has inhibited the face-to-face dialogue. The resolution spectrum places face-to-face, adult-to-adult dialogue at the heart of the modern organization.

In old money, this stage of conflict resolution sat within a grievance procedure and was referred to as 'informal resolution'. The term 'informal resolution' is vague and unclear – at precisely the time when the parties need clarity and focus. Informal resolution is often the part of the grievance policy that has the shortest description – a few lines or maybe, if one is lucky, a paragraph or two. In addition, the very fact that informal resolution sits as part of a grievance policy means that it is actually used late in the day when positions have already hardened and there is increasing polarization. To trigger it, the parties will have already prepared their missiles for an attack and, as a result, dialogue at the informal resolution stage of a grievance process becomes more difficult. In addition, there is often very little guidance available to the protagonists about how to get the best outcomes from informal resolution. Ultimately, opportunities are missed, which can increase the levels of frustration, mistrust and division.

The use of early resolution meetings presents an opportunity for the parties to reframe the conflict as functional rather than allowing it to become dysfunctional. During early resolution meetings, the parties should be encouraged to talk and listen to each other in a private space. It must be remembered by all parties that this is an informal meeting designed to secure a constructive and lasting resolution.

Resolution recommendations

Here are some guidance notes that can assist with the smooth running of the early resolution meeting:

- Remember, whatever outward appearances may suggest, the other person is probably feeling as nervous about meeting you as you are about meeting him or her.
- Make plenty of time for the meeting – don't rush it.
- Find a neutral, quiet location for the meeting – a safe space. If you are not sure, ask a manager, HR or a union rep to help you secure a venue.
- Be respectful and courteous to each other at all times; this is especially important if the meeting becomes a bit heated and emotionally charged.
- Give each other time to talk and avoid interrupting when the other person is speaking.
- Listen actively when the other person is talking.

- Use positive body language to demonstrate that you are being attentive (smiles, nods and eye contact).

- Ask open questions that elicit more information.

- Summarize back what you have heard.

- When you are speaking, depersonalize the situation and don't attack the other person – talk from the 'I'. This means starting your sentences with 'I' rather than 'you'.

- It may be hard but try to remain objective and impartial. This will prevent you from responding in a defensive manner as you are less likely to feel 'attacked'.

- Speak out and be honest about your feelings, your needs and your concerns. This is a golden opportunity to get your concerns and needs out into the open.

- Try, where possible, to see the situation from the other person's point of view as well as your own. Empathy can be incredibly powerful.

- When you are answering questions, be open and honest. This is a key part of building trust between you.

- Don't discuss the situation or the conversation with your colleagues. While being well meaning, they can sometimes inflame a situation. Gossip and Chinese whispers rarely assist the resolution process.

- Plan ahead for the resolution meeting and use this simple structure to help you say what you need to say during the conversation:

  - What have you observed occurring in the relationship.

  - Are there any relevant facts or evidence to support what you are saying?

  - What impact is the situation having on you and how has it made you feel?

  - What was/is your perception of the other person's intentions?

  - What are your underlying needs, goals, hopes, fears and aspirations?

  - What requests would you like to make to the other person to help move the situation forward. These should be framed as a request, *not* a demand.

- Seek areas for agreement and note these down as a shared action plan.

- Agree when you will meet again to review progress.

Barriers to the early resolution meeting and how to overcome them

The barriers to these kinds of conversations include:

I am fearful of approaching the other person in case of reprisals or recriminations.

They hold all the power.

I am worried that it will inflame the situation.

I am not sure if they will listen to me.

I don't feel confident enough to tackle them about their behaviour.

I don't trust them and I don't feel safe.

While these responses are understandable and valid, they are typical responses of people in the fight or flight mode and are broadly predictable. They are perception-based and, unless there is material evidence available to support the allegation, they are not adequate reasons to avoid a direct conversation with the other person. It takes courage and confidence to reject fight and flight and move into 'flow'. These are not easy conversations but they are critical. I believe that organizations can do a lot more to encourage this kind of direct communication at the earliest stage of a conflict.

What can employers do to promote early resolution?

Employees should be made aware from the day that they start work (or earlier if possible) that the organization promotes adult-to-adult dialogue and expects its employees and managers to engage in dialogue to resolve issues at the earliest possible stage of a conflict. We can't make dialogue mandatory, but we can make it a cultural norm and we can frame the rejection of dialogue as a rejection of common sense and of the core values of the organization. For instance:

- The organization's resolution policy (see Chapter 8) should promote early resolution and should engender a culture where adult-to-adult dialogue is the preferred route to resolution.

- The organization should encourage and where possible allocate 'safe spaces' for early resolution meetings to happen.

- The ability to hold a confident conversation with others should be designed into managers' role description and should feature as part of a manager's recruitment, promotion and appraisal processes.

- Managers should be trained and supported to have confident conversations and to be able to secure positive outcomes from early resolution meetings.
- A guide to holding a confident conversation should be included in the employee handbook and as part of personal development opportunities.
- HR and senior managers should coach and mentor parties to help them get the best outcome from a difficult conversation.

Resolution reflection

A member of your team has approached you wanting to discuss a difficult subject that has been causing them to feel upset and frustrated:

- How will you react?
- What considerations should you have about the venue for the meeting and the layout of the room?
- How will you prepare for the meeting?
- How will you start the meeting – what will you say?
- How will you demonstrate that you are actively listening?
- What body language should you be demonstrating during the meeting?
- What could stop you from being impartial and objective during the meeting?
- How will you handle any strong emotions?
- Why is it important to depersonalize the situation?
- How will you react if the other person criticizes you?
- How will you demonstrate empathy?
- How will you express your needs and goals?
- Why is it important that the agreement that you reach is based on shared needs and goals?
- How will you close the meeting?
- How will you follow up the meeting to keep the agreement on track?

It is reasonable to expect managers and employees to engage in constructive dialogue to resolve a conflict at work. If the employee or the manager is still unsure about the value of the early resolution meeting, it may be beneficial to remind them that the organization has adopted a values-based, person-centred, empowering, constructive and collaborative model of conflict management. In so doing, the employer expects managers and employees to engage in adult-to-adult dialogue as part of the resolution process – with a reasonable and adequate level of support provided. The resolution meeting can be used to define the various stages of resolution and to assess the levels of support that may be required at each stage.

CASE STUDY   Redefining resolution at the Royal Lancaster London hotel

An interview with Harriette Wolff, Employee Relations Manager

Our hotel opened during the heyday of 'Swinging London', and we have since witnessed the evolution of luxury hospitality. We were lucky enough to play host to many iconic moments from British culture, such as the launch party of 'Yellow Submarine' by the Beatles, and the filming of the original 'Italian Job'. In 2016 and 2017, we were selected as one of *The Sunday Times'* Top 100 Companies to work for and we have won many prestigious awards relating to our commitment to the environment and our local communities.

Why did you decide to change the way that you manage conflict?

When I started my career in HR, I did so because I wanted to make a positive impact on people's time at work. The Royal Lancaster London is a company that promotes care, respect and support, and our policies should always echo this. However, as my journey in HR progressed, I became very aware that a lot of my day was spent in investigations, disciplinary meetings and feeling like the 'hotel police'. I knew that I needed to change this to make the positive impact that I once dreamed about!

How did you first hear about mediation?

I had heard about mediation in passing conversations, reading online forums about HR and people's confusion of 'are they talking about mediation or meditation?!' I started to find ways of how I could use mediation in everyday scenarios at work. In August 2014, I did my research, looked at costs and figured out how many hours a week I was spending sitting in a disciplinary meeting, saying the same things to the same colleagues who I'd sat with in the same room, not more than a month ago, and then writing the same outcome letters with slightly more emphasis on needing to see a positive change in behaviour. It was costing the company approximately £900 of my time a month – it was time for a change in tactic!

In comes mediation. The first major milestone in our employee relations culture shift was getting buy-in from my strategy team, general manager and hotel director through devising a business case and a cost analysis tool. This highlighted how mediation can reinforce our company values to engage, support and encourage our employees to be the best they can be. The company supported the initiative and my training began as an in-house mediator for the hotel. Not only would mediation help us to embed behaviours like integrity and positive attitude in our empowered and inverted hierarchy, but it would also support our 'no blame culture' and nip issues in the bud.

How did you integrate mediation into the hotel?

I successfully trained as a mediator in 2014. In order to fully launch the new mediation procedure, I had to integrate the mediation scheme into the hotel's overall yearly goals to ensure that mediation played a vital part in our culture and so that senior managers used a proactive approach to conflict. New standard operating procedures (SOPs) were written and I talked about it at every possible hotel meeting and communication forum as well as offering it as an alternative to certain investigation outcomes.

What impact has mediation had?

Take-up of the scheme emphasized a new willingness from our colleagues to air issues more freely than before, and after just 10 months after its launch, I had conducted 16 mediations that would otherwise have been subject to disciplinary process: 14 reached positive resolutions with just two continuing to disciplinary.

In 2014 our yearly disciplinary total was 38. After implementing the mediation scheme, disciplinaries fell to just 15. In 2015 I carried out 22 mediations. In 2016, I prevented three large cases going to grievance and reached positive outcomes through our 'Resolution Request' procedure instead.

The Resolution Request procedure introduces mediation as a first step to resolve issues informally and encourages a no-blame dialogue to ease the parties into a positive working environment following their dispute. This can be done through their direct line managers, or involve myself as an objective party member; however, I always try to encourage the departments to tackle it internally first as this resonates more with the aggrieved parties.

How have you made mediation more widely accessible?

Our 'Mini-mediators' initiative was introduced to the strategy members in November 2016 to share a mediation skillset across our supervisory and management teams. What better way to resolve conflicts quickly than by giving employees the tools and understanding to tackle problems themselves? Mini-mediators across departments are trained by myself, sharing my knowledge and arming them with the tools needed to proactively solve low-level complaints and conflicts. This initiative has broken down the silos across departments and colleagues see HR as a trusting and safe environment instead of somewhere they come when in trouble.

What lessons have you learnt on your journey?

Although this all may sound straightforward and rosy, there is a lot of hard work, time and energy put into creating a procedure that fits with a company's culture. For the Royal Lancaster London, we needed something that showcased our value of 'We always care' and that would fully support our colleagues during a time of change and flux as we moved to a five-star hotel.

As a mediator, you have to fully believe in your own abilities to shift mindsets, engage in positive conversation even when the going gets tough, and always think about the bigger picture. I was lucky enough to have a strategic team and manager who fully believed in my vision, but being proactive and merging existing policies to fit within mediation is also key. If you want to have a business that develops and empowers your people, you must give them ownership to deal with their conflicts and overcome challenges constructively and collaboratively. Mediation not only does this, but it promotes trust, openness and an ability to enforce positive change in mindsets.

The changes that we have made across the hotel have brought me closer to the core reasons why I became a HR professional in the first place. Focusing on resolution and embedding a mediation-friendly culture has amplified the impact that I can have within this fast-paced and dynamic working environment.

Facilitated roundtable conversations

How to secure a collaborative outcome to a workplace conflict

Facilitation simply means the act of helping other people to deal with a process or reach a solution without getting directly involved yourself. A facilitated roundtable conversation (also known as an assisted conversation) is a highly effective way of bringing the parties together to help them to secure a collaborative and mutually acceptable outcome to a conflict or a dispute. It is typically used at an earlier stage than mediation and is an effective form of early resolution. For the parties, a facilitated roundtable conversation may feel less formal or daunting than mediation. As a result, organizations that use them generally see a significant take-up of facilitated conversations.

The facilitated conversation process is very similar to mediation and the principles that underpin a facilitated conversation are drawn directly from mediation. However, unlike mediation, where the mediation process is facilitated by an impartial third party, a facilitated conversation can be run by a manager, an HR professional and or a union rep.

Facilitated conversations apply the same FAIR Model™ that is used in the mediation process (see Chapter 9 for more details):

Facilitate

Appreciate

Innovate

Resolve

A facilitated conversation can be chaired by anyone who has the basic training required to do so. However, in many of the organizations that I working with to embed the resolution spectrum, facilitated conversations are jointly chaired by a manager and a union rep, HR and a union rep, or HR and a manager.

When to use a facilitated roundtable conversation

A facilitated conversation can be used when a request for resolution had been submitted to HR, or an approach has been made to a senior manager, union rep or other person. Facilitated conversations are a powerful and collaborative method for managing conflict. This joined-up approach models and promotes collaborative behaviour and mindsets. Most training for facilitated conversations lasts for a couple of days and covers the following:

- How to set up a facilitated conversation.
- How to run a facilitated conversation.
- How to conclude and evaluate a facilitated conversation.

Resolution reflection

Please describe the main points that facilitators should consider regarding the following stages of a facilitated roundtable conversation:

- Meeting the parties separately.
- Preparing the room.

- Getting the facilitated roundtable conversation started.
- Managing the exchange between the parties.
- Handling an impasse.
- Helping the parties to reach an agreement.
- Closing the facilitated roundtable conversation.
- Evaluating the impact of the facilitated roundtable conversation.

Mediation

How to set up and run a mediation session

I have been mediating for over 25 years and I am passionate about the role that mediation can play in resolving many disputes and conflicts within our workplaces and more widely across our society. Mediation is an incredibly effective means for resolving disputes and it surprises me that it is not used more widely.

People often ask me when mediation is not suitable. I am unable to think of a single situation where mediation cannot assist. The only factors that may make mediation unsuitable are where one or both parties rejects mediation in favour of avoidance or formal action (which should be actively discouraged in all but the most serious cases), or where one or both parties have a serious mental health issue (although there is a close relationship between conflict and mental health so this should not be seen to be a block in itself). When I am delivering presentations and work-shops, I still come across a lot of misunderstanding about what mediation is, how it works and what it can achieve. In some respects, addressing these factors has been at the forefront of my mind as I have been writing this book.

Mediation is a central tenet of the resolution spectrum. Chapter 10 focuses on mediation in greater detail, including the principles, the process and the practical applications of mediation. In that chapter, I also explore the many applications of mediation and I provide detailed guidance on the use of mediation within organizations: big or small, private or public.

Mediation is a well-established form of alternative dispute resolution (ADR). Mediation is a structured process used for resolving a dispute whereby a neutral third party assists the two or more disputing parties to discuss, identify and secure a range of mutually acceptable options for resolving their dispute. Many organizations are now using mediation including major international banks such as BNY Mellon. According to Amanda Essex, Head of Employee Relations, EMEA, at BNY Mellon:

> Mediation has enabled BNY Mellon to offer our people the chance to focus on their relationships, understand different perspectives and it has helped to foster trust and respect between colleagues. By proposing an impartial mediator before initiating a formal grievance process we have seen interactions improve, individuals become more engaged, and focused, on finding a positive outcome. The process enables employees to take ownership of their careers and address matters of importance in a timely fashion. The feedback from participants suggests that the 'mediation first' process is an encouraging one and something we can see our people are responding positively to.

Mediation core principles

There are some core principles that differentiate mediation from other dispute resolution processes such as arbitration, adjudication or litigation:

- Mediation is voluntary and confidential.
- Mediation is non-adversarial and the collaborative nature of the process encourages the parties to be less confrontational.
- Mediation is about mutual interest-based problem solving. It is not about allocating blame or identifying sanctions or punitive action.
- The outcomes in mediation are defined and agreed by the parties in dispute, not imposed by a third party.
- The mediation process generally takes a day or two as opposed to the weeks, months or in some cases years that the formal routes can take.
- Mediation is generally significantly less expensive than formal remedies.
- Mediation is a clearly structured process; however, it is less formal than other approaches.
- Mediation is a holistic process, ie it can deal with all issues raised by the parties. Other resolution approaches are narrow and only focus on the issues in dispute.
- Mediation is an increasingly popular method for resolving complex conflicts and disputes.
- Mediation is used in many different forms of dispute within organizations, large or small, across the United Kingdom, for resolving:

- workplace disputes as a means of restoring and protecting working relationships;

- employment disputes as an alternative to formal litigation;

- team and group disputes;

- disputes with consumers and customers;

- disputes arising from mergers and acquisitions;

- disputes in the boardroom, within partnerships and between family members in small family-run businesses;

- disputes with suppliers or other business partners.

Conflict coaching

Developing conflict-resilient individuals and relationships

Conflict coaching is a collaborative relationship between the coach and coachee. Conflict coaching may be undertaken by an external coach but the most powerful and sustainable models are those where people are trained to act as conflict coaches from within the organization. Conflict coaching can be used:

- As a precursor to mediation or a facilitated conversation to build confidence and to encourage reflection.

- To run alongside other resolution approaches such as mediation or facilitated conversations.

- Once a mediation or a facilitated conversation has concluded to help one or both parties develop resilience and sustain the agreements.

- As an outcome to a disciplinary or determination process to help one or both parties adapt their behaviours.

The coach works with their coachees to reflect on how they act, interact and react at times of conflict or change. The objective of conflict coaching is to develop a greater awareness of how the coachees behave during conflict, and to help them develop a range of alternative responses and behaviours that will yield better outcomes at times of conflict, change or crisis.

Conflict coaching is a highly effective tool for:

- Preventing and resolving workplace and team disputes.

- Addressing difficult or problem behaviours in the workplace.

- Managing change and responding to the aftermath from change or transformation processes.
- Developing resilience and confidence in managers and leaders where they are required to handle difficult situations at work.

CASE STUDY The police sergeant

I began working as a conflict coach over 20 years ago. In one of my first ever conflict coaching cases, I recall vividly getting a phone call from the HR department from a police force that I was working with. Apparently, an acting sergeant had received two complaints against him from members of the public for using undue force during arrests. These two complaints, while neither was upheld, were enough to cause concern about the officer's behaviour and how he reacted to provocation. It was also pointed out to me that an acting sergeant is required to take a leadership role and act as an example to other officers. It had already been made clear to him that this was jeopardizing his chances of promotion to sergeant.

After I met with HR and a senior police officer to understand what the organization needed from the conflict coaching process, I met the acting sergeant on three separate occasions for about two hours per session. The first meeting was about getting to know each other and building trust. He was already aware of the organizational objectives and he was signed up to the coaching process. I asked him what his objectives were and these acted as terms of reference between us. He wanted to: a) secure a promotion to sergeant, b) be a good leader and role model, and c) enjoy the camaraderie he experienced as a police constable.

Once we had discussed these, I then invited him to give me some background and I listened carefully while he set out his frustrations and concerns to me. I reflected back what I had heard and we then had a discussion about how difficult it was for him to be a new manager and to also be part of the old team of his mates. He began to recognize that his outward behaviours were a symptom of a more powerful inner conflict. One part of him was being pushed towards promotion and the other part of him was being pulled towards being part of a group of his old team mates. We would explore this inner conflict in more detail when we met next. Towards the end of the meeting, I asked him to reflect on what he had told me and to identify any areas for learning and personal development in readiness for our next meeting.

At our second meeting, we began to explore his inner conflict and his outward behaviours. He told me that he had made a decision after our last meeting – he wanted to go for promotion and he wanted the coaching session to support him to achieve this. This was a landmark decision for him and it represented the resolution of the inner conflict. We then explored ways that he could modify his approach when he was being provoked.

He was clearly a very intelligent and articulate person and I asked him what he needed from his leaders and which characteristics he respected the most. This is what he told me:

- Trustworthy.
- Sets a positive example.
- Open to new ideas.
- Communicates clearly.
- Stays calm under pressure.

We then used the facets and aspects of leadership that he respected from others to create a leadership model that made sense to him. At the end of that meeting, I asked him to think about how he would implement his new leadership model and what could hinder him from achieving his goals.

At our third and final meeting, we explored ways to make his objectives and ambitions a reality. He made a number of powerful observations about the kind of leader he wanted to be and we explored ways to implement these and evaluate his own effectiveness. At the end of the session, he told me he felt more in control, more focused and more resilient. Not bad for three two-hour meetings.

I stayed in touch with him for quite a while afterwards, He told me that he was awarded promotion to sergeant after about six months and that the conflict coaching process had changed the way that he thought about leadership and how he managed confrontation.

Team conferencing

Team conferencing, or team mediation, is a non-adversarial process for resolving disputes within teams or as part of collective grievances, and to resolve allegations of bullying or mobbing within a team. Team conferencing can be used to resolve all five of the team conflicts identified in Figure 2.2 in Chapter 2:

1 50/50 split.
2 All against one.
3 Meltdown.
4 Silo.
5 Inner core.

Team conferencing draws heavily on mediation and community conferencing. Community conferencing is a process of bringing an entire community together to address and resolve issues of conflict and incivility which affect the whole community.

Team conferencing can be defined by four core principles:

1 It is fully inclusive, ie everyone who is affected by the situation is involved in the conference.

2 It is non-adversarial and promotes collaborative and interest-based problem solving.

3 It is led by a neutral facilitator(s) who manages the process and ensures that all participants have a full and equal stake in the process.

4 It is confidential, ie anything that is said during the team conference will not be disclosed to anyone else.

The next section provides details of the team conferencing process. Naturally, no two teams are the same and the process will always be adjusted according to the situation and the unique needs of the team and the organization. However, the following description provides a broad overview of the team conferencing process.

Design phase

- Team agree to participate in a facilitated team conference to address the issues.
- Neutral facilitator(s) identified by organization.
- Facilitator(s) attend a scoping meeting with the sponsors of the process (senior managers, unions, HR, etc) to receive a briefing including the terms of reference, background to the situation, a chronology (timeline) of critical incidents, an organogram (organizational chart) and other relevant documentation.
- The team conferencing process is designed by the facilitator(s) and agreed with the sponsors.
- Any feedback and aftercare arrangements will be discussed and agreed beforehand.

Discovery phase

- Facilitator(s) contact all participants with a confidential questionnaire to gather data relating to their experiences, perceptions, emotions, needs and goals.

- Facilitator(s) attend an onsite meeting with the sponsors and all participants to the team conference, ideally at the team's location so that the
  facilitator gets a feel for the place of work. This is a chance for the team
  to meet the facilitators and for the sponsors to reinforce the importance
  of all parties committing fully to the conferencing process.

- All parties attend a private meeting with the facilitator(s) to explore their
  needs and goals for the team conference.

- If there is an inner core of protagonists, they will be invited to take part
  in a separate mediation process to resolve any underlying issues before
  the team conference commences.

Delivery phase

(At the team conference; usually one full day):

- Facilitator(s) prepares the room – a neutral venue away from the main
  place of work.

- Participants are welcomed, introductions are completed and ground rules
  are agreed.

- Objectives are set and some feedback is provided relating to the situation
  and the context for the conference.

- All participants are invited to provide an overview of their experiences,
  the impact of the situation and their needs and goals.

- A process of dialogue is facilitated during which the participants raise
  and discuss any issues that are important to them.

- Non-blaming problem statements are generated that are used for collaborative problem solving by the participants.

- The final stage of the conference is to develop a team action plan that also
  includes details of follow-up and aftercare.

Evaluation phase

- Action plans are distributed to all team members.
- The agreed follow-up and aftercare processes are initiated.
- Evaluation of the impact of the team conference is undertaken at inter-
  vals of one, three, six and 12 months.

The team conferencing process can be used in any size team from three
to 30 or more participants. I have successfully facilitated numerous team

conferences including some very complex cases between doctors and lawyers and within HR teams. One that I recall vividly was a team conference that I ran for a large call centre where eight 'pods' of telephonists were in a serious conflict and the call centre manager and supervisors were struggling to secure a resolution. The team was experiencing rapidly rising levels of absence, lateness and general antipathy. It was showing up on various metrics including increasing numbers of customer complaints, dropped calls and very low engagement scores.

After the initial discovery stage, all the members of the team met me for a short preliminary meeting, which lasted for about 10 minutes each. The conference itself took a full day. One of the notable elements was that, while the call centre team were onsite at the conference, the senior management team covered the calls. This built up a lot of trust in the management and proved to the team that they were being valued by the senior managers.

The conference was great fun – no one had ever done anything like it before and they participated fully and actively. They had a lot to say and a lot to get off their chests but they did so with great humour and a lot of respect. At the end of the day, the call centre had designed a series of statements that were produced as posters and screensavers for use across the call centre. The management team reported an immediate reduction in customer complaints and dropped calls and a marked improvement in terms of lateness, absence and employee engagement.

Early neutral evaluation

An early neutral evaluation (ENE) is a fact-finding exercise with a focus on identifying the best possible remedy to a situation – the route to resolution. It can be a useful activity to use as a precursor to a formal investigation and where the employer believes that a formal assessment of the situation by a neutral third party may provide insights about the best possible next steps. ENEs are particularly valuable for identifying the route to resolution in complex, long-standing and intractable disputes including multiple or counter-grievances, bullying, harassment and discrimination allegations.

The ENE is typically undertaken by an external neutral person or a trained and impartial manager. In some cases, it is carried out jointly by a manager and union representative, both of whom should be trained and competent to do so. The characteristics of an ENE are as follows:

- It is not a formal investigation and is not investigating specific allegations or gathering evidence to prove or disprove specific terms of reference.

- It is much quicker than an investigation and should last only a few days.

- It is evidence-based, but that evidence may be unsubstantiated and untested evidence, such as rumours, hearsay or word of mouth as well as material evidence that may be made available.

- The process will always align to your own policies and processes. Where a resolution policy is in place, this is made all the easier.

- The ENE process will introduce a wide range of restorative activities such as facilitated roundtable meetings, mediation and conflict coaching to the parties.

- The outcome from an ENE is a management report providing details for further action to remedy the situation.

- A determination, disciplinary action or dismissal *should not be* carried out solely on the outcomes of a neutral evaluation.

The five benefits of an ENE are:

1 The parties involved have control over the best way forward. The outcomes are designed by them, for them.

2 Neutral evaluations allow organizations to outsource the difficult and often contentious element of decision making to an expert third party.

3 It provides HR and managers with a series of practical options for the most appropriate route to resolution.

4 It is much faster and less damaging than an investigation.

5 It focuses on the entire range of resolution activities and will test the party's commitment to each of them.

Resolution reflection

- What was your initial reaction to the resolution spectrum?
- Do you currently use any of the elements of the resolution spectrum in your workplace?

- Are there any approaches that you don't currently use, and if so, why not?
- Which approaches will deliver the best outcomes for your employees?
- How do you currently assess which is the most appropriate route to resolution?
- What lessons can be learnt from the experiences of Harriette Wolff, Employee Relations Manager at the Royal Lancaster Hotel?

Conclusion

The resolution spectrum is a new approach for managing conflict. It brings together best practice from restorative justice, mediation and collaborative problem solving. It is not offered as a prescriptive model and organizations are free to adapt parts of it and to use in the way that is most suitable to their needs and context. However, where organizations are able to apply the resolution spectrum, it provides employees, managers and others with equilibrium, structure, clarity, consistency and reassurance.

The most effective way of embedding the resolution spectrum is to develop a resolution policy that either works alongside or preferably replaces your existing grievance, discipline and anti-bullying policies. The next chapter explains more and includes case studies from Capgemini and a large London Borough, both of which have embraced resolution.

Note

1 Opening address by Peter Cheese (CIPD, CEO), 2016, available at: https://www.youtube.com/watch?v=M67-Y23ZEhQ [accessed 10 April 2017]

Developing a resolution policy to replace your traditional grievance procedure

08

The formal grievance procedure does not have a primary objective of bringing parties together; rather it is there to reach a verdict: usually for one party or the other. In contrast, alternative dispute resolution offers parties the opportunity to find their own solutions within a properly facilitated environment. It is an empowering process and requires ownership of the issues by the individuals. (Victoria Pile, Head of HR Transformation and Services at Capgemini)

KEY LEARNING POINTS IN THIS CHAPTER

- The traditional grievance procedure is generally ineffective when it comes to resolving interpersonal disputes, conflicts and complaints.

- An alternative to the traditional grievance procedure is the resolution policy that is being embedded in numerous UK organizations.

- The resolution policy is a person-centred, values-based approach that provides a constructive, collaborative and highly effective approach for managing conflict at work.

- The resolution policy can be used to sit alongside or replace the traditional grievance procedure as well as bullying and harassment procedures.

- The focus of the resolution policy is on early resolution, dialogue building, mediation, facilitation and collaborative problem solving.
- The emphasis throughout the resolution policy is on taking personal responsibility, self-determination, empowerment and empathy.
- It also contains provision for managing more severe cases via resolution triage assessment, investigations and formal resolution meetings.
- The resolution policy meets, and exceeds, the requirements of the Employment Rights Act (1996) and the ACAS (Arbitration and Conciliation Advisory Service) Code on Discipline and Grievance.
- Organizations such as Capgemini and Newham Council, which have embedded a resolution policy, have reported a significant improvement in employee engagement, wellbeing and satisfaction and a shift from a blame culture to a resolution culture.

The inception, design and implementation of a resolution policy

By the spring of 2013, I had been working with organizations for almost 15 years trying to promote alternative dispute resolution (ADR). The biggest barrier that I came up against, time and again, was employees' and employers' seemingly irrational obsession with the grievance procedure. It was like a great big block to common sense, pragmatism and dialogue. It was a block to resolution. I had tried to work around it, I had tried to work with it and I had tried, without success, to encourage people to stop using it. It was time to do something radical – something that would shock employees and employers out of their fixation with this terrible document. I started work on a radical new approach for managing conflict. I called it the resolution policy.

On 17 May 2013, I launched my new resolution policy at the Law Society in London. Over 100 HR and ER professionals, along with numerous union representatives and senior leaders, were present at the event. My thesis was that the existing frameworks for managing conflict, in particular the traditional grievance and anti-bullying procedures, instead of resolving issues, were actually making them worse. A lot worse.

The initial response to my suggestion that the grievance procedure could be replaced with a more modern and more progressive resolution policy was one of disbelief. How could I possibly suggest that this key HR process – the cornerstone of modern employee relations, be anything other than valuable or that there could be an alternative to the cherished and much loved grievance procedure? As I explained to the audience then, as I have explained to many audiences since: at best the grievance procedure offers a mirage of justice. At worst, it is a deliberate attempt to apply rigid controls to the workforce under the guise of fairness and due process. Whatever it is or it isn't, it rips the heart out of a relationship and it undermines the very basis of the psychological contract – trust.

In case the audience were in any doubt about my position, I described the traditional grievance procedure as one of the most pernicious, divisive, harmful and damaging documents that exists in the modern workplace. Yet it is one of the documents that no one talks about. It is rarely, if ever, reviewed, its impact is not measured and it seems to have a mythical aura which means that no one dares to challenge its position in the HR and ER policy suite.

Let's not forget, this is the primary framework designed for resolving workplace disputes. In all my years of working with conflict, I have yet to meet anyone who has entered a grievance procedure and come out the other side with a smile on his or her face and a sense of relief that the dispute had been successfully resolved. This is what people tell me is the reality of the traditional grievance procedure:

- It is reactive and is often used at a late stage of a conflict rather than early on.

- It is intrinsically adversarial and it pitches people against each other from the outset.

- It is initiated with a finger of blame being pointed by the complainant, which provokes a defensive response from the person being complained about.

- It promotes and perpetuates the victim/persecutor paradigm (see Chapter 6).

- It follows a quasi-judicial model of justice that mirrors the worst of litigation.

- It is more concerned about facts than feelings, evidence than exploration, corroboration than collaboration, mitigation than meaning, rights than responsibilities and process than people.

- The use of informal resolution clauses or even mediation, which in themselves are positive attempts to resolve disputes, still operate within a formal grievance framework. Where mediation and informal resolution sit within a grievance procedure, they are doomed to failure.

- The relationship between the protagonists will be irreparably damaged and one or both parties will probably end up leaving the organization.
- The fundamental principles of mutual trust, respect and communication – the bedrock of good employee relations – will be destroyed.
- The protagonists will experience unreasonably high levels of stress and anxiety.
- The process will take inordinately longer than it should.
- Neither party will be happy with the outcome.
- If one party does 'win', it will be, at best, a pyrrhic victory.
- It encourages parent-child interactions that infantilize the workforce.
- It reinforces the notion that someone else is responsible for the cause of the problem, and someone else is responsible for fixing it.
- The parties don't have control over the process or the outcome.
- There are few, if indeed any, opportunities to generate empathy between the parties.
- They are often counter-intuitive – they don't offer a common sense approach to dispute resolution.
- They impede creativity and innovation, which are critical to business success and economic growth.
- They seek to mitigate the risk of future legal action rather than offer a genuine attempt to resolve a dispute.
- Opportunities for organizational learning, personal development and systemic change are impeded or lost.
- The very term 'grievance' is unhelpful as it has connotations of grief, blame, hostility, stress, betrayal, loss of control and negativity.

You can imagine some of the comments that I received:

'We have a statutory duty to have a grievance procedure, don't we?'

'ACAS tells us that we have to have a grievance procedure.'

'If we do not have a grievance procedure, we will be at risk of tribunal and we will lose.'

'If we don't have a grievance procedure, we will be removing a fundamental level of protection for vulnerable employees.'

'If we don't have a grievance procedure, it will be a green light for managers to behave badly and it will precipitate a culture of bullying and harassment.'

'Our unions will all walk out on strike if we proposed not having a grievance procedure.'

'If we don't have a grievance procedure, the sky will come crashing down and it could be the end of the world as we know it.'

All understandable I replied but all very, very mistaken. As the event unfolded, I began asking the delegates some critical questions. I invited them to engage with each other in a series of roundtable discussions so that they could begin to get to the truth rather than relying on these much-peddled myths. Their answers to these eight questions changed their view of the grievance procedure forever:

1 Does your grievance procedure align to your core values?

2 Does your grievance procedure deliver collaborative outcomes to workplace conflicts and disputes?

3 Does your grievance procedure drive the necessary behaviours for growth?

4 Does your grievance procedure promote adult-to-adult dialogue?

5 Does your grievance procedure deliver better working relationships?

6 Does your grievance procedure deliver a happier, healthier and more engaged workforce?

7 Does your grievance procedure actually work?

8 Would your organization be a better place without a grievance procedure?

The audience were spellbound as it began to dawn on them that, rather than resolving disputes and promoting better working relationships, their grievance procedures were damaging relationships, destroying trust, creating hostility and impeding business effectiveness. They were shocked. They had never thought about their grievance procedures like this before. As one delegate put it, 'It would appear that our current grievance procedure isn't an enabler of dispute resolution, it is a risk to our entire organization.' Yes, I replied, it is!

There is no statutory duty for an employer to have a grievance policy

There is a myth which abounds within the HR and legal community that organizations have a statutory duty to have a grievance procedure. There is no such duty. Nowhere in the Employment Rights Act (1996) nor the ACAS Code on Discipline and Grievance does it state that an organization should have a policy called a 'grievance procedure'. Section 3 of the Employment Rights Act (1996)[1] simply states that the employer must provide information to the employee within two months of commencing employment, as follows:

> a person to whom the employee can apply for the purpose of seeking redress of any grievance relating to his [sic] employment, and the manner in which any such application should be made, and where there are further steps consequent on any such application, explaining those steps or referring to the provisions of a document explaining them which is reasonably accessible to the employee.

It goes without saying that any procedure for addressing an employee's grievances should meet or exceed the ACAS Code on Discipline and Grievance. However, again, there is no legal or statutory requirement for an organization to have a document, a policy or a procedure called a 'grievance procedure'. The ACAS Code also suggests that:

> Employers and employees should always seek to resolve disciplinary and grievance issues in the workplace. Where this is not possible, employers and employees should consider using an independent third party to help resolve the problem.

Neither the 1996 Act nor ACAS defines what the policy should be called, how it should be devised or how it should be framed. In fact, many UK policy makers, including the Confederation of British Industry (CBI), the Trades Union Congress (TUC) and ACAS accept that an alternative term may assist the resolution process.

I interviewed Gill Dix, Head of Strategy at ACAS, Paul Nowak, Deputy General Secretary of the TUC, and Neil Carberry, Director for People and Skills at the CBI and they spoke with one voice. They explained to me that, irrespective of the title of the document, what really matters is that the organization creates a mechanism for disputes to be resolved constructively; that the mechanism must be compliant with the ACAS Code; and that the approaches must be consistently and fairly applied to all employees. Gill, Paul and Neil spoke about their support for a range of alternative resolution processes and expressed frustration that mediation is not used more widely when the evidence demonstrates that it is so effective at resolving workplace disputes. Who knows, maybe ACAS, plus the TUC and the CBI (which sit on the ACAS Council) may think again about the divisive nature of the traditional grievance procedure and consider promoting a more progressive policy framework for resolving disputes, such as the resolution policy.

CASE STUDY Capgemini develops a resolution policy

Victoria Pile, Head of HR Transformation and Services at Capgemini

For the past year Capgemini has invested in furthering our alternative dispute resolution agenda. This has included the development and launch of our 'resolution policy' for all UK employees. This is now the 'go to' policy for any conflict or dispute in the workplace. The resolution policy has not replaced the formal grievance procedure; instead it enables us to assess cases and, where possible (and appropriate) identify alternative forms of dispute resolution.

We genuinely believe (and have observed) that in many cases, despite our desire to have a constructive and supportive approach, a more formal process can lead to parties feeling 'judged', which in turn feels stressful and can act as a barrier to future good relations. This is because the focus in a formal grievance procedure tends to be on perceived 'wrongs' rather than on acknowledging differences and mistakes yet looking to the future and restoring the working relationship wherever possible.

The formal grievance procedure does not have a primary objective of bringing parties together; rather it is there to reach a verdict: usually for one party or the other. In contrast, alternative dispute resolution offers parties the opportunity to find their own solutions within a properly facilitated environment. It is an empowering process and requires ownership of the issues by the individuals.

We know from experience that this approach leads to more lasting solutions. Furthermore, we know that while there is demonstrable cost-benefit to successful informal resolution, of equal importance is the employee relations impact, ie for the individuals involved and for their colleagues who are also often impacted.

In the first year following the launch of our resolution policy we were able to resolve 49 per cent of dispute cases informally. We were able to evaluate the cost saving by looking at the average hours spent per grievance case from the preceding year. Without the resolution policy and the concerted 'push' to explore informal means in the first instance, most of these cases would have defaulted into the grievance procedure and quite possibly moved on to appeal stage. If grievance and appeal stages failed to deliver the result required by the employee, then their unhappiness would continue and inevitably impact them and their team. Failing to resolve such issues early on creates a far-reaching impact to the business, hence we regard early dispute resolution as a business imperative.

The next phase for us in further embedding alternative dispute resolution within Capgemini is to roll out training to our HR managers and to an identified pool of business managers. The training will be provided by an expert external organization and will be focused on equipping managers with the skills they need to effectively facilitate conversations between parties who find themselves in dispute. We believe this approach, when implemented by those in the business with the right skills and within a consistent operating framework, can be highly effective. We also recognize that some matters call for a different approach and we will continue to engage external mediators for cases where we feel this is a more appropriate resolution method. Equipping our managers with these transferable conflict management skills provides them with a great learning opportunity, which will positively impact our business far beyond the sphere of employee dispute resolution.

So far, this approach has been universally well received by employees, managers and employee representatives and we have direct employee feedback that demonstrates how much they valued the alternative dispute resolution approach, stating that it both alleviated their concerns and left them able to continue working within a cohesive and fully functional team. We will continue to monitor the impact of our approach and adjust and develop it as required. This approach also aligns with our core values of openness, honesty and trust and effects our desire to improve employee experience at all times.

The traditional grievance procedure destroys relationships

For many HR personnel, managers and union representatives, the grievance procedure provides a road map for managing disputes. However, experienced HR professionals, union reps and managers will do all they can to avoid the grievance procedure. They know it will be bruising and damaging so they make valiant attempts to resolve issues outside of the formal grievance process, applying a set of discretionary behaviours and activities.

This refusal to use the very process designed for resolving disputes is a damning indictment of that process – from people who know what they are doing.

Surely, as I have been told numerous times, one benefit of the traditional grievance procedure is that it provides consistency. Well, it does for some poor unsuspecting souls who are consistently stressed, harmed and damaged by it. But for those seasoned HR professionals, union reps and managers who know just how damaging and stressful the grievance procedure really is, it is actually promoting discretionary activity. I celebrate such discretionary activity, if it leads to a resolution. But surely discretionary activity is one of the biggest causes of inconsistency, which the grievance procedure exists to resolve. That's a paradox. Here's another paradox, which I call the HR paradox.

The HR paradox

The modern HR professional's role is to act as a strategic partner to the organization. The role includes finding, hiring and retaining top talent, creating meaningful reward systems, generating effective appraisal or review systems, embedding HR as a strategic function at the very top of the organization, aligning the workforce to the values, vision and strategy of the organization and vice versa, delivering effective internal communications and employee engagement activities, understanding the learning and development needs of the workforce, etc.

The reality for many employees, and particularly those in conflict, is not quite as positive or strategic. HR departments are viewed as the custodians of a policy suite that sends shivers down the spines of most employees and managers: a policy suite that promotes blame, division, confrontation, negativity, fear, betrayal, stress and antagonism. 'I will go to HR' or 'I will take a grievance out against you' is used as an existential threat against a colleague or a manager. HR, in these cases, become the Sword of Damocles hanging above people's heads. For many employees, the HR function is seen as the controlling parent, the police officer or the authoritarian arm of management. Therein lies the HR paradox. On the one hand, HR is an enabler and a strategic partner; on the other, HR and its associated rules and regulations is perceived as a threat.

At the heart of the HR paradox lies, you guessed it, the grievance procedure. However, there is good news, if I haven't depressed you completely, that is. It is possible to change and it is possible to reject the old paradigms and begin to embrace a new approach for managing conflict at work.

Instead of focusing on the grievance, focus on the outcome – resolution. It really is that simple. The case study from Capgemini provides solid evidence that change is possible.

Newham Council in east London is another organization that has made the transition to a resolution policy as an alternative to the traditional grievance and anti-bullying policies. Catherine Anderson, Organizational Development Manager at oneSource (which provides the back-office functions at the London Boroughs of Newham and Havering) expands:

> Anything that diverts a grievance is worth doing. They just take up too much time and they certainly, as far as I've seen, are completely ineffective. It's so important to get people to sit down and talk and that is the main thing that the resolution policy does. Our aim is to make dialogue the normal way for people to resolve an issue. Like if you had an issue in your family or with a friend or with a neighbour, I would like to think most people, well first thing you would do would be to have a chat. I don't know why we don't do that at work. It just makes good sense. The unions were fully on board as they knew that we had retained the formal elements of the old grievance procedure as well as promoting new routes to resolution for our employees. I suppose that you could say that we have lost nothing but we have gained absolutely everything. It's early days for the resolution policy but since it's been introduced (six months ago) there hasn't been a single grievance.

The benefits of developing and embedding a resolution policy

Clearly, there is an urgent need for a radical rethink of dispute resolution within our organizations. We need a new vernacular to define the issues and we urgently need a new way to handle and resolve conflicts and disputes. The resolution policy promotes and encourages positive relationships and constructive dialogue. It's about leaders and managers walking the talk. The focus of this new approach is on resolution rather than retribution, peace rather than polarization, dialogue rather than division.

What makes the resolution policy so effective?

- It links dispute resolution with your values and vision.
- It promotes and actively encourages positive and constructive behaviours in the workplace.

- It replaces your existing grievance and bullying and harassment policies with a single resolution policy.

- Employees, employers and unions can work collaboratively to achieve constructive resolutions to disputes and conflicts.

- It develops a conflict-resilient workplace and conflict-competent management and HR functions.

- It integrates the values and principles of mediation in your organization – mutual respect, openness, collaboration, fairness, etc.

- It gives control and responsibility for resolution directly to your employees and managers.

- There is a significant emphasis on mediation and early resolution.

- It offers a new name and a new focus for dispute resolution.

- It takes the grief out of grievances.

- It makes empathy, dignity and respect explicit features of dispute resolution.

- It reduces the amount of time HR professionals and managers spend on grievance case management.

- It will help your organization to transition from a 'grievance culture' to a 'resolution culture'.

- It includes a comprehensive resolution triage process that HR and ER professionals can use to assess the most suitable route to resolution.

- It is fully compliant with the ACAS Disciplinary and Grievance Code of Practice.

- In more serious disputes and in cases where there is a clear breach of your code of conduct, it offers the opportunity to escalate to an investigation or other formal action.

- There is an opportunity to offer mediation at each stage, even where the case has escalated to formal action.

- It gives greater control and offers greater flexibility to all parties.

- It supports return to work procedures following absence or suspension.

Conclusion

The resolution policy is concerned with restoring and protecting working relationships. It offers a holistic or total conflict management framework for resolving workplace disputes. It is proactive and values-based and it supports employees, managers and others at all stages of the conflict life-cycle (see Chapter 2).

The resolution policy has been designed by conflict management experts rather than civil servants or lawyers, and in that regard it is a practical policy framework that promotes resolution rather than a legalistic process aimed at reducing risk or generating profit. The resolution policy is designed to replace the traditional grievance procedure; however, as is the case with Capgemini, it can also work alongside it. The resolution policy is the proactive end and the grievance procedure is the reactive end of the spectrum. However you go about implementing a resolution policy in your organization, I wish you every success and I sincerely hope that you will contact me to let me know what impact it has had.

Note

1 Section 3 of the Employment Rights Act (1996) is available at www.legislation. gov.uk/ukpga/1996/18/section/3 (All references to the legislation made in this book were correct at the time of going to press.)

The TCM model resolution policy template

You are free to use the resolution policy template in full or in part to create your own resolution policy framework. All I ask is that you use the following acknowledgement somewhere in the document: This resolution policy is based on The Model Resolution Policy produced by David Liddle, CEO of The TCM Group.

Introduction and core principles

ABC organization is committed to fostering mutual respect and understanding with all of our employees: between colleagues, between colleagues and their managers, and within teams. This is even more important when we experience a conflict or a dispute in the workplace. We recognize that conflict in the workplace is normal; in many cases it is inevitable and when it is managed well it leads to healthy, resilient and positive relationships.

When conflicts or disputes do happen, we will foster a culture and a workplace where all parties can engage with each other constructively. We aim to support staff and managers to work together to resolve any disputes and conflicts constructively and speedily. This policy encourages early resolution and offers a collaborative system of dispute resolution that balances the rights of the parties with their interests and needs; it brings the core principles of mediation to the forefront of dispute resolution and encourages constructive resolution at every stage of a dispute. Any dispute should be treated in a fair and consistent way and dealt with quickly and supportively.

We recognize that a positive working environment and good working relationships have a positive impact on employee wellbeing, employee engagement and customer experience. A positive working environment can also lead to better performance, improved employee retention and reduced stress-related sickness absence.

This policy is a formal method for resolving disputes, complaints, conflicts and allegations of bullying or harassment. It may be used in individual disputes, team disputes and in collective disputes. This policy meets and exceeds the minimum standards set out in all relevant legislation and in the ACAS Code on Discipline and Grievance. The policy also reflects our corporate values which are *x, y and z*.

In summary, focusing on resolution is good for our organization, it is good for our employees and it is good for our customers. This policy draws on five core principles:

1 Dialogue – building dialogue between people to help them to resolve disputes, conflicts and complaints.

2 Fairness – giving all employees access to a fair and dignified approach for managing disputes, conflicts and complaints.

3 Mutual respect – recognizing that disputes, conflicts and complaints can be challenging and that we encourage a respectful approach at all times to assist with their resolution.

4 Collaboration – we actively encourage the parties in a dispute, conflict or a complaint to work together to identify, agree and implement a shared solution.

5 Timeliness – we will seek to resolve all workplace disputes, conflicts and complaints in a timely manner and will, wherever possible, avoid any unnecessary delays.

What does resolution mean?

The first meaning of resolution is that the situation will be resolved to everyone's satisfaction. The second meaning of resolution is that the parties involved in the process will be determined to implement the agreement – resolve.

We believe that a resolution that is secured by the parties themselves is more likely to be mutually acceptable and to endure over the longer term than one that is imposed – with one side perceiving that they have won and the other side perceiving that they have lost.

Applications of the resolution policy

This resolution policy aims to bring complaints, conflicts or disputes to a satisfactory and constructive resolution speedily and effectively. Wherever possible, the resolution policy places responsibility for the resolution of conflicts and disputes directly with the people involved. To assist resolution, the organization will provide such support as is required. The resolution policy is suitable for the following types of issue:

- Disagreements and disputes between colleagues.
- Disagreements and disputes within or between teams.

- Disagreements and disputes between managers and members of their team.

- Concerns or complaints about the allocation or distribution of resources.

- Concerns or complaints about the actions or inactions of the employer; about terms and conditions of employment; health and safety; new working practices; the working environment; and/or equality of opportunity.

- Disputes between local union representatives and managers.

- Allegations of bullying or harassment.

How the resolution policy works – a summary

Rather than submitting a grievance, we now refer to the initial stage of the process as making a request for resolution. A request for resolution should be made to an appropriate person: an HR professional or your line manager or your line manager's manager (if the issue is with your line manager) or a union or staff official.

The HR team administer the resolution policy, and requests for resolution will be communicated to the HR team and a copy of the request for resolution may be provided to them. The request for resolution may result in one (or more) of the following courses of action:

- Encouragement to engage in an early resolution meeting (direct face-to-face talks) between the parties.

- A resolution triage assessment of the case to identify the most appropriate route to resolution.

- Support from one of our team of resolution champions.

- A facilitated conversation chaired by one of the organization's HR team and/or a union rep and/or a manager.

- Independent mediation delivered by a fully trained and accredited mediator.

- One-to-one coaching.

- A team conference in the case of team disputes, collective grievances and collective disputes.

- A formal resolution meeting to offer a determination of the case in the event that the above steps are unsuccessful.

Resolution champions

Where possible, we will provide both parties with a nominated resolution champion once the request for resolution has been submitted. This person has been trained to work with all parties throughout the resolution process. He or she is not there to facilitate or to mediate. However, he or she will be able to provide impartial advice and guidance for all parties where it is required. Resolution champions do not give legal advice or undertake an analysis of the merits of the case. The resolution champion's role is to:

- support all parties throughout the resolution process;
- answer any questions that the parties may have about any element of the resolution process or this resolution policy;
- signpost the parties to any additional support that may be beneficial as part of the resolution process;
- provide support once the resolution process has concluded for a period of time that will be agreed between you and the resolution champion (typically three to six months).

Details of the approaches available within the resolution policy

Early resolution meeting

The resolution meeting is an early attempt to identify and resolve a disagreement, a conflict or a dispute. It provides an opportunity for managers, employees and colleagues to discuss situations in a supportive, constructive and empathetic forum.

Most workplace disagreements, disputes and conflicts can be resolved at the resolution meeting stage. Managers should be trained to be conflict-competent. In particular, they should receive training in the skills necessary to facilitate resolution meetings.

If the involvement or support of an independent third party is required, see the sections entitled 'Facilitated roundtable conversation' or 'Mediation' below for more details.

The resolution triage assessment process

The resolution triage assessment is an opportunity for a manager and/or the HR department to identify the most suitable route to resolution. The process commences once the employee has submitted a request for resolution and where early resolution has been unsuccessful or has not been attempted. During the resolution triage assessment, emphasis should be placed on early resolution, including the roles of roundtable facilitation and mediation. The employee should be provided with suitable information about facilitated roundtable conversations, mediation and additional resolution processes such as coaching.

The employer should encourage and promote mediation as widely as possible to ensure that it is viewed as a credible and constructive response.

The parties should be allocated a resolution champion where this role exists.

Facilitated roundtable conversation

The facilitated conversation or a roundtable meeting may be led by a senior manager, a union official or an HR professional. In some cases, it may be chaired jointly.

The facilitated roundtable conversation is a confidential discussion between all parties that draws on the same principles as mediation. However, it is less formal than mediation and can be used to bring parties together at an early stage of the dispute. The facilitator acts neutrally and creates the conditions for dialogue. The facilitator encourages the parties to engage in a constructive dialogue and to listen actively. It is a solution-focused process with the aim of helping the parties to reach a mutually acceptable outcome.

Mediation

Mediation is a non-adversarial way of resolving difficult situations. It is used as an alternative to formal or legal processes. The FAIR Mediation Model™ is the model most commonly used across UK businesses; it stands for:

Facilitate

Appreciate

Innovate

Resolve

The mediator is an impartial third party who helps the two or more parties have an open and honest dialogue, with the aim of identifying a mutually acceptable outcome: a win/win outcome. The mediator may be a trained line manager or an internal or external mediator. To ensure the highest quality standards, it is important that the mediator is trained to an accredited standard and engages in continuing professional development.

Mediation is different because it is about collaborating rather than blaming. Any agreement made during mediation comes from those in dispute, not from the mediator. The mediator is not there to judge, to say one person is right and the other wrong, or to tell those involved in the mediation what they should do.

Mediation is both *voluntary* and *confidential*. However, it is reasonable for an employer to expect employees to consider using mediation and to avoid rejecting it out of hand.

Investigation

An investigation can be invoked as a result of the triage assessment stage or when employees have a complaint or concern that they feel has not been resolved satisfactorily by a resolution meeting, a facilitated conversation or through mediation.

If an investigation is deemed suitable and necessary, the organization should follow its own internal investigation procedure. The key purpose of the investigation is to discover all the relevant facts and information in a fair, reasonable and objective manner.

Investigators should be trained in setting up, running and reporting on a workplace investigation. In addition, they should be aware of the role and benefits of mediation. In this way, should the need arise, the investigators can refer the parties back into the resolution process.

Recognizing that even the best run investigations can be challenging and stressful, mediation should be made available throughout the investigation process. The organization should have an investigation policy that provides a quality framework for all workplace investigations.

Conflict coaching

Conflict coaching is a solution-focused process that promotes empowerment, reflection and a focus on the future. It offers a safe space for managers or leaders to increase self-awareness and transform the way in which they handle conflict and change. Conflict coaches should be professionally trained and can come from inside or outside the organization.

Conflict coaching fosters a culture of collaboration and dialogue and complements the organization's resolution culture. Managers and leaders who are required to handle conflicts and change often benefit from one-to-one coaching.

Figure 8.1   The model resolution policy

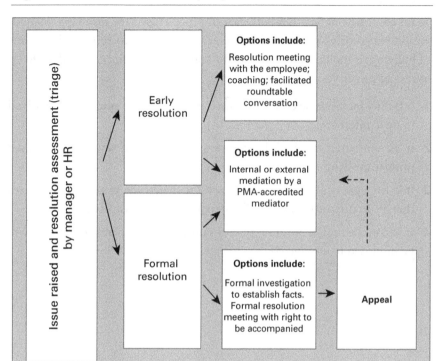

Formal resolution meeting

In old money, the formal resolution meeting is a grievance meeting. This is an opportunity for the employee to meet with his or her manager, HR representative and others to identify a suitable resolution to the situation. The meeting should be run with the same principles as early resolution meetings and, in particular, the meeting should be chaired by an HR professional or a manager who is trained in facilitation skills and/or core mediation skills.

The outcome of the meeting will be a formal recommendation for resolution and, in most cases, this will be agreed between the individuals and other attendees during the meeting. Employees are entitled to be represented at the formal resolution meeting if they wish.

Employees have the right to appeal the outcome of the formal resolution meeting. This should be made clear to the employee at the outset. In any event, if formal disciplinary action is taken, the employee will have the right of appeal as set out in the ACAS Code on Discipline and Grievance.

Team conferencing

Team conferencing is a non-adversarial process used for resolving disputes within teams or as part of collective grievances, and to resolve allegations of bullying or mobbing within a team. Team conferencing can be defined by four core principles:

1 It is fully inclusive, ie everyone who is affected by the situation is involved in the conference.

2 It is non-adversarial and promotes collaborative and interest-based problem solving.

3 It is led by a neutral facilitator(s) who manages the process and ensures that all participants have a full and equal stake in the process.

4 It is confidential, ie nothing that is said during the team conference will be disclosed to anyone else.

Mediation

09

An in-depth analysis

Mediation gives the parties control over the conflict and its resolution. You can physically see them change during the day. That's something, when we did the training, we didn't believe would happen. Even when we started out as mediators we didn't believe it would happen – it's something you can only see to believe. I can't see how anybody can lose using mediation, it's not going to make things any worse. It has the opportunity to make things a million and one times better. (Marie Coombes, in-house mediator with Royal Mail)

KEY LEARNING POINTS IN THIS CHAPTER

- Mediation is a voluntary, confidential and non-adversarial process of dispute resolution that generates win/win outcomes for the parties.

- The mediator's role is to help the parties engage in adult-to-adult dialogue and to explore and discuss their underlying feelings, needs, goals and aspirations.

- The mediator is an objective and impartial third party. His or her job is to facilitate the dialogue, not to impose or recommend a solution.

- Mediators can be from within the workplace or they can be accessed externally.

- According to the latest academic research, over 90 per cent of cases that go to mediation are resolved to the satisfaction of both parties (ACAS, 2015).

- The FAIR Mediation Model™ is an effective model of resolution and is the standard method used by numerous organizations in the United Kingdom and overseas. It stands for Facilitate, Appreciate, Innovate and Resolve.

- Mediation delivers significant human and business benefits. These include reduced time and stress, and increased engagement and productivity.

Introducing mediation

I first began mediating in the early 1990s. It is fair to say that, at that time, mediation was not widely known about. People often mistook it for meditation and, in some cases, people thought that I was talking about a new form of medication. They still do. Nonetheless, I managed to secure funding to set up a small neighbourhood mediation scheme in the northwest of Leicester. I was given an office and a phone in the local housing office and quite frankly, the local housing officers couldn't believe that someone was getting excited about dealing with the very issue that caused them the biggest headache – neighbour disputes.

I was surprised at how well mediation worked in some very challenging community disputes. That was when I first realized that mediation is full of surprises. I also learnt that mediation is an exhilarating, enjoyable and deeply rewarding activity. I was hooked. The local housing team were over the moon that they didn't have to deal with warring neighbours day in day out. It didn't take long for the local police to catch on, along with the local GP surgery, the local church and virtually every other local agency. Suffice to say that, in the next 12 months, I received 112 referrals for mediation in virtually every neighbour dispute across the north of Leicester. Our strapline was, 'Mediation works!' and it most definitely does.

Resolution reflection

Have you ever found yourself trying to mediate between two people – maybe two friends, family members or work colleagues?

- What worked well?
- What challenges did you face?
- What did you enjoy about it?
- What did you find frustrating?
- What do you wish you'd known?
- What did you learn from that experience?

Mediation has established itself as a driver of positive workplace relations

Over the past 20 years, the use of mediation to resolve workplace and employment issues has also been growing rapidly. Mediation is becoming a recognized profession with a professional body, quality standards, an accreditation scheme and annual awards. Mediation is now a key activity within a growing number of organizations and it is being used to resolve increasingly complex and sophisticated business disputes. Mediation is also being used across a wide range of people policy environments such as grievance, discipline, bullying, performance, absence, capability, whistleblowing and absence.

The 2015 CIPD report, *Conflict Management: A shift in direction?*, states: 'Our research shows that some big employers are wishing to make more, and more effective, use of mediation and mediation skills at an early stage.' The report goes on to say 'there is evident potential for such reforms to bring about a sea-change in the way employers manage workplace conflict'.

Furthermore, the principles, practices and processes of mediation are being embedded in the competency frameworks and the review processes for a growing number of managerial, HR and leadership roles. Greenwich University, based in the grounds of the Old Royal Naval College in London, has been pioneering the use of mediation and is one of a number of universities that have developed internal mediation programmes. Yvonne Walsh, Chartered FCIPD, HR Business Partner at Greenwich University, explains:

> For our organization, the use of mediation is proving to be a constructive and successful method of resolving workplace conflicts. Individuals who have taken part in a mediation session have reported that they feel empowered by the process as relations are repaired and the likely escalation of further conflict reduces significantly. We have the support of our senior leadership team who have seen the benefits of mediation. With their endorsement, we continue to raise awareness to ensure that mediation features high as a more productive and cost-effective alternative to initiating formal processes.

What is mediation?

Mediation is a structured process in which a neutral third party (the mediator) intervenes in a conflict or dispute to assist the parties in reaching a satisfactory outcome. Mediation is primarily used to resolve individual disputes, ie disputes between two parties – between colleagues or an employee and a manager. However, mediation is being used to great effect to resolve team or group conflicts along with resolving collective (union/management) disputes, discrimination allegations, consumer disputes, intellectual property disputes, conflicts arising from mergers and acquisitions, boardroom disputes and disputes with external stakeholders and communities.

As well as being used as a tool for resolving workplace and business disputes, mediation is widely used in family disputes, for resolving community disputes, in schools, for returning homeless people back to their families, in family businesses, in will and probate disputes, in the civil courts and to resolve multi-million pound commercial disputes. In fact, mediation is being used to resolve virtually every form of conflict that one can imagine. It is fair to say that you cannot fall out with someone in the United Kingdom without mediation being offered at some stage.

What do mediators do?

The mediator is the person who holds the process together. The mediator plays many roles during a mediation process: listener, critical friend, facilitator, referee, coach, timekeeper, chairperson and moderator. What mediators don't do is tell the parties what to do, allocate blame, propose solutions, force or coerce the parties to settle the dispute. This is what makes mediation so fascinating. As Barbara Browning, Senior HR Partner at Hastings Council, explains:

> As trained mediators we are able to offer an in-house response to a wide variety of workplace problems as well as to the community for other service-related problems (tax collection, planning issues) in a timely and cost-effective way. We are able to resolve workplace problems at a low level, satisfactorily, rather than risking elevation and legal action.

The qualities of a workplace mediator

Most people can be mediators. I would love to say that everyone could be a mediator but my experience has led me to believe that it's not right for everyone. Nonetheless, we are often called upon to moderate a dispute, perhaps between friends or family members. I do believe that organizations already possess copious amounts of mediation and diplomatic ability within their HR teams, management teams and amongst their employees. If we could get better at harnessing the inner diplomat that exists within so many of our people, perhaps our organizations would be a bit more harmonious, our employees a bit more engaged and our businesses a bit more productive.

The core qualities of workplace mediators are:

- Understanding of different situations and openness to other people.
- Able to learn from experiences and from others.
- Able to plan and organize a mediation intervention.
- Able to remain impartial, objective and dispassionate, especially when it is in a party's interests for the mediator to take sides.
- Awareness of own prejudices and assumptions and how their own triggers can affect their ability to maintain impartiality.
- Being flexible and able to balance various demands.
- Having a clear commitment to equality and equal opportunities.
- Analytical ability.
- Creativity and ability to facilitate a problem-solving approach.
- As part of a commitment to self-development, they demonstrate professionalism, seek areas for their own self-development and respond to professional practice standards.

James Wilson, internal OD consultant at the Victoria and Albert Museum, says:

> I first considered mediation as a skill to supplement my role. My particular interest has been in 'un-sticking' conflicts – finding ways to resolve seemingly intractable relational problems. Since then it is one of the ways I define my practice – I am a consultant, a coach and a mediator. This model is straightforward, understandable, clear and demonstrably effective. At the V&A, mediation has been used primarily when an interpersonal conflict starts to have an impact on colleagues, a project team or potentially, though rarely, external partners. Whilst mediation resolves conflict between individuals, for the organization the bottom line is business efficiency. As well as happier faces, there is usually a cost and time benefit to resolving conflicts.

The mediator's role is to:

- promote an early commitment to the mediation process from all parties;
- provide confidential impartial and non-judgmental support to all parties in dispute;
- foster a safe and constructive environment where the parties can engage in open and honest dialogue as a means of resolving their differences;

- encourage participants to transform their adopted positions by taking account of their personal interests and their underlying needs;
- test their unconscious biases and perceptions – particularly relating to perceived intent;
- provide full and equal opportunities for participants to consider and describe the causes and impacts of conflict upon themselves and each other;
- engage all parties equitably in the mediation process and ensure that all stages of mediation are managed in a safe and controlled manner;
- help the parties explore all the issues in full and support participants as they generate and evaluate a variety of opportunities for future working;
- handle impasses during mediation with sensitivity and compassion;
- develop opportunities for participants to create mutually acceptable outcomes to their conflict, complaint or dispute;
- support the parties to craft their own agreements to their conflict.

Resolution reflection

People often tell me that the skills and the qualities of the mediator are useful as part of their everyday roles as well as in the role of managing conflict. That mediation skills are in fact, useful 'life skills'.

Consider how mediation skills could support you in other aspects of your personal life and/or work life.

Introducing the FAIR Mediation Model™

I developed the FAIR Mediation Model™ over 10 years ago. The model is focused on helping the parties to transform their conflicts from dysfunctional to functional. FAIR stands for: Facilitate, Appreciate, Innovate and Resolve; see Table 9.1.

Tesco is another organization that has adopted mediation. The following case study explores how this major retailer has embedded mediation and is using it to drive better employee relations across the business.

Table 9.1 FAIR defined

Facilitate	Facilitate means to make something easier. The mediator's role is to make it easier for the parties to talk and to listen to each other. They do this by: • Creating a safe space during mediation. • Preparing the parties fully to meet each other. • Helping the parties to focus on their underlying needs and goals rather than the relative merits of their adopted positions. • Developing a set of ground rules that the parties sign up to for the face-to-face meetings: • Agreeing to strict confidentiality. • Being respectful. • Being open and honest. • Listening to each other. • Inviting the parties to talk without interrupting each other. • Helping the parties to focus on all stages of the narrative – past, present and future. • Reframing negative interactions and helping the parties to examine the positives and the challenges of their relationship.
Appreciate	Appreciation is a fundamental pillar of mediation. The mediator encourages the parties to look at the world through the other person's eyes and to appreciate what they have experienced, what they may be feeling and what they may need. This is about building empathy and having adult-to-adult interactions. The FAIR Model also draws heavily on emotional intelligence and positive psychology. During conflict, we often focus on the negatives and in some cases we actively seek out (and find) the worst in the other person. We may also catastrophize the situation and, for many disputing parties, the world is a pretty bleak place. Focusing on the positives provides a glimmer of light and some hope that all is not lost. It's somewhere from which we can begin building.
Innovate	Creativity is a key part of mediation. This is a different form of creativity – it's not about inventing the next Facebook; it's about crafting a new relationship and a new range of behaviours. If someone hasn't said good morning to you for two years, crafting an agreement where the other party will acknowledge you in the morning is an incredibly liberating and creative experience. This creativity seeds further creativity and it is not uncommon in mediation for the parties to explore issues outside of the relationship, such as business systems and processes. Mediation can seed future innovation that will carry on once mediation ends. Mediation releases immense human potential and who knows where that can lead…

(continued)

Table 9.1   (*Continued*)

Resolve	Resolve has two different but aligned meanings. The first meaning of resolve is that the conflict is resolved. It has shifted from dysfunctional to functional and the parties have agreed steps to prevent it reverting back into dysfunctional. This leads nicely to the second meaning of resolve. That the parties will have greater commitment to the agreement as it is forged by their own hands. The agreement in mediation is not imposed by the mediator or by anyone else. It is theirs and theirs alone.

CASE STUDY   Tesco embraces mediation

Tesco has been exploring the role of mediation as a means of resolving workplace issues for its colleagues. Leading this initiative is Pete Hodgson, its Head of Employee Relations.

Pete has a proven track record of providing ER and employment law support to senior directors across large multinational matrix organizations. He has extensive experience of consultation and negotiation with representative bodies in both unionized and non-unionized environments. Pete is also an experienced people manager and leader; he was responsible for bringing mediation into his previous employer.

'Mediation is a fascinating and an increasingly important area of work for us' explains Pete. 'Mainly because of the way that people behave when they are in work. The workplace creates an environment where people are forced to work together with people that they wouldn't normally choose to work with, and that creates friction.'

Pete believes that most workplace disputes start out as a minor misunderstanding that quickly escalate into a full-blown conflict. He suggests that these conflicts are often due to a misperception rather than malicious intent by one party or the other: 'The intention behind the situation is very rarely malicious but the way that it is perceived causes it to spiral out of control. People assume the worst. Because they are not communicating effectively, they are unable to challenge the intention behind the behaviour or to test their assumptions.'

Pete believes that mediation could help to address these kinds of interpersonal conflicts. He recognizes the harm that formal grievance procedures can do and he cites an example of a case he was involved in before he moved to Tesco of a dispute that lasted for a full year because a manager didn't make an employee a cup of tea. The situation escalated with counter-grievances being raised and a lengthy period of sickness absence, investigations and time spent by HR and managers. This situation was, in his words, 'an extraordinary waste of money and time'.

Pete also recognizes the importance of adult-to-adult conversations to help resolve workplace conflicts. However, he acknowledges that some people don't feel comfortable having a difficult conversation and that organizations can do a lot more to make the difficult conversation a less daunting prospect. 'Anything that an organization can do to reduce the fear of the conversation and make the parties feel comfortable to talk, the better' he explains. He goes on to add, 'In a conflict, the relationship between intent and impact can become very confused. The traditional grievance procedure does not address that.'

As a senior and experienced employee relations manager, Pete recognizes that ER needs to balance the need for managing the policy framework with a more proactive approach. 'ER has, in the past, been very much on the side of clearing up the mess after a grievance has been lodged,' says Pete. 'However, modern HR and employee relations should be moving towards thinking about the root causes of issues; identifying what steps can be taken to prevent conflicts; and helping our managers to deal with issues at a much earlier stage.'

Pete is aware of the challenges that this change presents for organizations. As he points out, 'Grievance procedures are deeply embedded into the psyche of organizations. Plus, in a big company people are often worried about getting things wrong and how it may be perceived by others. It's not going to be easy to move from classic ER to a greater focus on alternative dispute resolution (ADR). There needs to be a shift in focus from a reactive to a more proactive approach.'

Pete sees the use of a more values-based and person-centred approach as a great opportunity for the HR and ER community. 'We have loads of people policies and they all do their own thing – they may overlap a bit – but there is no unifying thread. This presents a massive opportunity for businesses to unify their people policies to the values of the organization and their overall HR strategy.'

Pete is a champion of mediation and he is committed to making it work within Tesco. 'Mediation is still an area that is being overlooked within HR and ER processes. I think that it is a fantastic way of resolving disputes.' Pete goes on to add: 'The ACAS Code, internal grievance processes and the employment tribunals – look for right and wrong or black and white.

At least one party leaves those processes feeling harmed and let down. There must be a better way and mediation is the best way that I have seen to help employees, human beings, connect with each other. Mediation allows them to explore what their underlying needs are, how they are feeling and what value has been trodden on. It is an infinitely better way of doing things than the old right/wrong way.'

Pete is passionate that the time for the change is right now: 'Everyone in HR should be aware of mediation. Mediation adds value to the HR function and it will help HR and ER deliver real value which, after all, is what the HR and ER functions should be doing.'

Pete has provided a series of hints and tips for organizations that are considering using mediation:

- Take the time to get the data and the evidence to build your business case for mediation. An evidence-based approach can help to win people over. This data also acts as a baseline to measure the impact of mediation.

- Secure buy-in from senior managers and leaders. It is vital to have their full support and for mediation to be resourced properly.

- Don't expect too much too quickly – take the time and have a plan with sensible and realistic objectives.

- Ensure that your front-line HR team are skilled in triaging cases and understand how to identify the right cases for mediation.

- Changing your grievance procedure and embedding alternative dispute resolution into your organization will take time – don't expect it to happen overnight.

Pete concludes that mediation is closely aligned to one of Tesco's core values: treat people how they want to be treated. 'This is an important value for us,' explains Pete. 'When people are comfortable to speak up and they know that they will be listened to it creates a more engaged, more productive and more harmonious workplace.'

The mediation process

Mediation comprises a series of private meetings followed by face-to-face talks. The process is structured in a way that allows the parties to have a constructive and non-confrontational dialogue. The mediator creates a safe environment where the parties are able to communicate and work towards the restoration of a positive working relationship. Mediation enables the parties to identify, consider and discuss their own and each other's feelings, needs and goals. The mediator encourages and facilitates open and honest communication which, in turn, leads to increased awareness, understanding and empathy between parties.

The mediator will contact both parties by phone prior to mediation to introduce him or herself and to answer any questions that the parties may have. They mediator will double-check that the parties are willing to engage in mediation and will address any blocks or barriers that may present themselves. Assuming that the mediation will progress, the mediator will send the parties a short questionnaire to complete and bring with them on the day of mediation, which will help them to prepare fully for the day.

Using the FAIR Mediation Model™, a typical mediation day would look something like this:

09.00	Mediator meets party A to explore the issues
10.00	Mediator meets party B to explore the issues
11.00	Mediator meets party A to prepare for the joint meeting
11.30	Mediator meets party B to prepare for the joint meeting
12.00	Lunch
12.30	Joint (face-to-face) meeting commences
15.30	Break
17.00	Mediation concludes

What happens in the mediation room?

The joint meeting is where the real magic of mediation happens. If you have ever seen mediation in action, you will know how powerful it can be. Below is a summary of what happens in the mediation room.

Opening the meeting

The mediator welcomes the parties and thanks them for attending. The mediator clarifies his or her role and sets out the objectives of the meeting as well as the process of the mediation session. He or she proposes a series of simple ground rules that will help to keep the meeting on track; these are approved by the parties. Finally, the mediator invites the parties to ask any questions about the process or the mediator's role.

Presenting the opening statements

This is a period of uninterrupted speaking time where the parties can speak to each other without the other person interrupting. It does not matter who goes first. Typically, I ask the person I met second at the private meetings to start. The parties are encouraged to talk directly to each other rather than through the mediator.

After each party has spoken, the mediator will ask a series of questions to elicit more information. Once all parties have spoken, the mediator will summarize what he or she has heard.

The exchange

After the mediator has summarized, the parties are invited to have a dialogue with each other. They are encouraged to ask questions, check, clarify, explain and discuss what they have heard. This is a more normal discussion and the mediator helps the parties to stay on track. The exchange phase of mediation is the longest, and is where issues are raised and greater understanding and insights can be formed.

Problem solving

This is the stage of mediation where the conflict moves into a transformational stage from ZONC (the zone of negative conflict) to ZOPA (the zone of possible agreement). The mediator will help the parties to articulate their underlying needs and goals. The mediator will map these and identify areas of convergence and divergence, which are used to create an agenda for problem solving. The mediator's role is to create a series of problem statements that relate specifically to the party's needs. For example:

- Both parties agree that they want to improve communication and to build a respectful working relationship.
- The manager needs the employee to improve the quality of his or her work.
- The employee needs to feel valued by the manager.

So, the agenda for problem solving will look something like this:

- How to improve communication.
- How to rebuild a respectful working relationship.
- How to address concerns about quality of work.
- How to ensure that the employee feels valued.

The mediator helps the parties formulate an action plan.

Concluding mediation

As the mediation process draws to an end, the mediator adapts his or her role to become an arbiter of reality. He or she checks that the agreement is achievable and tests the agreement against certain contingencies. In essence, he or she stress-tests the action plan to ensure that what the parties have agreed will work in practice.

In most cases, the action plan is written down. Verbal agreements are ok but they feel a bit 'light' considering how much work the parties have done to get to the outcome. If they are serious about the resolution, I believe that a written action plan is far better than a verbal one. The mediator will also develop a 'resilience clause' with the parties. The resilience clause in the action plan can be turned to by parties if the agreement begins to unravel or the parties begin to experience tension.

The mediator will destroy all notes from the mediation process and will ask the parties to do the same. The mediator will also check with the parties who, if anyone, needs to be aware of the outcome of mediation. While mediation is confidential, it is generally advisable for the parties' manager or HR to have sight of the action plan or to be aware of the broad outcome of mediation so that they can provide ongoing support. It must be stressed that, if the outcome is shared with management or HR, it should not be placed on either party's employment file. However, if the parties choose to do so, no feedback will be given to any external third parties and the process remains entirely confidential.

The mediator will also agree the level of follow-up required. Typically, the mediator will stay in touch for a full year once mediation concludes to check how things are going and to provide any support that the parties may require. This is generally very light touch.

CASE STUDY Gail's story*

I had worked for my company for over 15 years and with this manager for five years. It was a very stressful working relationship which culminated in having to initiate the grievance process. It was a gruelling procedure that started in the July 2015 and ended in December 2015 with my claim for the most part not upheld because of lack of witnesses.

Not wanting to leave the company, it was suggested by HR that we try mediation. I figured I would give it a go although I was not very convinced. It had been a problem five years in the making so how was mediation going to solve it?

How does mediation change people's behaviour and perceptions? I was really sceptical but I had nothing to lose.

Prior to the mediation, I was sent some paperwork to outline what I wanted from mediation and what my goals were. It helped me to focus on what the problem was. I felt safe during the face-to-face meetings and also talking to the mediator privately. The process was explained and I was able to ask questions. I felt that he took time to listen. It wasn't hurried. The whole process was extremely good. It surpassed my expectations. The day runs according to the progress you make, not according to the clock.

It was beneficial to listen and hear my manager's opinion on some of the choices I have made. I could appreciate how those choices may have looked to her. I know that her actions seen through my perspective has given her insight too. It gave us space to see each other's pain.

It has taken effort since the mediation to work on what we have agreed. I can truly say we have begun to understand each other and our improved working relationship has made our stressful job roles easier.

I have recommended mediation to a number of friends and colleagues because it has been a very positive experience.

I do believe though, that unless you come to mediation with an open mind and a desire to see the situation rectified you will not succeed.

*This is a verbatim record of a statement supplied by the individual. The name has been changed.

Mediation is not the easy option

One thing is certain: mediation is not the easy option. It is a brave and courageous decision by the parties to enter into a dialogue with the other person – their 'arch nemesis'. Somewhere along the line, mediation has been confused with 'soft skills' and a 'touchy feely' approach to people management. Hertfordshire police have been using mediators for many years. Vojislav Mihailovic from the Police Federation explains:

> It is often the case that when mediation is spoken of, questions arise such as, 'What's that?' and, 'Why should I do that?' I reassure the parties that bringing about a resolution through mediation and making sure all parties move on – whilst understanding each other's perspective about what they have been through – helps to build our organization into one that bases itself upon mutual respect, continuous learning and personal growth.

Just because mediators use terms such as empathy, compassion, emotional intelligence, forgiveness and dialogue – it does not mean that mediation is the soft option. Far from it. Mediation is really, really tough. It must never be entered into lightly and anyone who thinks that mediation can be used to tick a box or to be seen to be doing the right thing will experience the shock of a lifetime when they are confronted with the impact of their behaviour and the need to engage fully as the other party spells out the harm that he or she has experienced.

The mediator supports the development of constructive dialogue and helps the parties to reframe the conflict from dysfunctional to functional. In many cases, the mediation process will generate a significant transformation where the parties deepen their understanding of one another, foster a new working pattern, develop insights into their own and each other's responses to conflict, and modify how they deal with conflict and tension in other aspects of their lives.

Mediation is different from every other approach for managing conflict

For my entire life as a mediator, a leader, a husband, a parent and a friend, I have believed passionately in three things:

1 That dysfunctional conflict is harmful. It diminishes us and it is better to not have it in our lives.

2 That every human being has the capacity to resolve his or her own conflicts – if he or she is given the means and the opportunity to do so.

3 That all conflicts can be resolved constructively – if the parties choose to do so.

For me, mediation is simply the most effective way to resolve a conflict, a complaint or a dispute. There is no more powerful way to drive behavioural change than to understand the impact of what you have done, to have the opportunity to reflect and to be given the chance to make new choices about how to behave in the future. Mediation is as close to a panacea for resolving workplace disputes as it is possible to get. Mediation is the relationship equivalent of the antibiotic.

Many organizations that use mediation report a successful resolution in over 90 per cent of cases. This demonstrates that, when the parties are given the opportunity to engage in adult-to-adult dialogue, a solution can be found. Compare this with the damaging impact of our current approaches to handling conflict and the effectiveness of mediation becomes almost overwhelming.

The features, advantages and benefits of mediation

Mediation works in all areas of the workplace and the business environment, from international banks and retailers to a small business. Angie Juttner-Hart is a co-director of a boutique recruitment firm. She used mediation to resolve a dispute with her business partner and, as can be seen from this case study, mediation offers many advantages and delivers numerous benefits to the parties and the organization.

CASE STUDY Angie Juttner-Hart

We came into mediation because my business partner and I felt that we were unable to resolve a tough business issue between us. We didn't have the tools that we needed to resolve the conflict on our own. We were joint managing directors and equal partners. The work between us was not being handled equitably and this was showing up in the financial outcomes. It was creating resentment and frustration.

We sought mediation to help us to resolve the impasse. We were new to mediation but we absolutely loved it – it was such a great day. We knew that we needed to get this issue resolved and we were both on board with the idea to begin with. We loved our business and wanted to make it work. We were ready for the day and for whatever might be thrown against us. Mediation delivered all of the things that we were hoping for but it also delivered some unexpected outcomes. It has given us the tools that we need to run our business going forward.

The benefits of mediation have been dramatic – it's had an enormous impact. Since mediation, the path has not always been smooth but it has equipped us to deal with things as and when they come up. It's given us the tools that we need and it's given us some much-needed clarity.

What was surprising from the mediation was the importance of being true to yourself and to each other. We are very much more accepting of each other now and we are aware of our own strengths and limitations. I would advise anyone to try it – it is important to get perspective when you are in a conflict. If things are going well, you can analyse problems from a rational, analytical and logical point of view. That is not possible in conflict – that is lost. The mediation input can help you to assess and analyse what is going wrong and this is the bit that is often missing.

Mediation has given us the confidence to have tough conversations. It has played a strategically important part in the way that we run our business.

The business benefits of mediation are shown in Table 9.2; the human benefits of mediation are that it:

- promotes adult-to-adult dialogue at times of dysfunctional conflict;
- creates a safe space for parties to craft their own solutions;
- allows strong feelings to be aired and discussed;
- develops empathy, insight and self-awareness;
- enables the underlying root causes of a dispute to be examined and resolved;
- develops agreements based on the parties' mutual interests and needs; and
- develops resilience within the working relationship.

The core principles of mediation

Mediation is voluntary

Mediation is a voluntary process during which the disputing parties discuss and hopefully resolve their conflict. Voluntarism refers to the rights of the parties to enter the mediation process voluntarily, exit the process at any time and/or settle the dispute on their own terms.

This principle of voluntarism gives the parties control over the resolution process. However, it is important to stress that while it is voluntary, organizations are fully entitled to make it clear that their preferred route to resolution is via dialogue, which includes facilitation and mediation. When people choose to work for your organization, this should be made clear at the outset to avoid any future confusion.

Table 9.2   The business benefits of mediation

Less of this	More of this
Management and HR time	Productivity and performance
Time spent preparing and handling grievances	Goodwill and team working
Investigations (internal and external)	Managerial confidence and leadership
Legal costs, compromise agreements and ET costs	Wellbeing and engagement
Absence due to stress and stress-related sickness	Individual and team resilience
Absence due to suspension	Cohesion and collaboration
Recruitment and office cover	Customer experience

Mediation is confidential

Any notes from mediation are destroyed at the conclusion of the process. This allows the parties to have an open conversation with each other in a way that might not happen if they felt that the information they shared during mediation could be used against them in any subsequent proceedings. Any discussions held during face-to-face mediation and any exchanges of information that occur during private talks are done so on a without prejudice privilege basis. In simpler terms, mediation is held under the Chatham House Rule. (When a meeting, or part thereof, is held under the Chatham House Rule, participants are free to use the information received, but neither the identity nor the affiliation of the speaker(s), nor that of any other participant, may be revealed (https://www.chathamhouse.org/about/chatham-house-rule).)

Mediation is based on the principle of self-determination

Any agreement reached in mediation comes directly from the parties involved. They are actively encouraged to develop a 'sense of agency', ie the parties have full control over the *content* of the mediation and they control the nature of any final agreements or action plans.

However, the mediator is not a passive bystander – he or she has agency too. Mediators control the mediation *process* and they encourage the parties to think deeply about the conflict, its impact and its resolution. Mediators will also challenge the status quo and will invite the parties to consider a range of alternative options to the dispute. However, the ultimate resolution and the structure of any final agreement lies with the parties themselves, not with the mediator or any other third party.

Most mediations last one full day

The day contains a series of private and face-to-face meetings. The most common model of mediation used in the United Kingdom is the FAIR Mediation Model™ – see Chapter 9 for more on the model and the key stages.

Mediators are impartial and objective

Mediation can be undertaken by an internal or an external mediator. In either case, the mediator should have completed an accredited mediation skills qualification, should engage in regular supervision and continuing professional development (CPD) and should subscribe to a set of professional practice standards such as those developed by the Professional Mediators' Association.

Shirley Anderson, HR Director at Red Funnel, Isle of Wight Ferries, has embedded mediation in her organization. Shirley explains the benefits:

> Mediation has improved understanding in this business. It has encouraged greater self-awareness in individuals and respect and tolerance for differences generally within the culture. Whilst conflict is inevitable, it is now generally less threatening and can be managed positively to bring about necessary change and continuous improvement.

Resolution recommendations

Not everyone will want to engage in mediation and of course it is a voluntary process. However, an initial reluctance to sit down with the other party should not be used as a reason to forego mediation. If your organization has adopted mediation as one of its preferred routes to resolution, one must ask if it is acceptable for mediation to be ruled out of hand before it is even attempted.

To help you secure buy-in from reluctant or reticent parties, here are some hints and tips to help engage them in the mediation process:

- Listen carefully and let people know that you are hearing them by asking open questions and summarizing back. If people aren't being heard they may close down and it is hard to sell them anything, let alone the prospect of sitting in a room, face-to-face with someone they don't trust.

- Provide high quality information that demonstrates that mediation is not a whim or a fly-by-night solution. People don't want to be experimented on with some new-fangled management ideology. They feel vulnerable and cautious – as anyone would. Having clear information that confidently explains why your organization is using mediation, along with the benefits it can offer, will put many a doubtful mind to rest.

- Ask the parties to describe their needs and goals to you. By reframing their language and their mindset and focusing on needs rather than their adopted positions, they may realize that the need to be heard, valued, respected, trusted, etc is more likely to be met through dialogue than through a drawn-out process.

- Avoid asking straight away if they want to mediate. If they say no, it is hard to convert that to a yes. Ask them instead if they would be willing to speak to a mediator. No reasonable person would refuse to at least speak to a mediator, even if they tell you it will do no good.

- Explore the options (consequences) of not mediating. These are often referred to as:

  - BATNA: if you don't mediate, what's your best alternative to a negotiated agreement?

  - WATNA: if you don't mediate, what's your worst alternative to a negotiated agreement?

  - MLATNA: if you don't mediate, what's your most likely alternative to a negotiated agreement?

- Explain that your organization has adopted mediation and that it is a reasonable expectation of all employees to at least give the process a chance of working.

Conclusion

I ought to declare a vested interest – I am a mediator and I am passionate about mediation. I believe that mediation can work in almost every quarrel, feud, disagreement and dispute imaginable. There are no areas of the modern workplace where mediation can't deliver at least some benefit. With mediation, everyone wins and no one loses.

What I hope this chapter has demonstrated, and the case studies and quotes from mediators, HR professionals and those who have used mediation have shown, is that mediation is not just two people sitting down in a room having a cup of tea. It is a powerful and highly effective route to resolution for so many people.

Resolution reflection

- What role does mediation currently play within your organization?
- What can you do to make mediation more widely available?
- Do you measure the benefits and the advantages of mediation?
- In what kind of cases could mediation be used?
- What might some of the blocks and barriers to mediation be?
- How will you overcome these blocks and barriers?

References

ACAS (2015) *Towards a System of Conflict Management? An evaluation of the impact of workplace mediation at Northumbria Healthcare NHS Foundation Trust,* ACAS, London

CIPD (2015) *Conflict Management: A shift in direction?,* CIPD, London

How to develop   10
an internal
mediation scheme

Embedding mediation into our organization has brought me closer to the core reasons why I became an HR professional in the first place. Focusing on resolution and developing a mediation-friendly culture has amplified the impact that I can have within this fast paced and dynamic working environment. (Harriette Wolff, Employee Relations Manager at London's Royal Lancaster Hotel)

KEY LEARNING POINTS IN THIS CHAPTER

- More and more organizations are embedding internal mediation schemes.

- An internal mediation scheme provides the capacity and the resources to resolve issues speedily and efficiently.

- Internal mediation schemes are a clear message that the organization takes conflict and its resolution seriously. The message is even stronger when the internal mediation scheme is established as part of a broader conflict management strategy, developed by a wide range of stakeholders.

- Internal mediators are typically drawn from across an organization and are required to undertake a thorough selection and training process.

- Using an evidence-based approach and building a business case for mediation can have long-term benefits for sustainability, utilization and resourcing.

Introducing the internal mediation scheme

While Chapter 9 explored the role of mediation and the mediator, this chapter examines how organizations are embedding internal mediation schemes. It also examines the process that organizations go through to create a culture where mediation becomes an integral part of the values, systems and behaviours of the organization.

Mediation is generally delivered in one of two ways: by external mediators or by recruiting and training a team of internal mediators. These internal mediators may be a multidisciplinary team drawn from across the organization, or the HR team may take on the role of internal mediator. This is made much easier once the organization has created a resolution policy that addresses any residual concerns among the workforce about perceived conflicts of interest and the independence of HR.

Organizations may opt to use a hybrid of both internal and external mediators. Internal mediators manage the bulk of the cases that are referred for mediation. External mediators may handle more complex cases, team and group conflicts, or conflicts where the parties have subscribed to mediation but have requested an independent external mediator. This is particularly common in complex discrimination allegations or to negotiate settlement (exit) agreements.

Some organizations are pooling their resources to create regional networks so that organizations within the network share mediators. For instance, I have been working with the University of London to set up and coordinate a mediation network for use by various universities across London. These regional networks have the advantage of giving access to external mediators as and when required. However, rather than paying for an external mediator, the mediation is carried out on a *quid pro quo* basis. The additional benefit is that the mediators within a network bring a readymade understanding of the culture and the context of the organization.

Internal versus external mediators

There has been much debate about the pros and the cons of using internal versus external mediators. This debate has centred on the issue of trust – can an internal mediator be trusted to be impartial, objective and dispassionate? In the current dispute resolution climate, where grievance policies and associated processes undermine trust, and where unions, managers and HR commonly pull in different directions, I would concede that this could be an issue in some organizations. However, this is not a good reason not to embed an internal mediation scheme. Surely it is incumbent on our leaders, unions and HR teams to modify the systems and processes they have designed that are the drivers of mistrust. We need to go back to the root cause of the problem and transform that.

My experience has led me to believe that internal mediators are at least as effective at resolving a dispute as external mediators. Once they are trained fully, understand the boundaries of their role and have been given adequate levels of support and supervision, internal mediators have demonstrated time and again that they can deliver a dispute resolution intervention that is impartial, discreet and extraordinarily professional.

Which type of organizations set up an internal mediation scheme?

More and more organizations are creating internal mediation schemes and training internal mediators to support conflict management and complaints resolution. These approaches are aligned to the core values of major banks, retailers, insurance companies, manufacturers, pharmaceutical companies, hospitals, hotels, police forces, universities, postal delivery and logistics companies, airlines, Whitehall departments, councils, fire departments and ambulance services. All of these have embedded mediation programmes and have trained teams of in-house mediators to be available to resolve complaints and disputes anywhere in their organization.

It is not just big businesses and large public bodies that are creating internal mediation schemes. Small and medium-sized firms, small charities and other public bodies are increasingly training in-house mediators to act as office diplomats and to be available to resolve disputes and conflicts proactively and constructively. More and more professional bodies, institutes and trade associations are also recognizing the benefits of mediation for their members. One such organization is the Institute of Administrative Management (IAM), one of the oldest management institutes in the United Kingdom. Andrew Jardine is the General Manager of the IAM and has been developing an alternative dispute resolution (ADR) programme for members. Andrew explains:

At the Institute of Administrative Management we have a full range of members, from those just starting out in careers to CEOs and board members. We also have junior administrators all the way up to senior management. I believe that all IAM members benefit from mediation; from an understanding of the principles and practices of mediation to beyond that, and learning some of the skills of professional mediators. Conflict in the workplace can be daunting and can lead to an over-reliance on three styles – avoidance, compliance and domineering. While these have a place, if they are the only styles you know you will not be very successful, and in many cases can make a poor situation worse. Having access to a form of conflict resolution that promotes positive communication while leading to better resolutions is worth learning early in your career. It is good to know that there is an approach that reduces the threat of legal action and, in general, leads to greater follow-through from the participants.

If there were any doubt that mediation works, recent research suggests that as many as 90 per cent of cases can be resolved by internal mediators:

> The success of mediation was very high, with 9 out of 10 mediations resulting in an agreement. Most respondents who had been through the mediation process felt that their situation had improved as a result. Managers were generally positive about workplace mediation and almost 6 out of 10 managers also felt that mediation improved their ability to manage conflict. (ACAS, 2015)

The role of the internal mediator

I have trained internal mediators in hundreds of organizations, from small firms to major household names. Having access to a fully trained and accredited pool of mediators gives the organization a valuable resource to tap into when a dispute arises. Professional training should reinforce the importance of objectivity and impartiality and internal mediators should be required to be members of the Professional Mediators' Association (PMA) and subscribe to its professional mediator standards, which clarify the importance of impartiality and objectivity.[1]

The University of Westminster has developed an internal workplace mediation scheme for handling conflict in an informal and supportive way. Fehmeeda Riaz is an HR Manager at the University of Westminster and she explains more:

> We have a pool of professionally trained mediators amongst HR and union colleagues who are able to support mediation requests across the university. We always ensure that there is as much independence and impartiality as possible when mediation cases are assigned, so we don't mediate for our own faculties or departments.

Mediation works as part of a range of activities that we have in place to support staff and to try and resolve conflicts and disputes positively. This also includes coaching and mentoring and access to an Employee Assistance Programme (EAP). We have tried to raise awareness and the profile of mediation by setting up a dedicated mediation section on our intranet and by raising awareness through staff newsletters, wellbeing days, and through faculty and departmental meetings. We also use mediation techniques in team building and in organizational development interventions.

We use mediation skills and processes to build resilience and to help people to handle difficult situations. We mediate in around five to 10 cases of mediation per year, so whilst the numbers are not high, the impact has been significant. People who engage with mediation often say that they slept better at night, they felt more resilient and they managed to avoid a difficult formal grievance process. I think our internal workplace mediation scheme is enormously beneficial in dealing with conflict in a supportive, timely and informal way.

Using the FAIR Mediation Model™, mediations tend to last for one full day. The mediators receive a referral from HR and contact both parties to secure their commitment to mediate. Once this has been secured, the mediation happens quickly, usually within 10 working days.

In 2009, Arcadia Group decided that it wanted to identify innovative solutions to workplace conflicts and to provide an alternative route to resolution for its employees. Arcadia is the United Kingdom's largest privately owned clothing retailer, with more than 2,500 outlets and several well-known high street brands, including Topshop and Topman.

CASE STUDY Arcadia Group introduces mediation

Paul Forrest, Group Employee Relations Manager for Arcadia Group Limited

After the Dispute Resolution Regulations were repealed in 2008, we wanted to do things differently. We were concerned that the ACAS Code for handling a grievance was limited and that it did not meet the complex needs of our business. The grievance procedure is used as a hammer to crack a nut. It offers a one size fits all approach to managing conflict and, instead of resolving an issue, the formal grievance route often inflames it.

Our grievance process was probably much like many others: it was very formal and it followed several key steps. Ultimately, somebody must decide, on the balance of probability, whether something is believable or not. You often get a situation where no decision can be made, because there just isn't enough evidence. You end up with two very dissatisfied people who've been through the process and don't feel that they've got an answer. This can also lead to further breakdown in relationships, further grievances and an increasing cost to the business. We asked ourselves, is there not something we can do to address these issues in a more positive way before they get blown out of proportion?

The business case was built on cost savings from reducing the number of cases referred to the grievance procedure. We calculated that grievance cases typically took three weeks to resolve and required a significant input of HR and line management time – up to nine days. The cost of managing a grievance was around £1,000 per case and that was for straightforward ones. More complex cases took up a lot more time and were a lot more expensive. We were finding that most of the issues being dealt with by grievances related to miscommunication.

In August 2009, we decided to introduce a mediation pilot within the Topshop and Topman brands as a precursor to rolling out mediation across the entire business. In the first 12 months of the pilot, the number of grievances involving relationships between managers and subordinates at Topshop/Topman was down by 50 per cent, while it increased by 12 per cent across the group's other brands as a whole.

The mediation scheme now operates on a two-tier basis under which some cases are dealt with by accredited mediators who have undergone extensive training. Simpler issues are referred for local resolution by mediators who work across the UK. These mediators are drawn predominately from across our HR community.

The pilot had the unexpected benefit of getting across to employees the general idea that problems could be resolved by talking about them. This was a major shift from the belief that, if they had a problem, 'someone else' would be there to sort it out for them. Our mediation scheme fits well with the culture and values of Arcadia Group which, amongst other things, emphasizes employee wellbeing.

Putting in place a mediation scheme involves a lot of hard work for HR, unions and managers but it is worth the effort. Securing the buy-in from all stakeholders is vital from the outset. Mediation is an alien concept for many people and the scheme needs to be vigorously marketed. At Topshop and Topman there was some initial scepticism among employees, who saw that mediators were members of the HR team, which then raised the question, 'What was so different from the standard process for handling grievances?'

The HR team for the two brands responded with posters and leaflets emphasizing that mediation was totally impartial. Now that they are becoming more familiar with it, employees have confidence in the service. The group has undertaken a training programme for 30 additional HR professionals so that mediators are available to work across all Arcadia Group brands and the whole of the UK and Ireland.

We will continue to take the issue of conflict management seriously. Building on the success of the mediation scheme, we are now looking at developing a conflict management triage assessment process whereby all reported cases are referred to a central point. The most effective route for resolving those cases will be identified as quickly as possible. We want to see an increase in the use of approaches such as local resolution meetings between employees and their managers, an increased use of coaching and, of course, increased awareness and use of mediation.

We have proven already that HR have the capacity to mediate and that they can act impartially. Any initial suspicion about the role of HR has been dealt with. We now want to see managers resolving issues in the same way.

We are also introducing mediation into team and group conflicts and we are hopeful that we will see mediation contributing to team development and improving performance and wellbeing within teams. Of course, all of this will need evaluating fully; however, we are now well on the road to a very exciting and transformational cultural change across Arcadia Group.

The benefits of developing an internal mediation scheme

An internal mediation scheme delivers real, tangible benefits to any organization of any size within any sector. The total cost of training a team of internal mediators and embedding mediation across the organization can be less than defending one case at an employment tribunal. The return on investment (ROI) from embedding a mediation programme can be achieved very quickly and that's before considering the invisible benefits of mediation such as greater engagement, wellbeing, resilience, harmony, productivity, etc. (See Chapter 5 for more details about how to measure the cost of conflict to your organization and to help you develop tools for measuring the ROI of an internal mediation scheme.)

By creating an internal mediation scheme, organizations have a team of fully trained and accredited workplace mediators who understand the unique nature of their organization, its values, its culture and its structures. Developing an internal mediation scheme is not just about embedding an alternative form of dispute resolution, but also embedding the values and ethos associated with collaborative problem solving.

Bola Oginni is a specialist consultant who works with organizations to set up internal mediation schemes; he says:

> Organizations that establish an internal mediation scheme are putting relationships first. They are building on their commitment to ensure that everyone can work with dignity and with mutual respect. Employees, managers and other stakeholders can work in an environment where they can be confident that workplace disputes will be resolved constructively, effectively and speedily. Internal mediation schemes bring the core values of an organization to life in a really exciting way. In addition, the organization develops a culture and a reputation as a place where workplace conflicts are managed positively and resolved constructively – a place where people want to come to work and to be their best.

I set up an internal mediation scheme for a large London council. The cost of the whole approach was in the region of £40,000, which included selecting and training a team of 12 accredited mediators, embedding a case management system for the mediation scheme and designing and delivering one-day early resolution skills training for 300 managers, HR and union representatives. Shortly after the training had concluded, the HR director and I met and he mentioned in passing that one of the mediators had recently resolved a complex discrimination case. This, he explained, was heading to an employment tribunal and the time and the cost could have escalated very quickly to tens of thousands of pounds or even more. As he said to me, the cost of our entire mediation and dispute resolution programme was offset by resolving that one case.

Internal mediation scheme toolkit

Ten simple steps to help you to embed mediation in your organization

1 Choose a mediation partner who can work with you to embed mediation into your organization It is not an activity that can be taken lightly and having an expert partner working alongside you will help you to avoid many of the common pitfalls.

2 Gather evidence and build your business case for introducing a mediation scheme Chapter 5 provides details on how to measure the cost of conflict; at the end of that chapter there is a template to help you as you build your business case. It is important that the approach is evidence-based and that it receives sign-off from the board and/or the senior management team. The data gathered can also be used to evaluate the long-term impact of the mediation scheme.

3 Engage your key stakeholders Your key stakeholders (HR, managers, unions, work councils, occupational health advisers, etc) should be encouraged to play a key part in shaping and developing your internal mediation scheme. Some organizations develop a small working group who act as the responsible body for mediation. This group receives updates and provides quality assurance and governance of the mediation scheme.

4 Create a conflict management strategy and develop a resolution policy
Developing an internal mediation scheme as part of a wider conflict management strategy increases the likelihood that the scheme will be sustained and will be adequately utilized and resourced. Developing a resolution policy as an alternative to a grievance policy is a simple change and puts resolution at the heart of your approach to employees. It is important for mediation to feature in your employee handbook and within performance management, whistleblowing, absence, capability and other relevant HR and ER policies.

5 Recruit, select and train a team of internal mediators to an accredited standard The internal mediation team should, ideally, be drawn from across your organization. However, there are no hard and fast rules on this and each organization needs to consider who the right internal mediators should be. The mediators will be required to complete a selection process and attend accredited mediation training. They are also expected to participate in ongoing continuing professional development (CPD) activities.

6 Identify a mediation scheme coordinator The mediation scheme coordinator is the unsung hero of the modern workplace. His or her job is to manage the mediation scheme, organize the mediators, arrange the intake of cases and evaluate the impact of mediation. He or she may also play a role in sourcing rooms for mediation and will act as a champion of mediation and be responsible for promoting it as widely as possible. Typically, mediation scheme coordination sits within HR but again, there are no hard and fast rules about this.

7 Train your managers, HR teams and union representatives Unions, HR and managers are often at the front line of conflict and its resolution. Training them to possess the core skills for spotting issues early, listening actively, being emotionally intelligent, facilitating dialogue, overcoming impasses, being aware of their unconscious biases, setting goals, using interest-based problem solving and drafting an action plan will deliver significant benefits. Such training doesn't need to last for months: a one- or two-day course can be highly effective.

8 Ensure awareness and authorization are in place Ensure that internal investigators, disciplinary panels and appeals panels are aware of mediation and are authorized to refer cases to mediation. It's never too late to mediate. Mediation can be used after formal action and to return people to work after periods of sickness absence or suspension. Investigators should be actively encouraged to keep mediation in mind and, where the issues being investigated are relational, to seek opportunities to refer the case to mediation, particularly where the case is not clear and the issues are not black and white.

9 Communicate your new internal mediation scheme It is important to let everyone know that this is the direction your business is travelling in. The more people who share your vision and come on board, the more sustainable and credible your new approach will be. Typically, organizations promote their internal mediation scheme via leaflets and factsheets, roadshows, team briefings, videos, intranet pages and/or posters.

10 Evaluate the impact of mediation across your organization Using the data gathered during the set-up phase, it is possible to evaluate the impact of mediation over the longer term. The data gathered typically examines the impact of mediation on:

- Levels of cases of conflict, bullying and harassment, discrimination, etc.
- Time taken to resolve a complaint by managers, HR and others.
- Opportunity cost-benefits (ie how the time saved was used instead).
- Financial cost savings.
- Costs relating to settlement agreements, employment tribunals and other forms of litigation.

- As well as mediation's impact on:

  - employee engagement and staff satisfaction;
  - productivity and performance;
  - attendance levels;
  - attrition levels;
  - customer experience; and, where possible
  - employer branding.

CASE STUDY Embedding a culture of mediation within the Metropolitan Police Service (MPS)

An interview with Jaua Harris, Strategic HR Policy Lead at the MPS

Why did MPS consider setting up an internal mediation scheme?

We wanted to move away from a reliance on formal processes such as grievance procedures to resolve disputes. This is a slow process and not always successful. This is not helped by the fact that it has often been interpreted in a way that encourages individuals to think that they have either won or lost. This can be damaging to working relationships rather than improving them. We also wanted to change the language and the parties' mindset from grievance to resolution and we felt that mediation was an integral part of helping people to secure a positive and lasting solution.

In fact, it was an employment tribunal that brought this to life for us. An officer challenged the way that the Met dealt with complaints about how she was treated in the workplace. The employment tribunal agreed with the officer and highlighted shortcomings in the Met's processes, in particular the rigid way we dealt with discrimination complaints. To help us to better understand the problems, the Director of HR commissioned an external review of our complaints and dispute resolution processes. This was done by ACAS in collaboration with barrister Professor Roy Lewis. We wanted to demonstrate that we took the employment tribunal's findings seriously, were prepared to listen and committed to making changes to improve.

The review team made several recommendations in terms of how we could improve how we handle complaints and grievances, particularly discrimination complaints. The rigid method of deciding what could be dealt with within the grievance procedure needed to change. Where individuals made allegations of bullying or discrimination, we should listen to them, get some sort of understanding of the situation and decide on the most appropriate route to resolution. This was also a chance for us to embrace mediation within MPS.

What challenges did you face as you began implementing the changes?

The Met's working practices are governed by employment law and police regulations. The police regulations provide the formal mechanisms for how we deal with allegations of police misconduct, which can be different to employment law or conflict with ACAS best practice. This means that there is limited scope for holding a case within the grievance procedure for cases that have the potential to be considered as misconduct, ie discrimination, bullying and harassment.

Despite the challenges, we have introduced an approach which is more fluid. It's not so rigid. We have employed trained specialists who conduct initial scoping and triage cases much earlier. We are emphasizing the informal resolution routes to resolution to prevent the entrenched behaviour that happens when people let things fester. The message is that we now deal with things quickly, close to the business and close to where the problem happens in the first place.

What role is mediation playing in this new landscape?

We've invested a great deal in mediation, and that's how we got to know TCM, who have helped us to get a cadre of mediators in the business that can be activated or deployed quickly to resolve these situations when they arise. We have chosen a model of internal mediation whereby mediators have been selected from across the organization. This multidisciplinary approach is about giving parties in a dispute confidence in the mediation process and to ensure that they feel that they can trust the mediator as they are completely impartial and objective.

We have trained 50 mediators within MPS in the past six months and the feedback from the delegates has been incredibly positive. We wanted to drive the skills of mediation across the business, and evidence from other organizations and within MPS itself persuaded us that we should invest in mediation to make it a sustainable model of dispute resolution.

It's not about just putting initial investment into mediation; it's about having a whole system around having mediation, keeping it up to date, developing the practice, and reinforcing its use over time. That way it becomes the main way to resolve conflict.

What benefits has mediation delivered for MPS?

Sometimes people want to resolve issues but they need help. They want a third person there to keep the communication on track and to prevent behaviours from becoming unreasonable. It's about somebody who has no stake in the dispute listening to both points of view and helping the parties move into the middle ground.

The main benefit that I see is that it allows people to get on with their lives without the conflict hanging over them. They can get some sort of resolution that enables them to get what they want to achieve. It also empowers them to reach their own decision. In formal processes, it's pretty much taken out of their hands. This way, it gives them back control.

We also recognize the importance of gathering clear data about the financial and the human return on investment for mediation. It is still very early days for us and this is a work in progress. However, the overall experience of people who have been through mediation is telling us that it is working. We continue to gather data to demonstrate a wider benefit to the MPS. However, we have moved away from our black and white style of dealing with disputes. This was a major trigger for us and that has been a great improvement.

How did you get unions and staff associations to buy into this new approach?
I've worked with the unions, Police Federation and the Staff Associations (eg, Black Police Association) and I'm pushing on an open door there. They have a range of complex challenges to deal with – representing their members at all levels. Plus, with organizational changes generally, the demands on them are very high. There is an immense pressure on their limited resources. Any help to resolve cases and keep their members happy without calling on their limited resources is helpful. They have really supported this initiative and they have helped to push this new way of working.

Do you have any advice for organizations that are considering implementing a mediation scheme?
Yes. From senior managers' point of view, it's often about the bottom line. They are thinking in terms of productivity within the organization and how to get more with less. This is sometimes at the expense of focusing on the more human side of the organizations and how to repair relationships when they break. However, investment and real consideration should be given to making sure that, in this time of enormous change and reduced resources, we have properly resourced resolution processes and mediation programmes in place. The overall cost of disputes that are not resolved should not be underestimated and should form part of the business case for investment.

I would advise organizations to focus on developing things like informal resolution skills for managers and developing a network of resolution champions. Maximize the use of internal mediators to dampen down the fire as soon as it happens. Finally, think about embedding mediation across your organization and getting all the systems and processes right and the procedures in place and then build it up from there.

Note

1 www.professionalmediator.org/resources/Pictures/Image/The%20PMA%20 Professional%20Standards%202016.pdf

Reference

ACAS (2015) *Towards a System of Conflict Management? An evaluation of the impact of workplace mediation at Northumbria Healthcare NHS Foundation Trust*, ACAS, London

Tackling bullying and harassment 11

From process to people

The benefits that mediation has brought to our organization include providing an alternative means of resolving conflict to traditional grievance and harassment and bullying processes, that seeks to culminate in a win-win outcome for both the staff involved and our organization. Whilst mediation can be significantly challenging, when the staff involved say 'I didn't know you felt like that' to each other and then they take mutual steps to come to a new way of working between them, the effort of mediation is evidently worthwhile. (Lisa Neden, Equality and Diversity Specialist at The Royal Marsden)

KEY LEARNING POINTS IN THIS CHAPTER

- Workplace bullying is a serious issue with serious consequences for the parties involved.

- Bullying is another name for conflict at work and it should be part of a wider conflict management strategy.

- Allegations of bullying typically occur because the early warning signs have been missed, there are no routes by which the victims of bullying can speak out and managers have not been trained to spot problems and to intervene effectively and confidently when they do.

- Organizations and managers have become too reliant on formal processes for handling bullying, which creates a culture of fear within the organization.

- These policies are also reactive and apply the same rights-based methodology as the traditional grievance procedure. These approaches, while delivering 'procedural fairness' are woefully ineffective at tackling the root causes of bullying.

- Mediation and other remedies are proving to be highly effective at addressing bullying at work, yet such processes are significantly underutilized.

Introduction

Bullying appears to be a serious problem in our workplaces. Data from my own organization, The TCM Group, suggests that around 75 per cent of workplace complaints being referred for investigation or mediation involve an allegation or allegations of bullying, and the situation appears to be getting worse. More and more organizations are recognizing that bullying is a serious issue, often through external reviews or through issues being raised in internal audits or employee engagement or satisfaction surveys.

What are bullying and harassment?

There is no standard definition of bullying. However, the impact of bullying at work can be significant. According to ACAS (2014):

> bullying may be characterised as offensive, intimidating, malicious or insulting behaviour, an abuse or misuse of power through offensive, intimidating, malicious or insulting behaviour, an abuse or misuse of power through means that undermine, humiliate, denigrate or injure the recipient.

Harassment is defined in the Equality Act 2010 as:

> unwanted conduct related to a relevant protected characteristic, which has the purpose or effect of violating an individual's dignity or creating an intimidating, hostile, degrading, humiliating or offensive environment for that individual. Harassment is therefore unlawful and claims can be brought to the Employment Tribunal.

ACAS (2014) states in its guidance that:

> behaviour that is considered bullying by one person may be considered firm management by another. Most people will agree on extreme cases of bullying and harassment but it is sometimes the 'grey' areas that cause most problems.

My experience and the experience of many organizations is that it is precisely these grey areas that are particularly challenging to deal with. A 'black and white' approach for resolving issues does not work in these cases and ACAS is right to state that 'mediation can be a good way of dealing with bullying, discrimination or harassment situations depending upon the nature of any allegations'.

The resolution spectrum, which is explained in Chapter 7, extends beyond mediation and provides a range of remedies for tackling bullying and harassment at work – particularly those cases that exist in the 'grey area'. The use of resolution triage assessment, early resolution meetings and facilitated roundtable conversations can also be valuable in helping all parties identify the most effective route to resolution.

Examples of bullying and harassment

One high-profile case of an organization that has been in the headlines is London Ambulance Service (LAS). An investigation carried out by the Care Quality Commission (CQC) in 2015 found that there was a bullying and harassment culture embedded in the organization and identified numerous examples of verbal and physical abuse and harassment of staff. The organization's Chief Executive at the time, Dr Fionna Moore, publicly apologized for the problems, saying in a press statement issued by LAS that they would no longer tolerate bullying or harassment of any kind, at any level.

In 2016, LAS asked me to help address this issue and to develop and implement a bullying and harassment programme within the ambulance trust. The following case study shows how LAS used the principles of mediation and confident conversations training for their managers to tackle this complex issue.

CASE STUDY London Ambulance Service turns the tables on workplace bullying

An interview with Cathe Gaskell, bullying and harassment coordinator at London Ambulance Service

What led to London Ambulance Service (LAS) changing the way that it handled bullying and harassment?
In 2015, LAS became the first ambulance trust to be placed in special measures by the Care Quality Commission (CQC), and among the concerns raised were bullying and harassment. The trust took immediate action and recruited a

bullying and harassment specialist, nominated a non-executive director sponsor and set up a specialist bullying HR and OD committee. A phased action plan was developed and progress is reported monthly to the non-executive director, which keeps our resources, energy and focus on initiating cultural changes throughout the organization.

The trust has held 61 workshops to explore bullying and harassment and to explore potential solutions. To date, over 750 have attended these workshops.

How did you begin to tackle such a massive challenge?

I carried out some diagnostics, including conversations and interviews with as wide a range of staff as possible. I wanted to get a clear understanding of what bullying and harassment looks like within the organization. It became apparent very quickly that conflict was at the heart of the issue. Conflicts around what was communicated, how it was communicated and how messages were perceived. Because we are an emergency service, a lot of the communication can be issued in a very command-control style, because people are reacting to stressful situations. People wanted us to get much better at recognizing the early warning signs of bullying and creating processes for flagging up bullying behaviours as soon as possible. They wanted to see interventions such as roundtable meetings and mediation brought into play quickly to correct conflict within relationships before it turns into a protracted grievance or disciplinary process.

What steps did you take to address bullying and harassment?

We identified several areas to focus on which became the overall bullying and harassment programme framework:

- to raise awareness of the impact of bullying and harassment;
- to promote courageous conversations across the trust;
- to equip people with the skills to make the workplace more respectful;
- to set up and run roundtable sessions;
- to investigate bullying and harassment allegations more effectively; and
- to raise the profile of bullying and harassment with the HR team and with union and management colleagues.

What support did you receive for this transformation project?

We decided to partner with an external expert to help us to develop the training elements of the project but to also provide expert support and guidance. We wanted a partner who had the same values as us, and who understood what we were trying to do. We scoured the market place and ultimately we chose TCM to be our partners for this journey. We weren't looking for a traditional bullying course for a few people. Our aim was to train a large volume of staff, to equip them to use the practical skills of mediation – they would not be mediators but we wanted them to possess the core mediation skills that make mediation so effective at resolving workplace conflicts.

What where the objectives of the training programme?

The two-day training programme was designed to give delegates an understanding of the causes of conflict, as well as the skills:

- to nip conflict in the bud;
- to promote constructive and collaborative conversations;
- to build rapport with vulnerable people;
- to listen actively and with sensitivity;
- to act with compassion, impartiality and integrity; and
- to set up and facilitate a roundtable event for parties in conflict.

With this mass of trained staff, we talk a lot about better communication – shaping, not shaming. And there are 12 roundtable meetings being facilitated as I speak and many more in the pipeline. We try to facilitate open and honest conversations and we remember that when we're giving feedback – we're shaping, not shaming.

Who was the training programme aimed at?

People had to apply to attend the training and they went through a selection process. We have got people from all different parts of the organization: people who are working in offices, paramedics, people from HR, from patient experiences, from legal services, in fact all over the organization, learning these skills. To date over 70 people have been trained as roundtable facilitators and we are aiming to train a further 30 in the coming months.

One important point about making the training humanizing is that we trained in our normal clothes, not in uniform. It's very important for us to do that, because people are there not with their rank on show. Everybody's the same.

How was this approach different from other approaches that you have tried?

This approach was about not being adversarial. We've rewritten our grievance and our bullying and harassment policies, which now include more focus on courageous conversations, mediation and roundtables. We now make it clear that resolution will initially be sought via the roundtable process and potentially through mediation.

What happens during the 'day in the life' events?

LAS has held three 'day in the life' events over the past 12 months, which 120 employees attended. Teams opened themselves up to visits and questions for a week to encourage colleagues to spend time in services that they would not normally interact with, such as control rooms, legal services, NHS 111 and the hazardous area response team. This has been a powerful way of addressing the underlying sources of conflict, because people say, 'I never knew what you did.'

Is there any evidence to suggest that these new approaches are having a positive impact?

People are telling me every day that this new approach feels much better. They value the fact that LAS welcomes creativity and innovation and it is empowering people to find practical solutions to their own issues. We've got good evidence that staff turnover has been going down. That means that staff are staying, which is important, plus it's had a positive impact on our staff sickness levels. That means that there are now a significant number of people who are back in the workplace.

What we've done is let people know that we take it seriously. We don't want people to suffer in silence. The other thing is, we wanted to make it clear that staff have responsibility to speak up. If you feel you're going to take a grievance, you have a responsibility to speak up first.

These may be small, incremental improvements, but it's good that they're all going positively. Cultures take a while to change, because you can't change one overnight.

(A case study about how London Ambulance Service tackled bullying and harassment is available on the NHS employer's website.[1])

Resolution reflection

- What conclusions do you draw from the London Ambulance Service experience?
- LAS moved away from a process-led approach for tackling bullying and harassment to a people-focused approach – what were the key benefits to the organization of doing this?
- Courageous conversations are central to the LAS approach to tackling conflict – what is your experience of having to have a courageous conversation?

Why is there so much 'bullying' and what is going wrong?

I have met many hundreds of people who have initiated a complaint based on the bullying behaviour of another person. However, in virtually all of these cases, the situation began life as low-level, dysfunctional conflict of one form or another: a breakdown in communication, a misunderstanding, a poorly delivered management instruction, a clash of working styles, or a perceived slight about someone's personal characteristics – the list is endless.

Due to a lack of an intervention to address the issues at source, situations quickly escalate into a more serious conflict, with allegations of bullying and harassment being used by the parties to codify their situations. Henceforth the conflict becomes an impenetrable issue between the parties and the only solution (unless mediation is offered and accepted) is to apply a black and white policy framework which, everyone knows, is likely to inflame the situation.

Over the years I have spent an enormous amount of time listening to employees, managers and organizations as they describe their experiences and their reactions to what they describe as 'bullying or harassment'. It has become apparent to me that the terms 'bullying' and 'harassment' are being used as proxy terms for dysfunctional workplace conflict. These are situations where two or more people are engaged in a conflict with all of the associated negativity and complexity that it creates. These cases are serious – they deserve attention, they should be taken seriously and all necessary steps should be taken to resolve them effectively. However, they are not bullying, nor are they harassment. To describe them as such is disingenuous to those victims of real bullying and harassment who are often unheard and who experience real pain, real trauma and real harm.

Resolution reflection

Consider a bullying or harassment allegation that your organization has dealt with:

- What were the causes and the effects of the situation?
- Did your organization differentiate between dysfunctional conflict and bullying?
- What steps were taken to address the issues at an early stage?
- What action was taken to resolve the situation?

- Did this action work?
- With the benefit of hindsight, what would you do now to address the situation?
- How will you embed those insights if faced with future allegations of bullying or harassment in your organization?

The four reasons why bullying at work is such a big concern

The first reason is the impact of the uncertain state of the economy and the conditions in many workplaces. With things so tough in the economy since the financial crisis began in 2007/2008, people have been keeping their heads down at work, staying busy, trying not to rock the boat or cause any problems. Many people have felt fearful they could lose their jobs. That has meant that worries about bullying and conflict have been suppressed as other concerns took priority. Stress has been building in many workplaces and, much like a volcano, at some point that stress will erupt.

The second reason there appears to be so much bullying is the fact that it has become something of a catch-all term used to describe a wide variety of workplace conflicts. Due to the often confusing and incoherent nature of conflict management within our organizations, employees sometimes have no meaningful way of describing their negative experience, so they use the term they believe is the most appropriate to define the issue – bullying. This is not to undermine the fact that some people are experiencing bullying and that this will be having a traumatic and negative impact on them. However, the term 'bullying' is now greatly over-used, so much so it is at risk of losing its meaning.

In response, more and organizations have split their grievance procedure into two separate parts. One part deals with workplace issues where bullying or harassment are not cited; the other part deals with conflicts in which bullying and harassment *are* cited. These new procedures may be called Dignity at Work Procedures or Fair Treatment Procedures. The reality is that they are a grievance procedure, but with more teeth. Naturally, if one has been upset, by a manager say, one is are going to opt for the procedure with teeth.

By giving employees an à la carte menu of conflict management procedures to choose from, it may appear that we are doing them a service and taking the issues seriously. The reality, however, is that we are doing them, their peers, their managers and the organization a huge disservice. We are making it much more difficult to manage an already complex issue. Splitting up our already divisive procedures also divides our attention and our resources. The seeds of division are clearly being sown.

These fashionable, yet faulty, procedures are fuelling an over-use of the term 'bullying'. Many of the organizations that I have worked with to develop a corporate conflict management strategy and anti-bullying initiatives, do not have lots of different and confusing procedures to deal with different types of conflict. They have a set of clear values, a framework for management behaviours and a simple, all-encompassing conflict management policy – a resolution policy. This is all it takes to identify issues at the earliest stage, agree the most appropriate route to resolution, mediate those cases that warrant it and commence an investigation into the more serious or more complex cases.

The third reason we are seeing an increase in the use of the term 'bullying' is due to a lack of investment in our managers and leaders to help them to manage dynamic, complex and diverse teams of people. We assume that they have the skills to manage effectively and of course, many of them do. However, in some cases, things go wrong and managers are left dealing with a complex situation without the prerequisite competence, confidence or courage to react in an appropriate manner.

Some managers' lack of empathy, compassion, flexibility and self-awareness can come across as rudeness, hostility, abuse, prejudice and intimidation. These are of course, all classic signs of 'bullying'. For managers, though, being labelled a bully can be a career-defining moment. It makes everyone very fearful once the term is mentioned. The response by many is to deny the problem exists or to respond defensively when an issue is raised. These 'deny or defend' responses do little to help the organization deal with the issue or make sense of a series of complicated interactions.

The fourth reason is that, like it or not, the term 'bullying' itself is divisive. It conjures up images of an ogre, a villain or a playground thug stealing our crisps. This is simply not the reality of most workplaces. Anti-bullying initiatives need to be far more sophisticated than simply saying that bullying won't be tolerated. Not tolerating something, and then overreacting when something bad happens, is not the same as dealing with the actual problem.

Drawing on Transactional Analysis (TA) and the Karpman drama triangle (see Chapter 6 for more details), the term 'bullying' apportions clear blame and tends to single out one person as the 'persecutor' – the bully. It also puts the complainant into 'victim mode', which is hard to break free from and inhibits reaching a sensible, adult, resolution. As a victim, he or she wants to be saved by the 'rescuer' and for justice to be meted out:

- the bully to be sacked;

- an example to be made of the bully;

- an apology – in writing;

- recompense of some kind.

This drama triangle dynamic makes it much harder for the two parties to engage in that all important adult-to-adult dialogue.

In summary, the current systems for managing bullying at work are:

- Giving the impression that there is a hierarchy of conflict and that, for others to take their concerns seriously, the 'victim' needs to make sure that the behaviours of the 'perpetrator' are perceived as being as serious as possible. This can quickly escalate a situation and makes it much harder to seek a constructive and collaborative solution to the conflict.

- Causing 'victims' to fit their experiences into the organization's anti-bullying policy so that they will be taken seriously. This is at the expense of 'victims' describing their own experiences authentically and considering the most effective route to resolution in their case. This makes the situation less transparent and more divisive.

- Creating an environment where more and more negative interactions between colleagues, or between colleagues and managers, are being labelled 'bullying'. This has the effect of watering down the term and making it much harder to assess what is real bullying and what is an overreaction or a deliberate, or unconscious, misuse of the term.

- Undermining organizations' efforts to identify and respond to serious and damaging bullying when it does occur. This has the effect that most of the dysfunctional conflicts that are labelled as 'bullying' aren't being resolved and the more serious cases, which are deserving of a swift, robust and thorough intervention, are being lost in the quagmire.

- Causing managers to hold back from giving honest and genuine feedback to employees as they are afraid that this may result in an allegation of bullying and harassment being brought against them. This has the effect of inhibiting open and honest feedback that is delivered in the moment. As a result, issues that could be easily resolved at the time, build up and spill over, or may arise during annual performance reviews and annual appraisals.

Complex issues are being papered over by the term 'bullying'. In that sense, the term is a problem.

How to tackle bullying and harassment in the workplace

This part of the chapter provides guidance and support for all organizations to help them tackle bullying at work effectively.

Ensure that your values are visible and became a core part of your culture

Your values are the beating heart of your organization. Your people are your lifeblood. Carrying on this biological analogy, your systems and process are your veins and arteries, your culture is your conscience, and your strategy is the nervous system. Your organization is the entire being – the organism.

Your values are core to your organization's health and wellbeing – I would go as far as to say that they are the most important statement that your organization will make. It is vital that everyone in the organization understands the core values, recognizes their importance and lives them through their everyday interactions and behaviours. Much like good heart health, if your organization is going to be resilient, healthy, sustainable, successful and efficient, it is important to look after your values to ensure that they have meaning, that they remain relevant and that they are shared by all employees across your entire organization.

A report produced by the Great Place to Work Institute in 2014 suggested that: 'A strong values-driven culture is critical to the success of high performance organizations. Organizations with a culture of strong values are more likely to have better financial results than their peers.' The report includes several case studies from organizations and explains that 97 per cent of the best workplaces have values statements and attribute their business success to them. The report also states that, 'Strong values help build organizational resilience.'

Twinings is a great example of this values-based approach and provides a powerful testimony to the results it can deliver. According to Rajdeep Kaur-Hooper, HR Engagement Manager at Twinings:

> Values and the framework that sits behind them gives people a language to challenge their peers more effectively – both the tools to do so and for people to receive the challenge in the way it was intended. This means not taking it personally but to ensure best results for the team and the business. This is about empowerment. I've seen it at Twinings but not in other businesses. (Great Place to Work Institute, 2014: 8)

Define desirable and undesirable management behaviours

Values mean nothing if they don't drive the right behaviours. It is important to set out clear expectations of the behaviours of your managers and leaders, which should link directly to the core values of your organization. It is highly unlikely that your corporate values will promote abuse, harm and aggression. It is more likely that they will advocate mutual respect, integrity, innovation and collaboration. The required behaviours should be set out in a simple behavioural framework that includes clear indicators and contra-indicators. The contra-indicators name the undesirable behaviours and the indicators provide a clear preference for the positive and desirable behaviours.

These leadership behaviours need to be driven from the very top and cascaded throughout your organization. Managers and leaders need to 'walk the talk' and they need to be held to account for how they behave via regular performance reviews or appraisals. Bonus payments should be attached directly to the positive behaviours that the managers exhibit as well as their overall performance. After all, it is the leaders' behaviours that directly affect other team members' performance.

The preferred behaviours should be visible for all to see: they should be included on websites, on recruitment literature, as part of induction plans, in employee handbooks and on the walls and lobbies around the workplace. Negative, destructive and aggressive behaviour should be so counter-cultural that it rarely happens and, when it does, it is dealt with quickly and effectively. Employees, HR and other managers should be confident to call out any bad behaviour and know that they have a system for addressing issues via triage assessments, early resolution, facilitated conversations and mediation. Rather than jumping straight into a draconian response, organizations should apply positive psychology to help managers explore what has gone well and to build on the positives as well as to learn from areas of challenge or conflict. The London Ambulance Service case study reinforces the importance of providing mediation and training in confident conversations for key organizational stakeholders.

Create an open culture where people can speak up about their experiences

Whether it is staff surveys, regular meetings, focus groups, town hall meetings or other methods, it is important to gather data on a regular basis about what problems people are facing and what the root causes might be. This kind of proactive 'problem seeking' requires courage from an organization but will help to tackle issues early on. Being proactive is an enormous advantage.

Listening to your people and encouraging them to speak freely is important. Employee voice is vital to the overall health and wellbeing of your organization: Engage for Success place employee voice as one of the four drivers of engagement.[2] However, it is easy to listen to our people when the tills are ringing and the organization is performing well. It makes us all feel good when the cup runneth over. The true test of an organization is whether it listens to its people when they have tough messages to share and the organization and working relationships are under stress. This is genuine employee voice and it is this kind of dialogue that will ensure that underlying problems are spotted early and can be resolved.

Take a long hard look at your organization's grievance and anti-bullying procedures

Is your conflict management policy framework perpetuating a right/wrong, defend/attack, win/lose approach to problems in the workplace? The traditional approach to handling grievances is based on a litigation-inspired determination of who is at fault. This can often increase rifts in the workplace and rarely, if ever, uncovers or resolves the root cause of an issue. Reframing grievance and anti-bullying procedures to become a single resolution policy and using mediation and other restorative approaches can shift the focus to collaboration and collective problem solving when problems arise. Mediation, in particular, can be extremely effective. (See Chapter 8 for more on embedding a resolution policy in your organization.)

There is real benefit from having a clear statement about the organization's values and indicators and contra-indicators of acceptable management and colleague behaviour. If these are coupled with a well-developed resolution policy, there is no need to have a separate policy for dealing with bullying or harassment. Such policies do little more than sow the seeds of division, create confusion, infantilize the workforce and create a culture of fear.

Remember, bullying can be upwards as well as downwards

Often we perceive bullying as a top-down phenomenon: managers treating their employees unfairly. This does happen, of course, but bullying can be up, down, sideways and diagonal. It is also important to bear in mind that, in some cases, bullying allegations may themselves be an example of bullying.

Offer ongoing coaching, training and support

Coaching, training and support need to be available for managers on an ongoing basis. Not just 'sheep dip' training – everyone going on a one-day course before being left to fend for themselves. From the moment that managers are appointed, living the values, demonstrating the right behaviours, listening to employees and handling conflict need to be part of their core competencies so that they understand what is expected of them and can access the support they need. HR should play a coaching and mentoring role and should be available to support managers and assist them with the day-to-day management of the complex and diverse relationships and personalities that exist in the workplace. Emotional intelligence and compassion should be recognized as key managerial skills. Managers who don't feel they will be supported when dealing with conflict are more likely to ignore it or even suppress it.

Undertake a constant review of your approaches to ensure they are fit for purpose

As with any good practice, keep your approaches for managing conflict under constant review. They aren't something that can be set up and forgotten about. There needs to be active monitoring of their effectiveness rather than a passive approach that waits until problems arise. HR in partnership with unions can play a pivotal role in gathering data on the impact of your conflict management approach. The voices of people who experience your conflict processes should be sought and should be included in any future developments of your approach.

When bullying does occur respond robustly, swiftly and fairly

There are going to be conflicts that escalate and, in some cases, there may be specific incidents of bullying and harassment that fit the criteria of the ACAS (2014) guidance. In these cases, the resolution spectrum still offers a wide range of means for resolving the issues that need to be dealt with quickly and decisively. Managers need to have the right skills to set up and carry out investigations when necessary. They need to be objective and able to carry out factual assessments – but we also need to give employees and managers the skills to identify when the problem might be more subtle.

Use mediation and restorative justice if bullying does occur

The most powerful way to address and change behaviour is to confront it head on and face-to-face. As a restorative justice practitioner, I have brought victims and offenders together to help offenders understand the impact of their behaviour on real people – the victims of their offending. This also gives victims a voice in the justice process and an opportunity to look into the offender's eyes when they describe the impact of the offence upon them. The benefits of a restorative approach, above and beyond the dialogue itself, is the potential that it creates for understanding, reconciliation and forgiveness. I still use those restorative justice principles and processes in my work as a conflict management professional in the workplace.

Conclusion

It is important to remember that conflict exists in every single organization. It is a part of working life. Not all conflict is bullying and the labels of 'bullied' and 'bully' are often misleading and create rather than assist its resolution. Nonetheless, it is a very challenging area of work and when people perceive that they are being bullied, they should be supported, trusted and believed. It takes courage to speak out and to challenge bad behaviour.

Reactive remedies to bullying at work are just that – reactive. Successful anti-bullying strategies comprise proactive systems, processes and support that make bullying unacceptable and encourage people to speak out at the earliest possible stage. These systems, processes and training should be directly linked to the organizations' core values and they should reflect the competencies and behaviours their people are expected to demonstrate.

One of the key routes to resolution should always be dialogue. Behavioural change can and does come about when the parties can sit down together and discuss their situation, openly and honestly. For its part, the organization should be effective at doing five fundamentally important things:

1 Engendering a culture where dialogue is recognized as the primary route to resolution in all conflicts, including those cases labelled as bullying and harassment.

2 Providing the necessary resources for dialogue to happen. This may include, but is not limited to: accessing external mediators when required, developing a team of in-house mediators, embedding facilitation skills within HR teams, and providing training for leaders and managers to help them as they prepare for this new approach.

3 Creating systems for monitoring and evaluating the outcomes from dialogue and providing ongoing assistance where it is required.

4 In cases where dialogue is not possible, responding robustly, swiftly and fairly.

5 Listening to the voices of employees and managers who use the systems for managing conflict and fine-tuning the systems as required.

Talking about how you deal with bullying, harassment and conflict in general doesn't make you look like a bad employer struggling with a problem: it makes you look like a good one, dealing with a difficult fact of life. London Ambulance Service has more than ably demonstrated this.

Resolution reflection

- What does your organization do well with regard to managing bullying and harassment?

- What does your organization do badly with regards to managing bullying and harassment?

- Do you agree with the four problems with bullying that I have identified in this chapter? If so, why? If not, why?

- In this chapter, I propose that dialogue is one of the most effective ways to tackle bullying at work. However, some people propose that bullies should be treated via a punitive, sanctions-based approach. What do you think?

- If you had no constraints, what would you do to address this issue within your own organization?

- How could you make your answer to the above question happen in your own organization?

- If someone approached you tomorrow to discuss a concern about a colleague or a manager who was bullying them, what advice would you give them?

- What changes would you make to the policy framework in your organization?

- What support do your managers and leaders need to make these changes a reality?

Notes

1   www.nhsemployers.org/case-studies-and-resources/2017/02/london-ambulance-service

2   The four drivers of engagement are available on the Engage for Success website: www.engageforsuccess.org

References

ACAS (2014) *Bullying and Harassment at Work*, ACAS, London

Great Place to Work Institute (2014) *Organizational Values: How values can transform your business from good to great*, Great Place to Work Institute, London

Total conflict management 　12

A whole-systems approach for preventing and resolving conflict

The emphasis on mediation is of restoring relationships and harmony between people. The process aids communication between the parties, provides an understanding of the breakdown in that relationship and creates mutually beneficial solutions to develop a better working relationship. Mediation has the advantage of being a voluntary process, where staff feel their dispute may be remedied by discussion, thereby avoiding the negative and time-consuming aspects of formal processes. (Northumbria Healthcare NHS Trust's Dignity at Work policy)

KEY LEARNING POINTS IN THIS CHAPTER

- More and more organizations are adopting an integrated and holistic approach to managing conflict.
- These organizations are embedding constructive and cooperative conflict management into their systems and processes.
- The approaches are part of a holistic system for managing conflict called Total Conflict Management (TCM).
- TCM places positive relationships, constructive dialogue, mutual interest-based problem solving and dispute resolution at the heart of the organization.
- The TCM methodology integrates constructive and cooperative conflict management across organizations: governance systems, values, culture, leadership/management behaviours, employee relations, industrial relations, reward and remedial systems, policies

and procedures, customer experience, supply chain management, commercial relationships and Corporate Social Responsibility (CSR).

- Research suggest that these approaches are supported by managers, unions and HR and that they deliver tangible benefits to all stakeholders.

Introduction

So far in this book I have explored the nature of conflict, I have examined many of the causes and costs of conflict and I have considered the benefits to organizations that choose to promote mediation and embed a resolution policy. I have also provided details about a range of exciting new approaches for managing workplace conflict that include resolution triage assessments, early resolution meetings, facilitated roundtable meetings, mediation, conflict coaching and team conferencing. These approaches sit on a resolution spectrum that provides organizations with a substantial range of options to run alongside the traditional remedies to conflicts, disputes and complaints.

Numerous organizations are now making the shift towards a more person-centred, values-based approach for managing conflict at work. Organizations are rejecting the anachronistic, rights-based, litigation-inspired models and policies of the past and are embracing a more flexible, more humanizing and more common sense approach to conflict management. Those organizations are embracing approaches that develop dialogue, underpin understanding, drive dignity, improve insight, restore respect, encourage empathy and reframe resolution. However, many organizations are going a step further and they are embedding the principles of mediation, dialogue, empathy, interest-based problem solving and positive psychology across their organizations. These organizations are taking a holistic approach to resolution and they are embedding innovative and creative approaches that promote the effective management of conflict across numerous elements of their organizations. These integrated approaches are increasingly being described as Total Conflict Management (TCM).

As Jennifer Lynch QC, Former Chief Commissioner of the Canadian Human Rights Commission and leading advocate of integrated conflict management systems explains:

Integrated Conflict Management Systems are leading edge developments and are becoming a key part of organizational development strategies. An [ICMS] system has features that focus on the prevention of unnecessary conflict and (when conflict does arise) on managing conflict.[1]

This chapter draws on academic research and first-hand accounts relating to the development of a TCM system within Northumbria Healthcare NHS Trust. It also examines the benefits of the approach and how the Trust has overcome the many challenges and obstacles along the way.

What is TCM?

TCM is a whole-system approach for managing conflict; see Figure 12.1. I originally developed the concept of TCM in 1999 when I was studying Total Quality Management (TQM) as part of my MBA. I was fascinated by the development of TQM systems to drive efficiency within manufacturing organizations. TQM is now synonymous with processes such as Lean, Agile or Six Sigma.

I was also fascinated by the emergence of Integrated Conflict Management Systems (ICMS) and the ways that organizations could create the necessary systems and processes for managing conflict proactively, constructively and cooperatively. As a mediator, I am always seeking possibilities for collaboration: TCM emerged from a collaboration between TQM and ICMS methodologies.

A vision for conflict management

My vision is for organizations to develop the systems and processes that will transform how they manage conflict across their entire organization. This change should involve all organizational stakeholders in the process of designing, delivering and evaluating a conflict management system. This new system will provide the necessary proactive and reactive responses that prevent dysfunctional conflicts from occurring, and, when they do, transforming them into functional conflict and cooperative dialogue as quickly as possible. Ultimately, my vision is for organizations to move away from the rights-based, blame-oriented, win/lose systems and processes and to embrace a more compassionate and courageous system for resolving conflicts.

This is not rocket science

In a nutshell, what I am proposing in this chapter is institutionalizing common sense and putting human relationships and dialogue back into the core of our organizations; creating organizational cultures that reject dogma

Figure 12.1   Total conflict management

and division and embrace diversity and dialogue. This is not rocket science and I don't believe it is particularly radical. This is about using positive means to promote positive outcomes.

The case study in this chapter illustrates that these are not, in themselves, difficult changes to make. They do, however, challenge the status quo and the conventional wisdom that has developed within our organizations over the past 20 or so years – that all conflict is damaging and that conflict can be resolved by applying a policy. The case study demonstrates that the impact and the benefits organizations enjoy when they make the change to a system of TCM make the journey worthwhile. Northumbria Healthcare NHS Foundation Trust (NHFT) is now well on the way to developing a fully integrated approach for managing conflict across its organization which, the evidence suggests, is better for its employees, for its managers and for its patients.

Resolution recommendations

Developing a TCM system

One of the key stages for those that want to integrate a TCM system is to consider the parts of the organization that can: a) generate conflicts, and b) play a part in resolving them. I have attempted to map these out below:

- *Governance systems.* How organizations are managed, how they handle risk, how they develop a shared vision across the organization and how they create, implement and communicate their strategy.

- *Values.* The beliefs and principles that define the organization and act as the beating heart of the business.

- *Culture.* The embodiment of the shared values and beliefs that define how people behave. Culture is the way people behave when no one else is watching.

- *Leadership/management behaviours.* The expectations that an organization has of its leaders and its managers and how these influence the way that managers and leaders interact with their teams.

- *Employee relations.* The relationship between the employer and its employees.

- *Industrial relations.* The relationship between unions and management.

- *Reward and remedial systems.* How organizations reward those behaviours that are aligned to the values, vision and agreed behaviours, and how they address behaviours that are not aligned.

- *Policies and procedures.* The rules of the organization expressed through a policy framework and procedures. Policies and procedures generally provide a legally compliant framework for organizational activities. They support remedial activities and codify the nature and the level of punishment for breaches of company rules.

- *Customer experience.* The way that customer service is delivered and complaints are handled.

- *Supply chain management.* Managing and maintaining relationships with suppliers.
- *Commercial relationships.* Managing and maintaining relationships with partners and as part of joint ventures, mergers and acquisitions, etc.
- *Corporate Social Responsibility.* How the organization responds to external social factors, how it builds and maintains relationships with external communities and how it responds to environmental issues.

The impact of applying TCM

TCM means that organizations benefit from a sustainable, resilient and engaging system for managing conflict. Over the years, I have seen various attempts at integrating resolution being driven by an individual or small task force, only for them to leave the organization and for the approach to fail. In other organizations, I have seen vested interests, turf wars and power games undermine the good work put into embedding a resolution scheme. This is a shame: first, the hard work of the few is lost; secondly, the conflicts don't just vanish with them; and thirdly, it undermines the very core of what mediation and ADR is about – sustainability, resilience and engagement.

Applying TCM in practice

In 2010, I began work with Northumbria Healthcare Foundation NHS Trust (NHFT) to help it set up and embed a TCM system. NHFT provides acute and primary care services to over 550,000 people spread over a large geographical area in the north of England. This includes three district general hospitals and six community hospitals in addition to a wide range of primary care services provided in the community. In total, NHFT employs almost 9,000 staff.

The Trust has been a leading advocate of a fully integrated conflict management system and has been the subject of a rigorous evaluation by two world-renowned academics from the fields of management, economics, human resources and leadership: Professor Paul Latreille and Professor Richard Saundry. This is, to date, one of the most rigorous and forensic evaluations of an ICMS in the UK (Latreille and Saundry, 2015). Latreille and

Saundry's research, along with my own experiences and interviews with key stakeholders from the Trust, form the basis for the following case study. It is worth noting that, in a research paper published in the *Journal of Advances in Industrial and Labor Relations,* Saundry and Latreille, observed that in relation to NHFT, 'a systematic and integrated approach to identifying conflict and a range of coordinated interventions involving key organizational stakeholders can begin to embed a culture of resolution.' It is clear that this piece of work has got organizational leaders, academics and policy makers very excited and the following case study will provide a summary of the TCM principles embedded within the Trust.

CASE STUDY Northumbria Healthcare NHS Foundation Trust embraces TCM

Ann Stringer (HR Director) and Teresa Jennings (Consultant Clinical Psychologist) are the visionary drivers of change within Northumbria Healthcare NHS Foundation Trust (NHFT). Just like many of the innovators in the field of human resources, employee relations and conflict management, they are trying to make sense of numerous complex, dynamic and diverse workplace issues. As Ann put it:

> I kind of always have in my head this jigsaw puzzle and all these things: staff engagement, equality and diversity, mediation, health and wellbeing, they're all jigsaw pieces that fit together. They fit together to make sure that the staff are properly supported to be able to provide excellent patient care, and that's the model in my head.

Linking values to outcomes

Of course, it's not just in Ann's head at all. Ann and Teresa have spent several years embedding a well-respected and award-winning ICMS in the Trust. Ann and Teresa go on to explain:

> the trust's values are: everybody's contribution counts; respect; accountability and responsibility and putting our patients first. Our values are a great backdrop in which to say we all need to take responsibility for our individual relationships at work, and to treat people at work with respect and dignity. Our HR strategy says that if you support staff well and you're compassionate and caring, they in general will respond in the same way to patients. And the reverse is also true, so supporting staff to be able to resolve difficulties at work is one of those support mechanisms that's in place.

They have also brought the values to life in other areas of the Trust:

> we worked hard to build our values into the fabric of the organization and across systems and processes. For example, we changed our recruitment processes and trained people so that we had to use values as a way of recruiting. We put our values into the appraisal system as well so that you are reviewed every year against your behaviour. Our values have also been embedded into training and education within the Trust.

What were the drivers for change?

At the inception of the TCM strategy, a great deal of time was spent working with the Trust management team to help them understand and codify the challenges that their new approach would address. This fed into a system for gathering data that would be useful for future analyses of the impact of the new system. The coordination of the new approach would be undertaken by Teresa Jennings and she quickly built up a team of accredited mediators to work alongside her to make this new approach a reality. Teresa and I worked closely together to develop the most efficient pathways to make mediation work and we considered different ways to embed it within the Trust as part of an ICMS.

These drivers for change were identified in the NHFT evaluation report (Latreille and Saundry, 2015). In the report, the authors identified the four specific challenges within NHFT that had underpinned the design of the ICMS:

1 The most common causes of conflict were personality clashes and performance management. These tended to relate to either personal issues or difficulties in relationships between line managers and team members.

2 Wasted staff and management time was the greatest perceived cost of this conflict. There was also some evidence that conflict could have a direct impact on both performance and wellbeing of staff with potential implications for patient care.

3 The confidence of line managers in dealing with difficult issues was seen to be crucial. Managers were sometimes deterred from addressing difficult issues by the potential for escalation and employee grievances. In addition, operational pressures had the potential to 'crowd out' more creative approaches to conflict management.

4 Written grievance procedures were not seen to be conducive to conflict resolution. They were complex, time-consuming and stressful for all involved – and rarely led to clear and accepted outcomes or a sense of justice having been done.

The authors also exposed a view within the trust that the traditional grievance and anti-bulling policies were 'complex, time-consuming, and stressful for all involved, and they rarely led to resolution' (Latreille and Saundry, 2015: 17).

The problems with the traditional grievance procedure

As part of their evaluation process, the authors conducted interviews with key stakeholders across the Trust to explore the effectiveness of conventional grievance procedures. They spoke to an HR practitioner who explained:

> we were probably pretty poor in all that sort of stuff, so it used to get embroiled in formal processes. We'd have grievances that went on for ages because we were trying to solve interpersonal relationships with grievance investigations, where all you end up with is 'he said, she said' on a bit of paper. (p 17)

A Trust manager was highly critical of the time and the cost of the formal processes:

> If you, say, put in a grievance against someone because you have been bullied… after the investigation they've no feedback, you don't get any feedback in terms of what actually happened to that person. So yes, the process would have been carried out appropriately but the end result might not be satisfying to the victim… They end up with nothing to say this has been addressed… It gets dragged out a lot and it brings in a lot of people and it is quite expensive. (p 17)

One of the members of the Trust's mediation team explained:

> The problem with the grievance process is that you've normally got to come down on one side or the other… The person that was unsuccessful in the grievance always felt as though they hadn't been heard, not listened to, and it was a divisive action. (p 17)

The report's authors (Latreille and Saundry, 2015) also identified evidence that, prior to the introduction of the mediation scheme, workplace conflict was a significant problem for the Trust. Using data available from the 2005 NHS staff survey, the report suggested that NHFT suffered from higher than average levels of bullying and harassment (18 per cent of employees) and workplace stress (42 per cent of employees) (p 17).

Reframing the systems for delivering resolution within the Trust

The Trust revised its existing procedures and processes and included mediation as a preferred route to resolution. NHFT's grievance procedure now states that:

'only in cases where local resolutions cannot be found and mediation is not seen as viable should the formal grievance process be invoked'. In addition, an appendix to the procedure sets out details of the mediation service.

The decision was also made to redesign the existing dignity at work framework to include not only mediation but to acknowledge the importance of dealing with conflict at work. Once a concern has been raised under the dignity at work policy, a triage is undertaken and mediation is the first consideration. Employees and managers are advised that informal dispute resolution methods such as mediation should be attempted before resorting to formal procedures.

The policy framework within the Trust also advises that mediation is likely to be effective when there is a willingness by both parties to seek to resolve their differences. As Teresa Jennings explained to me during our interview: 'Our aim was to create a policy framework where dignity at work issues could be resolved through dialogue and, in particular, mediation would be made available in the cases that would benefit from that approach.'

Effective conflict management delivers better patient experience

NHFT's integrated conflict management system is part of a framework of activities that are underpinned by the belief that good staff experience equals good patient experience. Ann Stringer expands: 'These include, but are not limited to, quality improvements, transparency and openness, health and wellbeing, leadership behaviours, talent management, recruitment standards and broader employee relations.'

Setting up an internal mediation scheme within NHFT

Over the past seven years, NHFT has selected and trained an in-house team to a nationally recognized and accredited standard. The mediation team comprises consultants, managers, nurses, HR staff and trade union representatives. Ongoing CPD for the mediation team is provided regularly and the mediation team have been trained to resolve conflicts within groups and teams. The Trust also ran numerous stakeholder events to deliver presentations about mediation and to respond to questions, along with numerous mediation and conflict management awareness workshops for staff from across all the Trust's hospital sites.

Teresa Jennings explained to me why she believes that an integrated approach to managing conflict is so important:

> If you ask most nurses, doctors and healthcare workers, they would say the patient is their focus. The big thing is that people don't like conflict and it's uncomfortable. It's not a nice thing and I think people do want to find better ways of resolving it. If there's

less conflict there's better team performance and better outcomes for patients, but it's got a feel-good factor as well. It's distressing for people when they're not getting on. It affects teams when somebody's off sick, and people usually want to find a way to get through that as quickly as possible. It's like having a range of tools in the toolbox, really, mediation being one of them.

Latreille and Saundry's evaluation suggests that 90 per cent of cases that were referred to mediation reached a successful conclusion.[2] As Teresa Jennings explains:

we wanted mediation to be a first port of call, rather than grievances, because I think when I came into post and worked in Occupational Health we used to see a lot of people who were heartily sick that the only option for them was to go down a formal route, and often that was what they were advised by their staff-side rep who was also feeling pretty hopeless about that, as the only option too, causing stress and inordinate amounts of time off.

Driven by a desire to reduce the level of stress within the organization NHFT also embedded the Health and Safety Executives guidance[3] on managing workplace stress in their conflict management system: 'We also tied the conflict management programme into the stress management standards from HSE.' As Teresa explained during our interview. 'The relationship standard focuses on reducing conflict, bullying and harassment in teams.'

The relationship with the Trust's unions

The Trust worked closely with their union partners at all stages of the development and the implementation of the system. As one union representative said in the evaluation report:

Mediation was something that we were keen to look at because we were conscious that there were a number of grievances and disciplinaries that are incredibly time-consuming and incredibly expensive as much as anything else and we just thought that there must have been a way of trying to resolve things (trade union representative). (Latreille and Saundry, 2015: 19)

Latreille and Saundry identified a very positive factor within the ICMS – that union representatives were also encouraged to play a positive role in managing conflict within NHFT. As the evaluation report explains: 'Whilst managers reported that this could again depend on the individual approach taken by the representative, most felt that union presence, particularly in formal situations, was constructive.'

Collaborative working – the cornerstone of a TCM system

The research also recognized a key tenet of the TCM system – collaborative working. Collaborative approaches were a cornerstone of the design of the NHFT's integrated conflict management system. NHFT has exemplified this collaborative model over the years. As one participant in the evaluation of the NHFT scheme explained:

> there was a very strong sort of push towards partnership working and actually making that meaningful rather than just well we'll talk to staff side we do genuinely want a good relationship with them and want to involve them in issues and that I think has made a difference so that I suppose they have confidence that we're going to listen to them and try and resolve things but they take some responsibility as well and don't necessarily take the entrenched view anymore (HR practitioner). (Latreille and Saundry, 2015: 39)

The role of managers and leaders

The Trust has been embedding conflict management skills within the leadership and the management of the Trust to help address any residual concerns about the role of managers in managing conflict. The Trust has been developing facilitated roundtable conversations as part of the development of its TCM system. As Ann Stringer explained during an interview with me:

> it's about managers having the skills to set up and run facilitated conversations and to nip these sorts of problems in the bud so that the numbers of cases that we actually get to formal mediation should reduce. We actually have seen a reduction, and I don't think it's because they're ignoring it; I think it's because managers have got more skills and confidence to be able to deal with things at an earlier level, and I just see us continuing with that.

According to Latreille and Saundry's evaluation, managerial concerns about managing conflict stemmed from three main issues (2015: 16):

1 Some managers were worried that addressing poor performance or behaviour would escalate and potentially result in grievances from the staff concerned.

2 Several managers suggested that operational pressures could 'crowd out' the need to spend time talking to team members to uncover and resolve complex and difficult issues.

3 A lack of training was identified as a key issue in explaining levels of confidence in managing conflict.

Assessing the outcomes of the Trust's TCM system

Within their evaluation report, Latreille and Saundry explore the impact of the new TCM system on volumes of disciplinary and grievance cases. The authors note that over a five-year period there has been a reduction in the number of grievance cases that were triggered by accusations of bullying and harassment. The authors inferred from the data that 'conflicts which could otherwise escalate are being resolved at an early stage'.

Conclusion

In their evaluation report, Latreille and Saundry (2016: 44) draw a great many positive conclusions about the impact of the Total Conflict Management system embedded within Northumbria Healthcare NHS Foundation Trust. This is what they had to say:

> There are clear signs that the approach taken has had a number of positive effects. Overall, informal and early resolution appears to be embedded within the organization. Furthermore, the survey of managers found that the over-riding approach to conflict is one of collaboration. In addition, most managers feel well equipped to deal with conflict, and training both in conflict resolution and handling difficult conversations appears to be making significant inroads, at least within more senior managerial ranks.

In 2014, NHFT recorded the lowest proportion of staff reporting bullying and harassment from managers or colleagues among acute NHS trusts in the UK. This must be some of the most compelling evidence ever produced in favour of an integrated conflict management system within an organization.

The NHFT case study, along with numerous other examples of organizations that have embraced my vision for a fully integrated conflict management system, are better, happier, safer, more fulfilling, more engaging, more productive and more inspiring places to work. If I were applying for a job, one of my first questions to my new employer would be this: 'When I experience a conflict at work, as surely I will, what remedies do you have in place to support me to resolve it?' If they avoid the answer, or if they pick up their grievance and bullying procedures and say, here you go, I would walk out of the interview and go to an organization like NHFT. For it is organizations like NHFT that will be the employers of the future – employers where decent, hardworking people want to work.

Resolution reflection

- What have you learnt from the NHFT case study?
- Is your organization ready to embed a TCM approach?
- If your organization is ready, what are the next steps to begin the journey towards TCM?

Notes

1 Jennifer Lynch, Are Your Organization's Conflict Management Practices an Integrated Conflict Management System? available at www.mediate.com//articles/systemsedit3.cfm#bio

2 This figure is based on 54 cases out of 60 reaching agreement through mediation.

3 The HSE stress management standards are available at www.hse.gov.uk/stress/standards/relationships.htm

References

Latreille, P and Saundry, R (2015) *Towards a System of Conflict Management? An evaluation of the impact of workplace mediation at Northumbria Healthcare NHS Foundation Trust,* ACAS, London

Latreille, P and Saundry, R (2016) Toward a system of conflict management? Cultural change and resistance in a healthcare organization, *Journal of Advances in Industrial and Labor Relations,* 22, pp 189–209

Managing workplace and employment disputes

13

An international perspective

KEY LEARNING POINTS

- There are many varied approaches to the use of alternative dispute resolution (ADR) across many jurisdictions.
- While the use of mediation in civil and commercial disputes is becoming mandatory in more and more jurisdictions, its use to resolve workplace disputes remains discretionary.
- There are professional bodies and institutes in each jurisdiction that provide quality standards, training and resources relating to mediation and ADR.

Introduction

Due to its size and scope, this chapter provides just a brief overview of the emergence of mediation and ADR systems in four regions of the world: the United States, Canada, Europe and Australasia. This chapter examines the emerging role of ADR in workplace and employment dispute resolution with specific reference to the role of mediation. This chapter also includes a case study from an international courier and parcel delivery business,

Parcelforce Worldwide, which highlights the positive impact of institution-alizing an interest-based and collaborative approach to labour relations and conflict management.

The United States

Mediation is widely used across the United States as a means of settling disputes outside the court room. Workplace mediation (which aims to resolve issues and protect working relationships rather than negotiate settlement and severance terms) is a growing area within the United States. After a pilot, in 1999 the US Equal Employment Opportunity Commission (EEOC) expanded its mediation programme across the country. The EEOC offers mediation as an alternative to the traditional investigative or litigation process in discrimination allegations. Mediation is defined by the EEOC as:

> a form of Alternative Dispute Resolution (ADR) that is offered as an alternative to the traditional investigative or litigation process. Mediation is an informal process in which a neutral third party assists the opposing parties to reach a voluntary, negotiated resolution of a charge of discrimination. Mediation gives the parties the opportunity to discuss the issues raised in the charge, clear up misunderstandings, determine the underlying interests or concerns, find areas of agreement and, ultimately, to incorporate those areas of agreement into solutions. A mediator does not impose a decision on the parties. Instead, the mediator helps the parties to agree on a mutually acceptable resolution.[1]

A review of the EEOC mediation programme (McDermott et al, 2000) found that an overwhelming majority of the participants (91 per cent of charging parties (applicants) and 96 per cent of respondents) indicated that they would be willing to participate in the mediation programme again if they were a party to an EEOC charge: 'Participants, regardless of their satisfaction with the outcome of mediation, overwhelmingly indicated their willingness to return to mediation.'

The Federal Mediation and Conciliation Service (FMCS) provides a wide range of ADR services, one of which is 'repairing broken relation-ships'. However, many of the programmes offered by the FMCS focus on labour-management disputes. There is less focus on colleague to colleague or colleague to manager dispute resolution. This work tends to be under-taken by independent mediators working across the United States, one of whom is John Ford, a well-respected mediator, trainer, author and advocate of in-house mediation programmes.

John is based in San Francisco and founded a specialist mediation, training and coaching company called The HR Mediation Academy. John works with HR teams to help them to embed the principles and practices of mediation within their organizations. He explains more:

> HR professionals deal with conflict challenges every day. Ideally, they feel confident in their ability to help employees find lasting resolutions to challenging situations. Mediation is an effective tool for resolving workplace conflict, and is needed in addition to the investigation. The case for mediation for cases that leave the organization and go to the enforcement agencies and courts has been made – resoundingly. The opportunity for the future is bringing mediation in-house! Upstream away from the court house is where HR professionals can make a telling impact to the bottom line, by nipping conflict in the bud.

The US Postal Service Redress Program

The Redress mediation programme is one of the most evaluated of the mediation programmes in the United States. The US Postal Service (USPS) offers a transformative model of mediation that encourages employees to openly discuss their issues in a way that can 'transform' their working relationship. This open dialogue often helps employees recognize each other's viewpoint to determine how their dispute can be resolved. In transformative mediation, it is the disputing parties, rather than the mediators, who have the decision-making power to decide if the issues can be resolved. The mediator facilitates the discussion between the disputing parties, but does not determine who is right or wrong. According to its website, the USPS is convinced that:

> when employees are given the opportunity to participate in transformative mediation, they gain a better understanding of the conflict, and improve their ability to communicate with each other. Ultimately, conflicts in the workplace are reduced and communication is improved, leading to a better workplace environment.[2]

Canada

Canada is one of a growing number of jurisdictions that has made mediation mandatory. The Mandatory Mediation Programme is used to resolve civil litigation and estate matters and it applies in Toronto, Ottawa and Windsor. There is no such provision for the resolution of workplace and employment disputes. The workplace Fairness Institute has produced a white paper examining various conflict management activities currently in operation within Canada.[3] The ADR Institute of Canada also provides useful resources as well as a bi-annual journal (published in English and French) that is free to subscribers.

Europe

The European Foundation for the Improvement of Living and Working Conditions (Eurofound) publishes substantial analysis into the use of ADR (mediation and conciliation, etc) across Europe. In 2010, it produced a detailed analysis of the extent of ADR in workplace disputes entitled 'Individual disputes at the workplace: Alternative disputes resolution.'[4]

According to Eurofound, the European countries with medium or high usage of ADR include Austria, Cyprus, Denmark, Germany, Ireland, Italy, Malta, Norway, Spain, Sweden and the United Kingdom. Each country has different labour laws and in some cases, such as The Netherlands and Germany, these differ depending on whether the employer is in the private or public sector.

Germany

In Germany, labour courts are the principal mechanism of conflict resolution, in individual as well as in collective labour disputes. Labour law is applicable only to relationships based on private contract. The law on career public servants is considered to be a special section of public law. In Germany, disputes concerning career public servants are not settled by administrative courts.

German labour court proceedings aim to be simple, speedy and inexpensive, so every case brought before a court begins with a conciliation hearing, heard by the chair sitting alone. The purpose of the conciliation process is to achieve an amicable settlement – a compromise between the parties – without recourse to a formal hearing. At this stage both parties may also agree on a voluntary basis to independent mediation of which there are a growing number of providers across Germany.

Germany has been leading the way in the development of Works Councils, which play a vital role in the resolution of individual disputes before they escalate to litigation. In Germany, all employees have the right to have their grievances heard by the Works Council. A company-level arbitration committee with an independent chair may be established to hear the case. However, in most cases where a Works Council exists, it is able to resolve the matter with management, sometimes using informal mediation.

In regard to civil and commercial law, in July 2012, the Mediation Act entered into force in Germany. This was the first piece of legislation to formally regulate mediation services. The Act promotes mutual dispute settlement; for example, when parties bring a case in a civil court, they will have to say whether they have already sought to resolve the issue via out-of-court measures, such as mediation, and whether there are specific reasons for not considering this course of action. The court may furthermore suggest that the parties try to settle the conflict via mediation, or another form of out-of-court settlement. If the parties refuse, the Court may choose to suspend the proceedings.

CASE STUDY Parcelforce Worldwide

Parcelforce Worldwide (PFW) is a former public sector organization that operates a hub-and-spoke collection and delivery system with 54 depots across the United Kingdom feeding three highly automated tracking and sorting centres (two of which are in the Midlands and one in the North West).

While PFW has experienced industrial disputes and internal conflicts in the past, it has had a relatively positive track record for industrial relations. There have been no instances of industrial unrest in the last 15 years and the partnership between the Communication Workers Union (CWU) and management has been effective at resolving issues before they escalate. However, as Sharon Sherriff, Head of ER/IR, Commercial and Professional functions at PFW, puts it: 'We come from a highly unionized environment and often things can seem like a battle. However, we know that by working together, we can secure a joint agenda and a common goal.'

In recent years, there has been an enormous change in the industrial relations strategy within Parcelforce. Across the Group, there has been an increased focus on mediation in both industrial relations and bullying and harassment cases. The CWU has introduced mediation as part of its innovative 'Agenda for Growth' industrial relations strategy. PFW has been part of this change, but it was keen to develop its own approach that would be unique to PFW. In partnership with its union partners, PFW developed and embedded an industrial relations strategy entitled 'Table of Success' (ToS).

ToS is a unique industrial relations framework that was prepared jointly by the CWU and PFW management in 2008. The ToS principles were designed and agreed to strengthen strategic union/management partnerships within the organization. It recognized that the development of consensus and the sharing of ideas were vital for the organization's ability to meet its challenges and maximize success.

The ToS document delivered the purpose, the vision and the philosophy. In 2013/4, PFW and CWU jointly identified that the core competencies for delivering ToS needed to be developed across the organization. They began to work together to develop a mediation and collaborative problem-solving programme for managers and union representatives across the business that became known as the Table of Success Development Programme.

Sharon Sherriff argues that PFW's unique approach to industrial relations strategy and partnership working was important for three reasons:

> Firstly, it recognizes that we were starting from a different place. Secondly, that we are building upon a legacy of positive industrial relations within PFW. And thirdly, we are dealing with a different set of market pressures and levels of competition... so this allows PFW management to have different conversations with the unions about the unique nature of the market place.

A phased approach

The Table of Success Development Programme was aimed at building and maintaining strong relationships within Parcelforce. The programme has been rolled out across the business over three distinct phases:

> *Phase one* – delivering accredited mediation skills training to a joint team of senior managers and senior CWU officials from PFW.
>
> *Phase two* – two three-day joint CWU/management negotiation, mediation and collaborative problem-solving skills training courses. These courses were designed for area managers and regional CWU representatives.
>
> *Phase three* –15 two-day courses across the UK for local managers and CWU representatives.

Terry Pullinger, now Deputy General Secretary at CWU (Postal), was the CWU National Officer for PFW at the time that the Table of Success Development Programme was being developed:

> Parcelforce has grasped the opportunity to implement unique mediation and conflict resolution skills designed by TCM into the Table of Success approach. The Table of Success approach and the philosophy of Total Conflict Management

have collided into a perfect fit and our ongoing work is developing a genuine mutual-interest blueprint culture for any business.

Sharon Sherriff adds that in the early days there were plenty of doubts about the new training approach: 'There was lots of scepticism from people going in to it. People who had been here a long time weren't sure what new skills they could be taught. But coming out of it they all said that they'd got something out of it.'

By ensuring mutually supported change, the Table of Success framework is bringing about a profound cultural evolution within the organization, and Sharon Sherriff says people's behaviours have started to change:

> We found that people could really relate to the principles of collaboration and mutual, interest-based problem solving and see how it changed the way you approached things, how you consider the other party's point of view… This joint management/ union programme has made all sides more confident in being open during potentially difficult discussions and change processes. Some of those most sceptical about going into the process have become its biggest advocates. People are telling us that they've found the programme enlightening and they are coming back with something positive – irrespective of whether they are a manager or a union representative. Everybody has found that they got something from it.

Sharon Sherriff says that one of the most noticeable changes is a new willingness among people to talk without having a set solution in mind at the outset:

> It's about looking at things in a really different way and then to approach it in a different way. Subtle differences can make a huge, huge difference. Just the ability to have a discussion without feeling the need to have an answer and allow the discussion to generate the answer is, I think, quite an enlightened approach.

Terry Pullinger concludes:

> I genuinely believe that this has been the right way to go. The best way to create a successful company is by creating a genuine mutual interest culture, which means that the success of the company isn't just about pure profit and shareholders, but it is about taking everybody with you, and everybody shares in the success of the company. The Table of Success Development Programme and in particular the use of mediation skills has put the focus onto people's lives and it has meant that joint problem solving and collaborative problem solving are now embedded across PFW. This is all about life skills. If people more generally held these kinds of skills, then it could really help all processes of engagement.

Australasia

In New Zealand, mediation services are provided through Employment New Zealand, which is part of New Zealand's Ministry of Business, Innovation and Employment. While mediation is voluntary, a very useful guide to mediation[5] published by the Ministry of Business, Innovation and Employment states that:

> Mediation is voluntary; you don't have to go to mediation. However, if the other party asks for mediation and you choose not to go, and the other party has a legal claim, they might complain to the Employment Relations Authority (ERA). The ERA can require you to attend mediation. Going to mediation to try to resolve a problem can show you are acting in good faith in the employment relationship.

In addition, the Employment Relations Authority, which is an independent body set up under the (NZ) Employment Relations Act 2000, can investigate employment disputes that are not resolved via mediation: 'If you have not resolved a problem through mediation, the Employment Relations Authority can formally investigate issues, determine whether mediation could help, and rule accordingly.' According to its website, the Employment Relations Authority helps to resolve employment relationship problems. It does this by looking into the facts and making a decision based on the merits of the case, not on technicalities.

In Australia, workplace mediation is primarily undertaken by private mediators or law firms. There is a National Mediation Accreditation System (NMAS) which is run by the Mediation Standards Board.[6] The Australian Mediation Association, Australian Dispute Resolution Association and Resolution Institutes provide valuable resources and support for parties considering using mediation, be that civil, family, or indigenous dispute resolution. The organizations provide details of mediators and can signpost training in all forms of ADR.

Notes

1 https://www.eeoc.gov/eeoc/mediation/facts.cfm

2 See https://about.usps.com/what-we-are-doing/redress/programs.htm (accessed 17 April 2017)

3 See http://www.workplacefairness.ca (accessed 17 April 2017)

4 See www.eurofound.europa.eu/sites/default/files/ef_files/docs/eiro/tn0910039s/tn0910039s.pdf

5 Available to download at www.employment.govt.nz/assets/Uploads/tools-and-resources/publications/using-mediation-services-effectively.pdf

6 The NMAS standards are available at www.msb.org.au/sites/default/files/documents/NMAS%201%t20July%t202015.pdf

Reference

McDermott, E P *et al* (2000) *An Evaluation of the Equal Employment Opportunity Commission Mediation Program,* https://www.eeoc.gov/eeoc/mediation/report/index.html

PART THREE
Resolution resources

A quick conflict health check

I have designed this quick conflict health check to help you to assess your own organization's current approach to conflict. The health check will help you to establish your organization's responses to conflict and what, if any, steps may be required to help you to manage conflict more effectively in the future.

Health check instructions

For each of the 16 statements in the following table, place a tick in the box if you agree with it. The following pages include an answer grid and explanation plus recommendations.

Table P3.1

Statement	Agree
1 My organization has a conflict management strategy that we use for shaping our policy framework and our responses to conflict.	
2 My organization collects data and evidence relating to the cost and the impact of conflict.	
3 Our grievance procedure is divisive, it takes too long and it damages working relationships.	
4 My organization refers to mediation in relevant HR policies (grievance, performance, etc).	
5 Our HR team receives conflict management training.	
6 Our managers usually avoid dealing with conflict – until it is too late.	
7 Mutual respect, collaboration and fairness (or similar) are stated values of our organization.	
8 We have lost good employees due to unresolved conflict.	
9 Over the past 12 months we have seen an increase in the costs associated with managing conflict (such as investigations, settlement agreements, litigation and employment tribunals).	
10 Stress and sickness absence is a problem for our organization.	
11 Important organizational changes are hampered by disagreements and disputes.	

(continued)

Table P3.1   *(Continued)*

Statement	Agree
12 We regularly review our grievances and bullying cases to identify patterns and opportunities for learning.	
13 We have access to mediators when we need them (either internal or external mediators).	
14 Our reputation is damaged as a result of conflict.	
15 Our employee engagement levels are unaffected by conflict.	
16 Employee relations is often reactive and confrontational.	

Health check analysis

Please circle the answers that you agreed with in the table below. Each answer in the left-hand column is worth 3 points; answers in the right-hand column are worth 1 point. Add up the total for your answers. An explanation of your organization's conflict management approach is set out in the table.

Table P3.2

If you agreed with these statements, each answer is worth 3 points: 1 2 4 5 7 12 13 14	If you agreed with these statements, each answer is worth 1 point: 3 6 8 9 10 11 15 16

Score 0–11

Analysis	Recommendations for action
Your organization may be experiencing the negative effects of dysfunctional conflict. For those employees and managers experiencing or witnessing a conflict, it is a potentially unhealthy or negative experience. Your business performance could be undermined and some offices or departments may be tense and negative.	This is an opportunity to reframe your approach to resolution. Undertaking a more detailed conflict analysis using the tools in this book will be a useful starting point.
The culture of conflict is likely to be 'them and us' and conflicts that could be resolved earlier often fester and take weeks or even months to resolve.	Training your managers, HR teams and others to spot and resolve conflicts constructively will deliver immediate results.
You may have the odd case that has gone on for a year or more. Unresolved conflict is significantly undermining your efforts to enhance your attrition, attendance, engagement and wellbeing levels.	Developing a resolution policy framework as outlined on page 171 could help to reduce confrontational and adversarial responses to disputes and conflicts.

Score 12–21

Analysis	Recommendations for action
You are on the right track and you have some innovative systems in place for tackling workplace conflicts. However, some dysfunctional conflicts are not being responded to as quickly or as effectively as they could be and this is putting a strain on your organization. Conflict management is still a bit	The conflict analysis tools in Chapter 5 will provide valuable data about what is working and not working. Increasing access to mediation and promoting early resolution more widely could help you to develop adult-to-adult dialogue at times of conflict. Training managers and others to handle

(continued)

Table P3.2 *(Continued)*

If you agreed with these statements, each answer is worth 3 points: 1 2 4 5 7 12 13 14	If you agreed with these statements, each answer is worth 1 point: 3 6 8 9 10 11 15 16

Score 12–21

Analysis	Recommendations for action
ad hoc and this may be having a detrimental impact on your attendance, attrition, wellbeing and engagement levels. Employees and managers may not feel confident to raise or deal with issues and this is creating stress and eroding trust.	conflict assertively and confidently could assist you to nip more and more issues in the bud.

Score 22–30

Analysis	Recommendations for action
Your organization has embraced functional conflict. You appear to have a very positive working environment where dysfunctional conflicts and disputes are responded to in a positive and constructive manner.	You have proven that it is good to talk. The challenge for your organization going forward is to embed the positive culture as widely as possible and to sustain it during periods of uncertainty and challenge.
You have embraced approaches such as mediation and, as a result, formal grievances and complaints are likely to be relatively low. Your culture is one that embraces diversity and encourages people to talk openly to each other about their concerns and disagreements.	You will benefit from articulating your values and ethos clearly and encouraging and rewarding the necessary behaviours across your organization.
Your attrition rates are probably relatively low and your attendance rates will be very high – as will your engagement and overall wellbeing levels.	You may benefit from investing in future leaders and promoting the development of conflict-competent leadership and the development of policies, processes and procedures that actively promote collaboration and dialogue building.
Your line managers feel confident that they can address issues without it becoming a 'them and us' situation and they feel supported by a senior management and HR function that drives a coherent and strategic approach for managing conflict.	You may also benefit from extending the use of mediation and associated dispute resolution process across other aspects of your organization.

Working with feelings during conflict

Below is a table of some of the feelings that we may experience during conflict.

Table P3.3

Dysfunctional	Functional
Lonely	Calm
Vulnerable	Optimistic
Sad	Relaxed
Angry	Reasonable
Betrayed	Engaged
Frustrated	Excited
Anxious	Optimistic
Confused	Hopeful
Tired	Exhilarated
Attacked	Full of ideas
Disengaged	Refreshed
Worried	Heard
Fearful	Valued
Stressed	Trusted
	Respected

Feelings worksheet

- How do you feel when you are in conflict?
- How do your feelings impact how you manage the conflict?
- How do you address your feelings?
- How do you react when someone gets emotional in the workplace?
- What are the benefits of helping people to describe their feelings and emotions when they experience a conflict?
- How can you help others to express their feelings?
- What can you do to react empathetically to people in conflict?

De-escalating strong emotions

One of my favourite techniques for de-escalating a tough situation is what I call the four As:

1 *Acknowledge* how the person is feeling and help him or her to name his or her feelings. It is amazing how often we think that we are talking about feelings but in reality we are dodging talking about them. By naming our feelings out loud, they become real and they become almost tangible. The mediator should reflect the feelings back to individuals so that they can hear them and to let them know that they have been really heard and acknowledged.

2 *Affirm* their feelings and let them know it is ok and perfectly understandable to feel angry, frustrated or betrayed, etc. At this stage parties may say things like, 'I must sound pathetic', or, 'I can't believe how petty you must think I'm being.' Mediators should affirm that the situation is neither pathetic nor petty and that what the parties are saying is valued and valuable.

3 *Ask* a variety of questions to identify the root cause of the situation. The questioning techniques used by mediators encourage deep reflection by the parties. I have often been told that my curious nature in mediation has defused a difficult situation and my use of open but searching questions has given the parties a new area to focus on.

4 *Alternatives.* Invite the parties to tell you what alternatives they can think of to move the situation forward. These alternatives should meet underlying needs and interests. Asking, 'What do you want to happen?' will elicit a positional retort, while asking, 'What do you need to happen?' gets under the surface and helps the parties think about what is really important to them. As they open up to you, summarize back what they are saying and avoid judging or evaluating. Slowly, the situation will defuse and they will have given themselves one or more alternative strategies for dealing with the situation.

Ten-minute active listening technique

A guide for a busy person

Active listening is a valuable skill and is one that I use during a mediation process to engage with the participants and to hear and understand what they are saying. It allows the talkers to feel that they are being heard and to feel affirmed and valued. However, I hear many people complain that they just don't have the time to sit down and engage in a dialogue. This can be even more challenging when there are strong emotions, where there is a conflict or where the relationships are remote.

This 10-minute guide to active listening is designed for use in time-poor environments and for use during video calls or phone calls. By the way, remember that were given two ears and one mouth – it is vital that we use them according to that ratio during the conversation.

Preparing for the conversation

Make the room comfortable and provide a glass of water or a cup of tea.

Think about the seating. People don't like to be sat with their backs to the door if they feel a bit unsure or unsafe.

If the meeting is likely to become emotional (as is often the case in a conflict) have some tissues to hand. Running out of a meeting in a blind panic trying to get hold of some tissues isn't ideal.

Minute 1

Put down your phone, turn the screen of your PC off and give the talker your undivided attention for the next 10 minutes. Turn and face him or her.

Minute 2

Invite the talker to tell you what he or she needs to say. Be relaxed, look at him or her while he or she is talking and smile – look interested and avoid interrupting.

Minute 3

Thank the talker for sharing whatever it is he or she has said and check if he or she has anything more to add. Remember to demonstrate empathy, ie you can imagine what it must be like for him or her. It does not mean agreeing with him or her or being sympathetic (which is empathy with a judgement attached).

Minute 4

Summarize back what you have heard.

Minute 5

Ask the talker a series of open questions to get more information. These tend to start with who, where, when, why, what or how.

Rudyard Kipling wrote a short poem outlining a powerful set of questions:

I keep six honest serving men

(They taught me all I knew)

Their names are What and Why and When

And How and Where and Who.

Minute 6

Thank him or her again for answering your questions fully. Reflect back what you have heard and highlight any critical points. Remember that empathy is vital here. The more you can do to put yourself in the talker's shoes and demonstrate that you are doing so, the better the conversation will go.

Minute 7

Check with the talker if your summary is accurate and if he or she needs to add anything else.

Minute 8

You are beginning to wrap up the conversation now. Check and clarify with the talker if there is anything more that he or she needs to tell you so that he or she has said everything that he or she wanted to share with you.

Minute 9

Agree what needs to happen next and by when.

Minute 10

Thank the talker for taking the time to discuss the issue with you and summarize back the actions that you have now agreed. Wrap the meeting up with a positive and inspiring formal comment.

Ten-factor Conflict Model™

While there is a lot going on for us in any conflict situation, people are not mind-readers, however much we may think that the situation must be obvious to them. Our observable, outward behaviours are a symptom of a lot of things going on inside our minds and bodies. The problem is this: unless we can sit down and discuss what we feel is going on and listen to what is going on for the other person, the situation will not get resolved. If these things in our minds – the stories and the narratives – could be shared and understood, they would unlock the conflict. What is needed is dialogue and the parties should be given every opportunity to tell their stories.

Having mediated in numerous conflicts and supported thousands of organizations to embed mediation programmes, I have identified 10 specific psychological and behavioural factors at play in any conflict. I call this the Ten-factor Conflict Model™

1 Context	6 Perceptions
2 Observations	7 Communication
3 Feelings	8 Behaviours
4 Needs	9 Adopted positions
5 Loss	10 Aftermath

Each of the 10 factors presents a risk but also a great opportunity for resolution. While the individual's experience is wholly unique and should be treated as such, the 10 factors are common in virtually all conflicts, ie they can be broadly predicted, so approaches can be designed and replicated for managing them.

The ability of the person managing the conflict to be aware of the 10 factors, to ask appropriate questions to elicit the necessary detail and then to develop an empathetic and compassionate level of rapport with the individual, will define whether the conflict will continue down the path of dysfunction, or whether it will become functional and constructive.

Whether I am mediating a conflict, training mediators, setting up resolution triage assessment, coaching a manager, or developing a company-wide conflict management strategy, these 10 factors are central to my approach.

Practical applications of the model

Let's imagine that I am using the 10-factor conflict model to address a conflict between an employee and a manager. The table below presents a series of questions that I would ask during the meeting with the employee. I would use a similar range of questions during my meeting with the manager.

Their responses will provide a steer towards the best route to resolution for the parties. If the intervention is done quickly and it is supported by a resolution policy and a conflict-competent culture within the organization, these questions can potentially be a precursor to a powerful dialogue between the two parties.

The model provides a framework that is designed to run through any organizational conflict management strategy as well as any conflict management training for managers, HR, unions or others. It can be used as a basis for resolution triage assessments or conflict coaching and it is a powerful methodology for mediators to use and should be the foundation of any mediation training and practice.

Table P3.4

Factor	Questions
1 Context	• Describe your working relationship and focus on the positives and the strengths as well as the challenges. • What has changed? • What do you enjoy about your working relationship with your manager?
2 Observations	• Thinking about a recent team meeting, can you describe what you observed happening during that meeting?
3 Feelings	Take yourself back to that meeting: • How did the situation make you feel? • How do you think your manager was feeling at the time? • How do you feel now? • How would you like to feel?
4 Needs	• What did you need to happen during the meeting? • What do you need to happen now? • What do you need to happen to resolve this situation with your manager?

(continued)

Table P3.4 *(Continued)*

Factor	Questions
5 Loss	• What impact has this conflict had on you (self) and why? • What impact has this had on your manager (other) and why? • What impact has this had on the relationship (situation) and why?
6 Perceptions	• How did you perceive the manager's behaviour towards you? • What assumptions did you draw from the behaviours? • Have you been able to check these assumptions with your manager? • If you could imagine a positive intention by your manager, what would that have been?
7 Communication	• Can you describe the communication between you during the meeting and subsequently? • What currently works well in terms of how you communicate? • If the manager were sat here now, what would you say to him or her?
8 Behaviours	• How did you behave during the meeting and what reflections do you have on those behaviours? • What were your actions, interactions and reactions before, during and after the meeting? • If you could go back in time, would you do anything differently?
9 Adopted positions	• Did you adopt a position in the conflict? • Can you describe it to me?
10 Aftermath	• What has been the consequence of the conflict? • What have you learnt from the conflict? • What needs to happen to resolve the situation satisfactorily?

Managing conflict in teams

Some handy hints for managers and leaders

Team conflict can be profoundly destabilizing and hard to deal with. Here are some helpful tips for managers and leaders who are experiencing a conflict within their team:

1 First and foremost, be reassured that having a conflict in your team is not a sign of failure. It is perfectly healthy and a normal part of team functioning. In fact, the process of transforming the conflict from dysfunctional to functional could make your team stronger and more effective. Remember that asking for help is not a sign of weakness: these issues are complex and it is important that you seek guidance and support from a colleague, an HR professional or a senior manager.

2 Listen to all the members of the team in a private meeting. Give them time to talk to you one-to-one about what they are experiencing and the impact it is having. Show that you are empathetic and ask a wide range of open questions. Encourage each team member to tell their story and don't be afraid to check with each member of the team about how they are feeling and what they need to happen: feelings and needs are the currency of resolution.

3 Avoid making judgements about the situation and remain impartial and objective. Don't let the outspoken person, the charismatic team member or the wily fox impact on your ability to take a dispassionate approach to the situation.

4 Bring the team together to discuss their concerns. Your role is to lead this meeting and to allow everyone to have their own time to speak out and to be heard by their colleagues in a safe, constructive and supportive way. Such a meeting could take a few hours so make sure that you give yourselves enough time.

5 Engender a future focus during the meeting – invite the team to explore, a) what a great team looks like, b) what needs to happen tomorrow, and c) how they can resolve their differences collaboratively.

6 Be clear what role you are going to play as leader going forward and also what you have learnt from this situation and how it will help to make you an even better leader. Set out your own expectations and needs for the future of the team. This is a chance to set out your own vision, goals and aspirations. It is a great opportunity to inspire the team with your vision.

7 Wrap up positively and summarize the agreed goals and objectives for the future of the team.

Mediation: frequently asked questions

How can I use mediation?

Mediation can be used by anyone who is experiencing a conflict or a dispute at work. If you wish to use mediation, it is generally advisable to speak to your manager, a union official or HR officer who can make the necessary arrangements.

How long does mediation last?

Mediation tends to last for one full day. However, in more complex cases or cases involving more than two parties, it may last slightly longer.

Do mediators tell people what to do?

No. Mediators do not tell parties what to do. Mediators do not judge who is right or wrong, nor do they impose a settlement or solution.

Can I have someone with me during workplace mediation?

While it is recognized that parties may wish to have someone with them, the mediators will create an environment where parties do not need to have anyone else to support them.

Is workplace mediation voluntary?

Yes. The mediator will check with you at the outset that you have entered into the process freely and voluntarily. Mediators do not force, trick or coerce people to engage in workplace mediation. However, it is reasonable for an employer to expect employees to give due consideration to mediation and to avoid rejecting it out of hand.

Is workplace mediation confidential?

Yes. Parties are asked to sign a confidentiality agreement before mediation commences. Mediators do not disclose anything that has been said during mediation, unless given permission to do so by both parties.

Where does mediation happen?

Mediation takes place in a neutral venue. Each party has his or her own private room for the entire day, and there is a separate room for the joint meetings.

Why does the mediator meet the parties separately?

Having separate meetings with the mediator gives all parties the chance to talk about the conflict from their point of view. The mediator listens to what all parties say and explores how the parties feel, what their concerns are and what their underlying needs and interests are.

What happens at the end of workplace mediation?

At the end of mediation, the parties will hopefully have reached a resolution to the dispute, including a number of points of agreement.

Does mediation really work?

Yes. However, for mediation to work it requires a commitment from all parties. If all parties enter into mediation with the right mindset – with the willingness to listen to each other; to be mutually respectful; to challenge and be challenged; and to seek a new way of working together – there is a very good chance that mediation will succeed. Recent research from ACAS suggests that mediation is successful in 90 per cent of cases.

Developing a conflict management strategy and embedding mediation

Business case template

This business case template can be adapted and developed in accordance with the unique needs and context of your organization.

1 Vision and objectives

What are you trying to achieve and why?

How does this fit into your wider corporate/HR/IR strategy and objectives?

How does this align with your values and leadership behaviours?

2 Current context

What is the reason for introducing mediation?

What are the key drivers for change?

3 Evidence of the need for change

Quantitative and qualitative data gathered on the costs of conflict: visible, hidden and intangible costs.

Data from the cost of conflict calculator.

Triangulated data from existing internal sources: grievance, wellbeing, engagement.

4 Benchmark data

What are other people in your industry doing?

What are CIPD and other relevant organizations advocating?

What is your trade body or professional association advocating?

5 The key stakeholders

Unions/works councils/employee reps

Management

Board/C-suite

Diversity and equality groups

Occupational Health

Lawyers

Organizational Development

Change agents

L&D

Employee engagement/internal communications

6 Internal factors

What are your policies, procedures, etc?

Are you considering introducing a resolution policy or a similar protocol for using mediation?

How does this align with your activities on equality and diversity? On stress and wellbeing? On employee engagement? On customer experience?

7 External factors

How does this align with the regulatory and compliance framework?

How does this relate to Brexit?

Are you considering using mediation to resolve disputes with customers, suppliers, etc?

8 Project plan and key milestones

Think about what success will look like.

Where do you want to be in one, two, three, four and five years' time?

9 Resource requirements

How much will the scheme cost and what other resources are required?

10 Potential return on investment (RoI)

What impact could this have?

How will you evaluate the cost benefit of this new approach?

11 Overcoming resistance

What are the potential blocks and barriers and how you will overcome them?

12 Your resolution partner

How will you identify and secure the right organization to partner with you and to support you on your exciting journey?

How to set up a facilitated (roundtable) conversation

This section provides detailed guidance for setting up and running a facilitated roundtable conversation. However, there is a health warning attached. This guidance only covers the basic details to facilitate a meeting successfully; proper training should be sought. If you are in any doubt, seek advice from a professional mediator or facilitator.

I'm going to assume that a resolution triage assessment has been undertaken and the parties have received information about the facilitated conversation process.

Prior to the meeting

- Secure a venue for all meetings – a safe space.
- Meet both parties privately (by phone or in person in the safe space) before you commence the facilitation process.
- This meeting will last for approximately 15–30 minutes.

At the private meeting

- Thank the parties for considering a facilitated roundtable conversation.
- Introduce yourself(s) and explain what a facilitated roundtable conversation is.
- Provide a positive and enthusiastic overview of the facilitation process.
- Clarify your role:
  - You will aim to be neutral and impartial.
  - You are a facilitator, not a decision maker.
  - You will not make judgements or attribute blame.
  - You will encourage the parties to identify their own solutions to the conflict.
  - You will help the parties to reach a resolution that is mutually acceptable to each of them.
- Confirm the timings for the meeting and details of breakout areas, toilets, etc.

- Explain that the meeting is voluntary and confidential, ie. the parties can ask for a break at any time and anything that is said during the meeting is held under the Chatham House Rule.
- Notes of the discussion will be destroyed at the end of the meeting and only the action plan will be retained.
- Invite questions from the parties.

Bear in mind that the parties may have a variety of questions and concerns that they want to discuss with you during the private meeting. There are broadly four areas of concern that parties may have:

1 *Psychological* – their emotional wellbeing, their fear and feelings. They may also want to discuss issues that are personal to them such as their need for safety, to be heard and to feel respected.

2 *Physical* – physical issues and their need for any reasonable adjustments to be made to ensure that they have full and equal access to the facilitation process.

3 *Substantive* – the issues in conflict and the main focus for the discussion.

4 *Procedural* – the process that will be used to resolve the conflict. Parties will want to know that it is a sound, robust and fair process and that you are able to manage it adequately.

It is vital that you allow the parties to describe their concerns to you and that you listen carefully while they talk. It is advisable to remain empathetic at all times during the private meetings (and the subsequent roundtable meeting). Once they have told you what they need to say, you may wish to:

- Reflect back what you have heard.
- Acknowledge and affirm what they are saying as being valuable and important.
- Ask open questions, ie ones that require more than a yes or no answer.
- Offer reassurance where you are able to do so.

Ultimately it comes down to this: do they trust you and do they trust the process? If they do, they will generally be happy to proceed to the next stage – the facilitated conversation. If not, you will need to probe their concerns in more detail and continue the meeting/discussion until such time as they feel ready to proceed or they decide to withdraw from the process.

At the end of the private meeting, I encourage the parties to prepare a short opening statement for the roundtable meeting. This is not a long statement and I generally advise them to prepare a few bullet points. This way, the parties can be confident that they will have a full opportunity to say what they need to and that, in the heat of the moment, they won't forget to say something that is important to them.

How to run a facilitated roundtable conversation

This is where the parties come together to discuss the conflict and agree a way forward. It is a wonderful process. It can be daunting, challenging, fun, exhilarating, tiring and extremely rewarding. We are, after all, working with real people with real feelings, real concerns and real needs. However, the process works well and any fears that you may have about running a facilitated conversation will soon dissipate as the process develops and the parties begin to engage.

Setting up the room

I advise facilitators to arrive early for the meeting, before the parties do. That way, you can prepare the room, arrange refreshments and ensure that you are mentally prepared to run the session. If you have a circular table that is the best layout. In any event, set the room up so that everyone can see everyone else.

Setting up the meeting

Welcome the parties and set out the objectives for the meeting. These objectives should refer directly to the parties' needs and also focus on reaching a resolution.

Establish some ground rules for the meeting:

- Be respectful.
- Be open and honest.
- Listen actively.
- Be brave – speak out and use this opportunity to get issues out into the open.

Uninterrupted speaking time

- This is a chance for the parties to talk to each other without being interrupted. For the person listening, it is chance to listen carefully to the other person as he or she describes his or her concerns, feelings, needs and goals.

- Invite one of the parties to start the process. Usually the aggrieved party starts but it doesn't really matter who goes first as both parties have an equal opportunity to say what they need to say.

- Each party should read out their opening statement and provide a detailed analysis of the situation from their point of view. Encourage each party to direct their opening statements towards each other rather than to you, the facilitator.

- The facilitator should make notes – these need not be a verbatim record but will be used for the summary once both parties have spoken.

- Once each party has finished speaking, ask a series of questions. At TCM, we call these the INCA Questions™

  - *Impact.* What effect has this had on you and how has it made you feel?

  - *Needs.* What do you need to achieve from this process?

  - *Consequences.* This question is asked in two parts. It is important to ask it in the following order: 1) What would the consequences be of not reaching an agreement today? 2) What would the consequences be of reaching an agreement today?

  - *A good day.* Describe to the other person what a good day would look like.

- After the first party has spoken, acknowledge him or her and thank him or her for the contribution. Thank the other party for listening and acknowledge that listening without interrupting is not easy.

- Now swap over so that the second party has the opportunity to speak before you summarize back.

So far, the meeting may feel a little contrived. However, for the parties, it is a powerful stage in the resolution process and it should have already delivered some considerable benefits:

- The parties are experiencing flow as an alternative to fight, flight, freeze or fall.

- They have got issues off their chests – catharsis.

- They have talked and listened to each other and feel heard.

- They have reflected on the situation in each other's presence.

- They have a better understanding of each other's points of view.

- They have begun to map out their needs and goals and they may already recognize that some of these may be common and shared.

- They may be a little more empathetic towards one another.
- They may already be getting a sense of a possible future working relationship.
- Trust, mutual respect and direct communication are replacing mistrust, fear and anxiety.
- The stressor hormones (adrenalin and cortisol) are being replaced by happy hormones (dopamine, serotonin, oxytocin, and endorphins); see Chapter 6 for an overview of the neuroscience of conflict.
- The atmosphere and tone of the meeting may be a little more 'can do'.

Managing the exchange

The next part of a facilitated conversation is the exchange phase. This is more like a typical discussion between two adults. Once you have summarized, hand the meeting over to the parties. This is a chance for them to:

- ask each other questions;
- provide explanations;
- check and clarify any issues;
- clarify intentions;
- explore the impact of the situation in more detail.

A few facilitator dos and don'ts

Table P3.5

Do	Don't
Ask open questions that encourage the parties to think deeply about the issues.	Interrupt the flow of the conversation.
Acknowledge any progress points during the conversation.	Offer your suggestions or potential solutions.
Summarize regularly to capture key points in the discussion.	Interrupt a silence – silence can be golden. Silence gives the parties time to process the issues.
Check if it appears one of the parties has not heard something important.	Make judgements about the issues or the parties. This is particularly important when the conversation gets challenging and the parties become emotional.
Remain empathetic at all times and encourage the parties to constantly put themselves into one another's shoes.	Panic if the discussion becomes confrontational – simply check with the parties how they are feeling and what is going on for them.

Towards the end of the facilitated conversation, the facilitator's role is to help the parties move forwards: to begin to identify solutions and to help them to craft an agreement that is mutually acceptable. During the facilitated conversation, problem solving often requires a bit of lateral thinking, or thinking 'outside of the box'. It is not advisable for the parties to resolve their conflict by doing more of the things that created the conflict in the first place.

The specific items on the agenda for problem solving are defined by the parties; however, the agenda should be structured as follows:

1 *Convergent factors.* These are factors that are shared and common – often referred to as 'common ground'. Convergent factors may include: improving communication, rebuilding respect, restoring trust, valuing each other's work and improving day-to-day interactions.

2 *Complementary factors.* These are factors that are mutually beneficial and support a win/win outcome. For example, the manager wants to see an increase in performance and the employee wants to feel more valued.

These two factors are complementary in as much as the manager may agree to adopt a more supportive and appreciative management style. This may lead to a greater level of motivation and sense of wellbeing for the employee. Ultimately, these two issues complement each other and the manager gets the increase in performance he or she needs and the employee gets the motivation and the sense of being valued that he or she needs.

3 *Divergent factors.* These are factors that relate to differences between the parties – diversity. They can include any personal characteristic, belief, religion, etc that is not shared by the other party. The discussions in this case are about greater awareness, understanding, insight and respect. They are not a negotiation or a compromise. The discussion is about recognizing and valuing our differences.

How to conclude a facilitated conversation

The end of the meeting should feel much better than how it was at the beginning. This is how to wrap up the meeting in a controlled and compassionate manner:

1 Summarize the progress made.

2 Reflect back the challenges that they have overcome.

3 Ask the parties to feed back to each other and to you what they have achieved from the meeting.

4 Ask the parties if there is anything more that they need to say to each other.

5 Identify any outstanding issues and agree the next steps for resolving them.

6 Confirm any follow-up arrangements.

7 Thank the parties for attending.

8 Close the meeting.

How to run a successful focus group

1 Welcome, introductions and objectives

Begin the focus group by providing participants with coffee and tea plus, where possible, biscuits or cakes. Food usually gets people into a positive mood and creates informal interaction before the group session begins.

It is important that the focus group should be a positive experience for all attendees. Progress will not be achieved if one person speaks too much, if people talk over each other, or participants are disrespectful towards each other, so it is worth setting and agreeing four ground rules at the outset:

a respectful language;

b courtesy towards each other;

c all comments are valid and valued;

d confidentiality – the Chatham House Rule applies.

Open the meeting by thanking people for their attendance and going round the room to do introductions – ask people to be brief. Also, state any house-keeping issues and highlight fire evacuation procedures and the location of toilets, etc.

Clearly state the reason for the meeting. You could use a phrase similar to this:

> Thank you for taking the time to attend today's focus group. The purpose of this meeting is to obtain your feedback about how xyz organization manages conflicts and disputes. We also want to listen to your ideas for ways of improving conflict management within the organization. The data that you share with us today will be used as part of a conflict management strategy that is being developed. Unless you give us specific permission to do so, we will not identify anyone in this room within the report. However, we will use what you say today to highlight specific points in the strategy and, where required, to highlight the need for any changes to the way that we handle conflict.

2 Conflict: context and analysis

For this part of the focus group, ask the participants a series of open and probing questions such as:

- Please describe your experiences of conflict in xyz organization.
- What are the causes of conflict in xyz organization?
- What kind of conflicts have you observed?
- What impact does conflict have – human and organizational?
- How is conflict generally managed?
- On a scale of 1 to 10 (10 being excellent and 1 being very poor), how effective is xyz organization at handling conflict?
- How effective is the current grievance/anti-bullying/disciplinary procedure for resolving conflict?
- On a scale of 1 to 10 (10 being excellent and 1 being very poor), how effective are the following roles at spotting, managing and resolving conflict? (Identify any roles that are relevant to your organization, eg HR, managers, unions, occupational health.)

For each question you ask, allow the group to engage in follow-up discussions and encourage them to share specific experiences or stories that illustrate the points they raise. However, time is limited so maintain the momentum and keep the discussion moving forward.

3 Testing potential conflict management solutions

Ask the group a series of questions relating to the following five approaches (for more information and an explanation about each of these approaches, see Chapter 7 on the resolution spectrum):

The five approaches

- **a** One-to-one coaching for people who are in conflict (conflict coaching).
- **b** Face-to-face meetings directly between the conflicting parties, often referred to as early resolution or local resolution.
- **c** Roundtable meetings facilitated by an HR officer, union official and/or a line manager.
- **d** Mediation undertaken by an internal mediator.
- **e** Mediation undertaken by an external mediator.

The questions to be asked of each approach

Are you familiar with the approach?

How effective do you believe it is/could be?

What are the strengths and the weaknesses of each approach?

Do you believe that xyz organization should use this approach more or less?

4 Wrap up, next steps and close

Close the focus group by thanking the participants for attending. Let them know that their comments are taken seriously and describe the timescale for producing the conflict management strategy. Generally, participants at the focus group are given access to the strategy as part of the consultation stage.

Conclusion

If this book has demonstrated anything it is this. The way that conflict is managed is a vital sign of a healthy organization.

Where conflict is acknowledged, where it is treated as a strategic priority by senior leaders; where a balance of proactive and reactive remedies is available; where there is an organization-wide emphasis on early resolution; where mediation, facilitation and coaching are actively encouraged; where adult-to-adult dialogue, empathy, insight and flow are valued; where line managers are equipped with the confidence and the competence to manage conflict; where HR processes reflect the values of the organization; where rules and regulations encourage, rather than impede, trust and common sense; where HR, unions and managers pull together and demonstrate a genuine commitment to pluralism; where lessons are constantly being learnt; and where all people (including alleged wrongdoers) are treated as human beings with real feelings and real needs – the impact on employee experience, on managers, on culture, on customer experience and on the bottom line can be beneficial and lasting.

Conversely, where conflict is treated as an afterthought or it is ignored; where having a conflict in your team is viewed as a sign of failure; where a resolution process only starts once the parties have dug their trenches; where managers lack the confidence, the courage or the competence to handle conflict effectively or they are afraid that doing so will result in career-damaging accusations; where the parties are subjected to cumbersome and divisive HR processes; where the organization treats disputing parties like naughty children or helpless victims; where blame and division are an accepted by-product of conflict; where HR, unions and managers pull in different directions; where terms like 'dialogue', 'empathy', 'insight' and 'flow' are widely misunderstood; and where the reliance on expensive litigation-based remedies is seen as being an acceptable cost of conflict – the impact on employee experience, on managers, on culture, on customer experience and on the bottom line can be damaging and lasting.

We should be better than this by now

It is over 10 years ago since the Gibbons review was published, resulting in the repeal of the Dispute Resolution Regulations (2004). Michael Gibbons made it clear that a shift in public policy and organizational culture towards a more person-centred and values-based approach for managing conflict would deliver real benefits across our organizations. He offered significant evidence to support his assertions and undertook rigorous consultation with key public policy makers. However, over the past 10 years, public policy in this area has tinkered around the edges of conflict and has focused primarily on reform of the tribunal system and the use of early conciliation (or late conciliation, as I call it) to mop up cases that can be prevented from going to tribunal. Little, if any, focus has been given to the management of conflict in the workplace and the resolution of disputes via alternative dispute resolution (ADR). The preservation, or restoration, of the psychological contract and the promotion of a truly collaborative system for delivering lasting business results is notable by its absence from almost every HR or ER policy that I have ever read.

Public policy, instead of offering clarity for HR, unions and business leaders, has created confusion and sown the seeds of disharmony. Public policy, which is reflected in most HR policies, perpetuates a reliance on litigation-style remedies while promoting a risk-averse and reactive system of employee and industrial relations. It is no wonder then that so many of our employees are so disengaged, so unhealthy, so unhappy and so unproductive. The root cause, I have argued throughout this book, is a systemic failure by our leaders, business and political, to send out a clear message that conflict is a strategic issue and should be treated as such. Moreover, the book has delivered significant evidence that the effective management of conflict can transform it from a dysfunctional phenomenon into something that is valuable, constructive and functional. We just need to reframe our understanding of conflict. We need to focus not on the risk but on the resolution.

This book sets out some simple challenges about managing conflict. Trying to consolidate those challenges into a simple phrase, I would say this. Organizations need to go back to basics. They need to find ways to get people talking and listening to each other – nothing more complicated than that. Dialogue. Mutual, respectful and honest dialogue. Our leaders need to be less afraid of the difficult conversation and they need to learn how to react less defensively when tough issues are raised. They need to institutionalize systems and behaviours that promote collaboration, empathy, insight and flow. They need to remove those systems that are divisive, risk-averse and damaging. I can't say for sure that this will change things overnight. This is not a silver bullet. This is a process of substantial cultural change that may take many years to implement and to realize in full. However, the numerous case studies in this book demonstrate, time and again, that the journey is worthwhile and that it delivers real and lasting benefits.

To succeed in today's global environment, we need our people to be happy, to be healthy and to be in harmony; to be human. Our current systems for managing conflict are woefully ineffective and they simply don't deliver against these four objectives. It is time for them, and for us, to change.

GLOSSARY

active listening   A communication technique that is particularly effective for managing conflict. It requires that the listener fully concentrates, understands, summarizes and then remembers what is being said. The listener asks a range of open questions to assist the person who is talking to tell his or her story.

alternative dispute resolution (ADR)   A range of non-legal remedies to a dispute, including conciliation, facilitation, mediation, arbitration and early neutral evaluation.

amygdala   A small almond-shaped part of our brain that affects how we react to a perceived threat by triggering the release of hormones and neurotransmitters. Believed to drive the 'fight or flight' response to conflict.

appreciative inquiry (AI)   A process of managing conflict and change during which greater focus is placed on what is working well and on our strengths, rather than what is not working and our weaknesses. By building on strengths and the positive elements of relationships, parties are empowered to drive growth and to secure a constructive resolution to a conflict.

arbitration   A process of dispute resolution in which the dispute is presented to a third party who makes a binding determination (outcome).

bullying   Actions by another person that are perceived to be deliberately intimidating, abusive, dominating or harmful. When bullying is carried out by a group, it is often referred to as 'mobbing'.

collaborative law   A term used primarily within family law to describe a network of lawyers who subscribe to a non-adversarial system for resolving family disputes, such as divorce and separation, avoiding the need for formal court processes and costly litigation. This approach could very easily be applied to employment law if more employment lawyers subscribed to a collaborative employment law network.

conciliation   A process of ADR that is very similar to mediation. It follows similar principles and processes to mediation – mediation is a conciliatory process.

culture   The shared customs, beliefs, values and assumptions that define the way people behave within an organization.

dialogue   A constructive conversation between two people where ideas are exchanged and insights are shared in a constructive and supportive way.

drama triangle   A useful way for analysing the roles that people adopt in conflict and the relationship between victim, persecutor and rescuer.

dysfunctional conflict   Damaging and harmful conflict that can be hard to resolve due to the entrenched and often dogmatic positions adopted by the parties.

Organizations wrongly assume that all conflict is dysfunctional and they design policies and procedures for managing it rather than promoting the dialogue and collaborative problem solving that can transform it to functional conflict.

emotional intelligence (EQ) A term made famous by Daniel Goleman in the 1990s. EQ focuses on the ability to be aware of our own emotions (self-aware) and the ability to develop empathy with others. If organizations valued EQ in in the same way that they value cognitive intelligence (IQ), I would not have needed to write this book.

emotions A set of complex reactions to a stimulus or series of stimuli (an incident, a relationship, a piece of music or art, an object, etc) that will define how we feel and how we will react to that stimulus or stimuli. Emotions can affect our mood and our levels of motivation.

empathy A vital part of emotional intelligence and central to effective conflict management. The ability to perceive the world through another person's eyes, often referred to as standing in another person's shoes. Not to be confused with sympathy, which is like empathy but with a judgement attached.

employment contract A legal statement supplied by an employer to employees on the commencement of their employment.

facilitation The process of making something easier. In conflict management, the facilitator is often thought of as an impartial third party who helps to make the process of dialogue easier.

FAIR Mediation Model™ A highly effective mediation framework that stands for Facilitate, Appreciate, Innovate and Resolve.

fight, flight, freeze or fall Our innate and instinctive response to a perceived threat. Also known as the 'fight or flight' response. Driven by powerful chemicals and hormones.

flow Drawn from positive psychology: a state of mind and associated behaviours at which times we are open to new ideas and prepared to consider a wider range of alternative outcomes to a conflict above and beyond our own adopted positions. Being in a state of flow is thought to make us happier. Mediation generates flow between parties: a flow of ideas, of insight and of empathy.

functional conflict This is healthy and constructive conflict. It is generally achieved during dialogue and at times of high flow and low fight or flight. Processes such as mediation are designed to transform dysfunctional conflict into functional conflict. Functional conflict is generally cooperative, supportive and constructive.

grievance A traditional way to codify a complaint against an employer or against a colleague or manager. May be lodged as part of a 'grievance procedure'. A widely used but generally unhelpful and negative experience that perpetuates dysfunctional conflict and results in greater harm and distress for all parties. Grievances are modelled on a litigation model that focuses on the rights and wrongs of a conflict rather than the underlying needs and goals of the parties.

hormones   Chemicals that deliver messages around the body. Examples of hormones in conflict include adrenalin and cortisol, which are released by the adrenal gland at times of a perceived threat.

impartial   The ability to remain objective and dispassionate (not to take sides) during an emotionally charged situation such as a workplace dispute. HR, managers and unions can act in an impartial way if appropriate training and support are provided.

Insight/Change Model™   A model in which change is managed by engaging all people affected and giving them a voice to explore its impact. This dialogue during change results in shared insights that can be used to enable the change process to proceed successfully.

leadership   The role of an individual or group of individuals to provide direction, vision, objectives and a coherent structure within an organization or a team.

litigation   The legal process of resolving a dispute where two advocates (lawyers), or the parties themselves prepare and present a case to a judge who will rule on the outcome.

mediation   A voluntary and confidential process of dispute resolution during which an impartial third party (the mediator) enables the two or more disputing parties to achieve a mutually acceptable outcome.

mindfulness   Being aware of what is happening in our own bodies and around us at the present moment. It is closely linked to meditation and is thought to enhance mental health and wellbeing.

narrative   *see* story.

neuroscience   The scientific study of the brain and neurosystem plus associated chemical reactions that drive our behaviour.

neurotransmitter   A chemical such as dopamine or serotonin that acts as a messenger between neurons (nerve cells).

online dispute resolution (ODR)   The process of resolving a dispute remotely via the internet. ODR is growing rapidly and is used in situations where the parties are unable/unwilling to meet in person or where it is not financially viable for them to do so.

positive psychology   A branch of psychology popularized by Martin Seligman in the late 1990s. It is future-focused and it aims to reinforce our positive experiences, traits, and relationships rather than trying to treat the negative elements. It also aims to create flow.

principled negotiation   A process of negotiation made famous by Roger Fisher and William Ury in their seminal text *Getting to Yes* (revised edition published in 2012 by Random House Business Books, London). The objective of principled negotiation is to help the parties to achieve a mutual gain or a win/win outcome by focusing on their underlying interests and needs rather than trying to negotiate their relative positions (which is known as positional bargaining).

psychological contract   The unwritten contract between an employee and his or her manager. It is used to foster a trusting, mutually respectful relationship. The breakdown of the psychological contract can be a trigger for conflict.

reframing   To help the parties in a conflict to modify their perception and how they communicate it from destructive (blaming or attacking) to constructive (self-aware and supportive).

resolution policy   A highly effective framework for managing conflicts and disputes within organizations. Focuses predominantly on resolution triage assessments, early resolution meetings, roundtable facilitation, mediation, team conferencing and early neutral evaluation. It also includes provision for formal action where this may be required. The resolution policy is being used as an alternative to traditional grievance procedures and it meets and exceeds the requirements of the Employment Rights Act (1996) and the ACAS Code of Practice on Discipline and Grievance.

safe space   A designated space within the workplace that can be used to promote dialogue between two parties. Generally, it is a neutral space away from the main place of work.

story   In conflict, everyone has a story to tell. Actively listening to a person's story, valuing it and giving it meaning is an important stage in the resolution of a conflict. It is important that we neither judge nor undermine people's stories – they are personal, they generate insight and they hold the key to the resolution of the conflict.

total conflict management (TCM)   Created by David Liddle in 2001 as a hybrid of Total Quality Management (TQM) and Integrated Conflict Management Systems (ICMS), TCM is the process of embedding a conflict management system across an entire organization.

transactional analysis (TA)   A system for understanding human interactions (transactions) developed by Dr Eric Berne in the 1960s. Berne identified three ego states: parent, adult, and child, which define the roles that people will adopt during conflict. The common transaction that exists at times of conflict is an unhealthy parent-child relationship. The aim of mediation, facilitation and other ADR approaches is to enable the parties in a conflict to engage in healthy adult-to-adult dialogue.

union   An organization that represents the needs and the rights of a group of workers regarding, amongst other things, wages and working conditions. Unions also provide a valuable role for consultation and representation. Unions are a key partner in the development and implementation of a conflict management strategy.

works council   A group of employees who work with management to negotiate on behalf of the workforce and to provide a formal channel for consultation and communication. Used predominantly in non-unionized environments. Since 1994, employers in EU member states (with over 1,000 employees from those states) must provide the right for their employees to establish a European Works Council (EWC) within their organization.

zone of negative conflict (ZONC)   The place that many people experience when they are driven by the fight or flight response. Can result in high levels of stress, anxiety, fear and insomnia, which drive dysfunctional conflict and result in higher absence levels, staff turnover and associated financial costs of conflict.

zone of possible agreement (ZOPA)   The place that the disputing parties can experience at times of dialogue, flow, insight, empathy and understanding. A place where disputes can be resolved. It is often achieved with the help of a third-party facilitator or mediator. Can best be achieved at times of functional conflict.

INDEX

Note: Chapter notes, chapter references *and* 'key learning points' are indexed as such; page numbers in *italics* indicate Figures or Tables; 'resolution recommendations' and 'resolution reflections' are indexed as such.